UNIVERSITY OF
DREAMS
FOUNDATION

CARVED BY GOD, CURSED BY THE DEVIL

A True Story of Running the Sahara Desert

Ted Archer

Redwood City, California

University of Dreams Foundation
2010 Broadway Street
Redwood City, CA 94063

University of Dreams Foundation Press hardcover edition January 2009.

Edited by Brianne Webb
Layout and Design by Maida Design
Manufactured in the United States of America
ISBN: 978-0-9770735-3-5

For Miss Bell (if I may call you that):

I would run the entire Sahara if you were waiting on the other side.

Contents

Preface

This is one man's true story of competing in the 2008 Marathon Des Sables, a 153-mile, six-stage self-sufficiency running race through Morocco's Sahara Desert. The week-long event requires runners to be self-sufficient—which meant that we ran with backpacks filled with food, clothing, a sleeping bag, and any other luxuries that we were willing to carry. The temperatures ranged between forty and 120 degrees, and at times we were blinded by sandstorms. We slept on the Saharan hardpan, ate what we could, and did our best not to dehydrate.

Every attempt has been made to accurately recount the details of the event; however, this book is not a journal. It is a story about friendships that were formed under the most painful of circumstances. For this reason, simply logging each day's events would be hollow. My hope was to recreate some of the feelings and emotions that were passed between haggard souls; to do so, I have recounted, as best as I can remember, our conversations, exasperations, moments of strength, and pleas for help. In doing so, I acknowledge that it is impossible to claim that every quotation is 100% accurate. Yet, while the quotes may not be exact in every respect, I feel confident in saying that they represent the spirit of the conversations, and in this sense, are a truthful account of my 2008 experience.

There is no need to grab your running shoes. You may wince, but you can enjoy the "Marathon of the Sands" from the comfort of your couch.

Ted Archer

June 2008

1
Pain

Tacky to the touch, the soles of my shoes had begun to melt. Or so it seemed, but I couldn't be sure—the heat was so suffocating that I struggled to think. Yet another runner passed me, and within moments the heat waves had distorted his frame so that all I could see was a blur.

I wanted more air, but it hurt to breathe. I needed more water, but even the action of drinking was difficult. I put a salt tablet in my mouth, but as I tried to swallow, my gag reflex shot it out onto the ground. As my feet shuffled along the black, rocky terrain, my goal was simple: just keep moving. At one point I thought to myself, *I want to die*. Paradoxically, this gave me strength. I knew that I would live—despite all of the pain and suffering—and I was determined to finish the day's twenty-five-mile run through the Sahara Desert. My mind was resolute, but my body wanted to shut down.

How in the hell did I get here?

The temperature was approaching 120 degrees, my feet were beginning to blister, I had sores on my waist from the twenty-two-pound backpack I was carrying, and my insides were churning. It was misery at a level that I had never before experienced.

But there was one simple fact that I could not dispute: I had voluntarily paid thousands of dollars to do this.

It was the second day of the Marathon Des Sables, affectionately known as "the world's toughest footrace." A 153-mile, six-stage running race through Morocco's Sahara Desert, this year's edition had attracted more than 800 competitors from thirty-two countries. I was one of the people stupid enough to have become consumed by the mystery of the event.

That morning, race director Patrick Bauer had stood atop his Jeep and proclaimed that the second stage was the easiest of the event. Nearly four hours into the stage, my eyesight disrupted by the delirium, I wanted to argue the point with him. But he was nowhere to be found. It was my job alone to suffer and my responsibility to succeed or fail. With only a couple of miles remaining, I knew that I would complete the stage despite the consuming sensation of disgust.

***

My journey had actually begun two years earlier. In my discomfort during that second stage, I remembered it quite well. Sitting in my air-conditioned office, I looked out my window at the squirrels jumping from branch to branch. It was early spring. With new foliage and improving temperatures, it had become perfect running weather. Looking at the slits of sunlight shimmer between the oak leaves, I was counting the minutes until I would head out for a half-hour jog.

My computer chirped and an instant message window popped up. A colleague from down the hall, Mike Newton, had sent me a Website link.

"Look at these crazy people," he wrote, with no other explanation.

I clicked the link, opening a Webpage of photos. They were of people I had never seen, all carrying backpacks and wearing strange clothing. They were running, walking, and sometimes even crawling over the most unforgiving terrain imaginable: sand dunes, scorched salt flats, jagged boulders, and small thorn bushes. Were it not for the obvious suffering, the photos were beautiful; the landscapes came from paintings and Hollywood movies.

It was a juxtaposition of beauty and suffering that I had never seen. It was disturbing and painful, but fascinating. It was pleasurably voyeuristic to be sitting in the comfort of my high-backed chair while looking at people who were struggling to survive.

Then came the pictures of the feet. Some were taped, others blistered. Yet others had ceased to be feet except in the strictest definition. They had swollen, turned black and purple, been sliced, and were further disfigured from obvious infection. And yet, despite their condition, the next photos showed these warriors continuing, walking on nubs that any sane doctor would have sent to the emergency room.

"Those are crazy," I wrote back. "What in the heck are those from?"

"I don't really know . . . some friend sent me the link. It's some race in Africa somewhere."

"Is this recent?"

"Oh yeah, it just happened," he wrote back. "It's happened for years. Every year, I think. People have died doing it."

"Did you see these?" I asked. I sent him a link to pictures of more mangled feet.

"Yeah, I think that I looked at all of them."

I clicked through to other pages and read a few of the press releases announcing a particular stage's results. I then came across what looked like a child's hand-drawn maps, complete with a legend. The maps had little lumps and symbols, complete with labels for "sand dune," "salt flat," "tree," and other. They were absurdly simple renderings for such a dangerous event. *Was this all that the race organizers gave these runners as they struggled to survive in the Sahara?*

"Holy cow! Did you read those press releases?" I asked. There was no response, but I continued: "Check out this link to the hand-drawn maps. Those things are hilarious. Can you believe that's all they get?"

I remained in my own little world for a few moments, staring at photos and marveling at the insanity of the event. I was so consumed that I failed to notice Mike's response: "You're thinking of doing it, aren't you?"

I sat and simply stared at his response. I had only ever run three marathons and certainly had never considered something of this scale. I was the Director of Marketing for a Silicon Valley technology company—not some adventure racer or outdoors freak. It made no sense, but there was no denying that I had decided that I wanted to be one of those "crazy people."

***

Jolted back to the realities of the Sahara, I looked around. I wiped the sweat from my eyes and shook my head as I could see the end of the second stage off in the distance. I thought back to that initial conversation with Mike and felt sick at how spontaneous the decision had been.

The entire training and preparation process came into focus and seemed like a blur.

As I remembered packing and repacking my backpack in the months before the race, I felt a blister pop on my back.

As I recounted my excited conversations with my roommate about how cool it would be, I felt the not-so-cool straps on the front of my pack rub my chest.

I thought back to the number of times I had excitedly explained my upcoming trip; I had become even more animated in response to my friends' looks of disbelief and horror. As I shuffled along, I scolded myself for my naiveté.

I apologized to God for my hubris.

Sweat dripped from every pore but would evaporate moments later, forming crusty salt streaks down my body. My calves began to cramp. My left quadriceps muscle felt as though it had been pierced by a knife. My eyesight blurred, and my back buckled. My feet ached each time I stepped on a rock. Never before in my life had I been so uncomfortable, so much in pain.

I was loving every minute of it.

2
Amy

As I boarded the plane to Morocco, I thought that there was a fifty percent chance that my sister would commit suicide while I was away. Her alcoholism had progressed so rapidly during the previous six months that none of her family members could believe the extent to which she had ruined her life.

She had gone from being a tall, well-built, gorgeous gal with modeling experience, a college degree, and awards as a company's top corporate salesperson, to a disheveled, strung out, acne-faced alcoholic lying in a pool of her own urine.

She was twenty-five.

My brothers and I sat with her in late February, more than six hours following her most recent binge. She could barely put together a coherent phrase and needed assistance just to lift her own head. With the few sensible thoughts that she did offer, she expressed jealousy at my success, anger at my father's infidelity, sadness at her lack of connection to her siblings, and regret over her fallen condition. Mostly, however, she simply offered the rants of a madwoman: words ran together in a near-endless exercise of free association.

I have no idea when her alcoholism began to take over. Sure, her entire family was aware of certain youthful indiscretions dating back to middle school. But, despite pain and anguish stemming from our parents' divorce, she seemed to persevere relatively well, completing her college degree and involving herself in a series of go-get-'em companies. It was September 2007 when she admitted for the first time that she was an alcoholic. Less than twenty-four hours later, she recanted, claiming that certain members of our family were trying to control her life.

During the first few months of her crisis—coincidentally, the first few months of my full-time Marathon Des Sables training regiment—things appeared to stabilize. Dissention within our family had enabled my sister to justify not entering an inpatient facility. As loved ones are wont to do, we all denied the gravity of her addiction. She entered an outpatient program and succeeded in convincing our family for some time that she was undergoing a healthy transformation.

Despite my (some would say unhealthy) cynicism and skepticism, not even I considered the depths to which she had fallen. In every sense, her life had become a lie and a manipulative game. While actively working to destroy their lives, addicts nonetheless pour incredible amounts of energy and devotion into creating the impression that their lives are in order. The sneaking, the cover-ups, the alternate explanations, the health problems, the missed appointments—all are a result of the addiction, and yet all get explained away in a complex web of deceit.

***

As I checked my luggage with Royal Air Maroc, I recounted the events of my sister's life over the previous six months: hospitalization with a near-death .4% blood alcohol level, participation in three inpatient treatment facilities, family members' flights around the country to try to help her, alienation of her boyfriend, and countless drunken stupors even while under supervision. All the while, she had fought treatment; she wanted nothing more than to try to return to a normal life. In her protests to family, she recounted her life's successes and criticized us for questioning whether she was capable of succeeding. It never occurred to her that she had lost herself completely to her disease—that we were not questioning her abilities, but rather pointing out that the person with those characteristics no longer existed. "Get clean, or you'll die," we would say. But the last elements of her capable, confident, prideful self refused to acknowledge that alcohol was steering her ship.

In a perverted way, I look at my sister's disease as being inextricably linked to the Marathon Des Sables. That statement is absurd on its face, of course. There is no causal link or any connection at all, except that my mind has fused the two. The reason is a shallow one: My awareness of her disease began as my formal training began. In the six months leading up to the race, training and my sister were the most powerful, painful, and dominant forces in my life. I could escape neither, for I was powerless over my sister's disease, and I was too obstinate to succumb to the ever-present desire to back out of the most grueling physical process I had ever contemplated.

Because these two forces served as my yin and yang for the better part of a year, I increasingly ruminated on the similarities, differences, and connections. So many days began with phone calls to crying family members, included runs longer than a marathon, and ended just as they had begun—with crying and pleas and confusion aimed at righting my sister. My energies and thoughts while dealing with either of these elements always caused me to cycle back to the other.

It goes without saying that it takes considerable commitment, dedication, and perseverance to train for the Marathon Des Sables. I think that it takes similar traits to be an alcoholic. I do not in any way want to conflate the two, but as they have been so intertwined in my mind, I cannot help but do so—despite the fact that the former is a positive pursuit and the latter a life-shattering process.

Think of the sacrifice required to prepare oneself for a 153-mile run through the most godforsaken terrain on the planet. To a large extent, I had to put relationships on hold. Every Saturday and

Sunday, I would awake, often in darkness, and proceed to ignore those that I love. As I planned to run the entirety of Sacramento's American River Bike Trail or to the top of Black Mountain in San Jose, I had to brush aside the invitations that I had received. I know the excuses that my girlfriend and family members made for me.

"No, he can't join us; he's got a long run."

"I'll leave in the middle and pick him up, and we'll return after he showers."

"We'd love to, but Ted's got to run hills this weekend, so we won't be in town."

"Sure, we'd love to meet for dinner, but could we do it a bit later? Oh, and are you okay if Ted won't be able to walk much?"

Good friends are resilient, patient, kind, and understanding. I was fortunate enough to have people in my life who did not understand my pursuit, but were nonetheless willing to accommodate my twisted quest. Nonetheless, my avoidances did at times strain our relationships. Friends tried to support me but at times grew weary of my excuses: "Oh, okay. Well, it's sort of a once-a-year thing, but I guess we can just meet up another time."

My sister's alcoholism has been a similar string of excuses that have decimated her relationships. As I rose to run, Amy no doubt lay in bed, passed out from a night of drinking. Family and friends no doubt called, but she was too sick to pick up. Her mornings, and then late mornings, and then afternoons—all succumbed to her drinking. And, just as my friends remained loyal despite their disappointments, Amy received unconditional love from so many.

But after a while, friends just stopped calling. I was fortunate enough to maintain my friendships despite my training schedule, but I know that some invitations just stopped arriving. People can only hear "no" so many times. My sister's alcoholism pushed everyone around her away. What began as a social activity on nights and weekends became a life-consuming parasite. Her decision to drink came with an enormous price tag: she shattered relationships in order to appease the bottle.

In addition to sacrifice, both my pursuit and my sister's disease share another common element: we both had to exhibit unwavering commitment and dedication to achieve our ends. It would have been so much easier to stop training. I could have slept in, participated in other social functions, and shared time with those that I love. To sacrifice these relationships—albeit temporarily—took an incredible amount of resolve. Through pain and suffering, I had to conclude that an event months in the future was worth the price that I had to pay on any particular morning. My legs would ache, my back would hurt, and my body would have blisters throughout—and still I would have to run, even though every physical and emotional part of me would have preferred to give up. My goal mattered so much to me that I sacrificed, even against my own wishes. It required an unsurpassed level of commitment and dedication.

My sister made the same choice.

I am not a mental health professional, and I recognize that I will never fully comprehend the severity of alcoholism as a disease. I fully admit that my choice to train for the world's toughest footrace was more of a choice than my sister's unrestrained binge drinking. Nonetheless, each of our experiences required commitments with severe consequences. In her case, death may be the ultimate price.

It is from this perspective that I marvel at my sister's problem. I realize the mental strength that was required to persevere in my training toward a sixteenth-place Marathon Des Sables finish. I know the allure and strength of so many forces that tried to derail that process. And I know that it was only inner mental strength that enabled me to persevere in the face of so many contrary emotions and desires.

However involuntary my sister's drinking has been, it nonetheless has required a considerable sacrifice. And, to continue the way she has, she has had to, at some level at least, choose to reject and leave behind so many of the people that she loves. As someone who found the internal strength to counteract so many intense internal drives, it is painful and disheartening to see someone I love give up so much and get only destruction in return.

My commitment was born out of pride; Amy's was born out of loathing.

My perseverance was fueled by strength; Amy's was fueled by weakness.

My pursuit was an attempt to savor life; Amy has embraced death.

I am not judging my sister, though I have little doubt that she would disagree if she were to read these words. It is just that this has been an indescribably painful experience for everyone around her, and nothing I have ever experienced comes close to helping me understand the pain and turmoil that she has been living. If only in concept, then, I think that training for this event gave me a small window of insight into what one loses as alcoholism begins to win.

My sister and I share the inability to explain to friends *why*. Neither of us had an explanation or reason that makes sense, but both of us were driven, forced, by something that pushed reason to the background. The difference here is that my obsession was a mostly healthy one that has served to inspire my loved ones, while her spiral is killing her. I wonder to myself: Where is the inner strength and confidence that I know she has? How is it that she cannot find a way to tap the support and strength within herself, and of those around her, in order to beat this illness? Why is it that she continues to suffer so much and receive so little in return?

***

After returning from Morocco, I learned that my sister was still alive. She had entered her third inpatient treatment facility, an alternative adventure-oriented outdoors program. Immediately upon her arrival, she began trying to convince family members that "this program is not for me." But the more she protested, the more we prayed that something about the experience would awaken her to her desperate reality.

We both left for the desert on March 22, 2008—I for Morocco and Amy for Utah's backcountry. I was not searching for anything in particular but knew that I wanted to find it nonetheless. Like Billy Crystal's character in the movie *City Slickers*, I returned from my adventure in the great outdoors able to hold one finger in the air: I had found that something, that miracle, that indefinable peace that places the rest of life in perspective and promises hope and satisfaction for the future.

I can only hope that Amy too will be able to emerge changed—in whatever way, shape, or form is necessary.

3
Arrival at the Bivouac

Nature does not care.

It does not coddle, nor does it seek to punish.

It simply acts how it will and feels nothing about the consequences.

Nature is not irreverent; no, this would imbue it with too much soul. It is simply uncaring, immovable, unswayable, and entirely unconcerned with any and all human whims.

***

Seven of us lay huddled in Tent 77 at the base of Erg Chebbi, North Africa's tallest sand dunes. The whipping winds stirred up sand and bits of rock, and try as we may, none of us could sleep.

"This sucks," someone uttered, the voice muffled by the sleeping bag and gusts of wind.

"I hope it's not like this the entire time," another cocoon exclaimed. "Could you imagine?"

We had prepared ourselves for lots of running on uneven terrain. We had trained wearing twenty-five-pound backpacks. Some of us

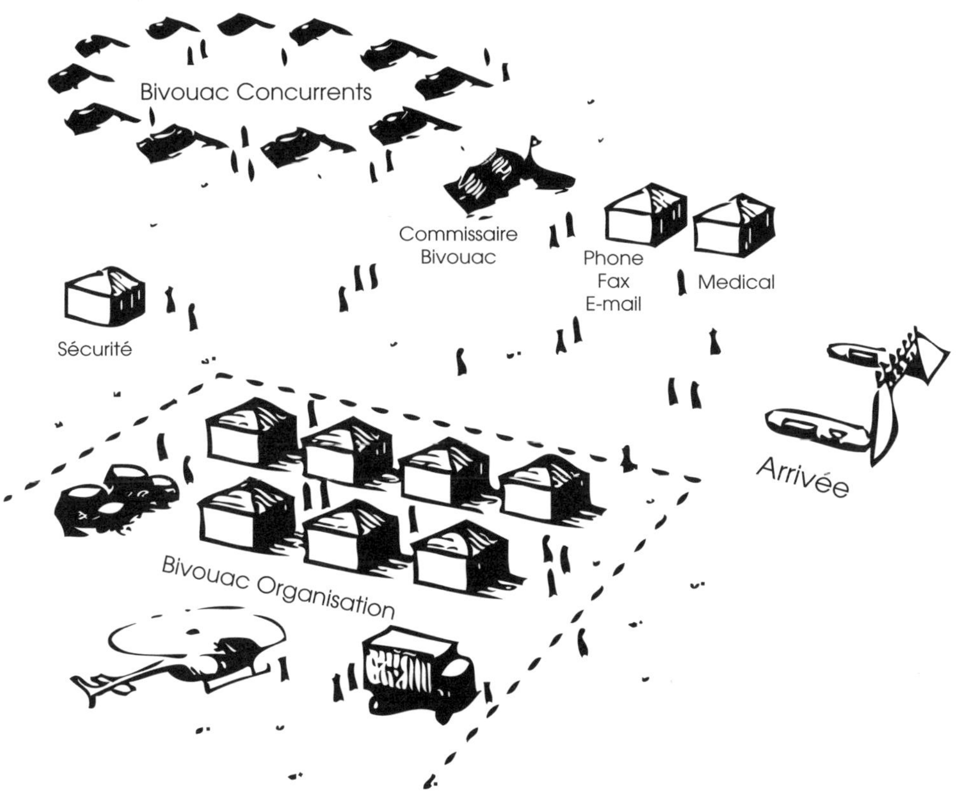

had even sat in saunas to learn how to brave the heat. But none of us had ever considered trying to sleep in front of an industrial fan spewing sand into our faces. We realized during our first night in the Sahara that this would not have been a bad training strategy.

Our time in Ouarzazate had been pleasant. Temperatures topped out at eighty-five degrees, we shopped for poorly made jewelry, and we visited movie studios on the edge of town. Following a six-hour bus ride into the middle of the middle of nowhere, the niceties had ended. With two days to acclimate to the unforgiving Sahara prior to the start of the race, we were indoctrinated quickly.

***

As we stepped off the bus, the experience began to feel real. Padded seats and air conditioning behind me, I stepped into the dust and looked out into the distance. Miles and miles of parched earth stretched out, and the Erg Chebbi dunes stood ominously a mile away. Hundreds of meters high and countless miles long, the dunes resembled a scene straight out of a Hollywood production. We knew that we would be running through them on the first day of the event, but all of us tried to believe that there had been some sort of mistake.

"This is surreal; unbelievable," someone said.

"This is *awesome*!" I screamed. Only moments before I had been despondent, terrified of the event. I had gulped as our bus left the poorly paved one-lane highway and drove over unmarked, bumpy dirt. My sudden manic rush was part of a pattern of recent mood swings. I let a scream go at the top of my lungs. It felt great to be terrified by the desert.

"Ted's back!" someone exclaimed. A few people chuckled as they dusted off their packs and started walking toward the camp.

The "camp" was nothing more than a flat, dusty plain. The race organization had set up a horseshoe pattern of 120 dual-sided, Berber-style tents, which we were to call home for the following nine days. In the distance, set aside from our makeshift homes, was a series of sturdy, finished tents. In direct contrast to the black rags under which we were to sleep, the white tents were off limits to competitors. Complete with electricity, water, and mattresses, these dwellings would be moved from bivouac to bivouac so that race officials, doctors, and members of the press could be comfortable as they helped us suffer. Off to another side was an enormous inflatable structure resembling a forty-foot-high orange spider, which would be used as our dining hall for the first two nights. Until the race began on Sunday, we would be fed by a French catering company. The magnitude—and stupidity—of the event was clearly before me, but with enough creature comforts still at hand for the next few days, I quickly returned to schoolboy anticipation.

As I walked toward the ring of black tents, a slight breeze stirred enough dust to produce a slight haze. Warm but not hot, the air was the very definition of dry. A group of Americans approached a sign with instructions that would point us toward our tents. Like high school athletes trying out for the football team, dozens of people fought for position so that they could find out if they had made the cut. We all had, of course: we had paid our money. But finding out our meaningless tent number nonetheless filled us with excitement.

I could hear a different language being spoken in every direction. The locals ("Berbers") spoke Arabic or French, the dominant language at the camp, with more than a third of all competitors and most volunteers hailing from France. Yet, within five minutes of stepping off the bus, I had heard Spanish, Dutch, Korean, Japanese, Italian, and a host of other languages that I could not place. Thirty-two countries in all would be represented in the twenty-third running of the Marathon Des Sables.

The Spanish, with their cheers, chants, and celebrations, were by far the loudest—until the bus with the Italians arrived. It felt like the pre-game party before a World Cup Soccer match as people chanted, waved flags, and yelled allegiance to their country.

As we meandered toward Tent 77, the atmosphere was electric: a mild dust storm, multiple languages, arriving buses, a few camels, and hundreds of temporary tents—all randomly set in the middle of a dust plain, in the middle of the Sahara Desert, with enormous sand dunes in the distance.

I arrived at my tent and reacquainted with my tent mates. I was a bit nervous because I had irresponsibly forgotten to check tent assignments, so I was uncertain who would be forced to subject themselves to my company for the following week. Aside from Brendan, a mellow forty-one-year-old Canadian who wrote for Lonely Planet Guide Books, I had known the others for some time. There was Andrea, a Canadian and self-proclaimed wine goddess who would carry a box of wine for the first five days so that she could enjoy a glass following the long stage; Karen, our third Canadian, whose radiant smile and energy instantly picked up everyone's spirits; Jeff, originally from Atlanta but now living in Switzerland, the "former fat kid turned Ironman"; Michelle, from Colorado, the most experienced ultra-runner in the tent, having won a few fifty- and hundred-mile races back in the U.S.; Georgia, an Alaskan who had trained in positively miserable conditions and the only one of us who had already signed up to run this event the following year; and me. I was the guy that a lot of folks referred to as fast but was rapidly earning a reputation as a smart-aleck who would spontaneously sing country music (logical, given my California roots).

As the seven of us tossed our bags beneath the flaps of our Berber tent, that became home. Those bags would be our only means of subsistence over a seven-day event.

"These tents are pretty nice, eh?" Karen offered, echoing a thought many of us had.

"Eh?" I asked, poking fun at the Canadian stereotype.

Not missing a beat, Karen went into a sarcastic but professorial explanation, "Oh, sure. The 'eh' is great, eh? It can be used at the beginning, middle, or end of a statement. It's so flexible, eh?"

We chuckled as everyone shook hands to reacquaint or meet for the first time.

"Did you guys see those dunes?" Jeff asked.

"Those things are ridiculous!" Georgia responded.

"They can't make us run through the middle of them, can they? I mean, we'll sort of run to the side, don't you think?" Karen looked at us, hoping.

"They can do whatever the heck they want!" said Andrea. "And I'll bet you that, just to piss us off, we'll be forced to climb to the very tops of all of them."

After a few minutes of shuffling around in the tent, tossing our bags from side to side, and making general observations, we realized that the waiting had officially begun. It was Friday afternoon, and the race would not begin until Sunday morning. Back home, we would have gone to a movie, taken a walk, or planned to meet up for drinks. But, stranded in the middle of the desert with forty hours to kill, the challenge became finding ways to entertain ourselves. Anyone for a game of "toss a rock into the dust?"

"Anyone know what time dinner is?" Jeff asked. All of us had become ravenous in recent days, as if our bodies had finally been informed of what they were up against and had decided to try to pack on a little extra weight.

"I think that I heard 7 or 7:30," I offered.

"Or 8 or 8:30," Karen quipped, poking fun at the race organization's penchant for flexible timing. That morning alone, we had been told to be ready for a 9 a.m. bus pick up at our hotel. Our promised five-and-a-half-hour bus ride actually took an hour longer—once we left the hotel at 11 a.m.

"Whenever it is, I am going to eat a ridiculous amount," I promised. "I might just eat twenty of those little French cheeses that are so popular around here. And then I'll eat twenty more."

"They'll probably prepackage your meal in a little bag and slap your hand if you try to take more," Andrea threatened, a subtle reference to the bagged lunches they had passed out on the bus. All of us were beginning to learn to use humor to confront the uncomfortable life that lay before us.

Suddenly, our food discussion was interrupted. "Are any of you guys Americans?" a woman asked enthusiastically with a thick British accent.

"We're all Americans—or at least residents of the fifty-first state," I joked, looking at my Canadian companions to see if I could get a rise out of anyone. No one flinched.

"Oh, great," the lady responded. "We're with ABC, and we're trying to find Jay. Do any of you know where Jay is?" She was referring to Jay Batchen, the representative for the U.S., Canadian, and Australian contingent—and the man who had been playing father to all of us confused, running children.

Jeff introduced himself and pointed about twenty yards away, guessing at the approximate location of Jay's tent. Each of us, in turn, said hello to Clarissa and the two men lingering over her shoulder.

"Clarissa," she stated, smiling with hand extended.

"Ted ... Archer," I responded, shaking her hand and smiling back.

"Oh! Ted *Archer!* You're Ted Archer?!"

I looked nervously from side to side, my eyes darting around to search for context cues. The last thing I expected upon arriving in Morocco was to have my reputation precede me—whatever that reputation might be. Now I was staring at someone from one of the nation's largest media outfits, worried that the camera would swing in my direction and grab footage of my dumbfounded expression.

"Uh, maybe . . ." I droned, staring slyly at her in hopes of figuring out why exactly she had heard about me. I had spoken with someone from ABC weeks earlier when their producers had called a number of Americans to research the event, but it had been a relatively routine discussion. It had never occurred to me that I had made any sort of impression.

"Wait, I'm confused," Clarissa confessed. "You're Ted?"

"Yes, I guess. It depends." I stalled; Clarissa obviously did not understand my breed of humor.

"Oh, great. We're looking for you, too. Bruno, our producer, has been getting the pre-race e-mails that you've been sending. They've been great, so we're looking forward to talking with you, too."

Relieved, I explained to her that I had forgotten that I had included Bruno on a series of thoughts, musings, and rants in the run up to the race. It made sense now: ABC did not know me, but rather knew of me, having read a few of my half-witted e-mails.

"Matt, this is Ted Archer. Let's get a shot of him with the camera." Matt, an unassuming and normal-looking man—normal except for the massive black camera that seemed to have "We embarrass people on national TV" written all over it—swung my direction and stuck a giant black, glassy eye in my face.

"Can we get your name for the camera?" he asked.

Throughout the past few weeks, I had been aware that ABC might have a crew on-site. But nothing had prepared me for that one moment where self-consciousness took over and caused me to think, *Ted, it's time to be interesting. Are you interesting? Be interesting. Do something or say something interesting.* I looked into the camera and offered a weak wave and a smile.

"Uh, hi. I'm Ted. How's it going?"

Real interesting, Ted.

For the next few hours, the joke became that ABC had sent "Ted's camera crew." My tent mates chided me for the attention that I had received. Their presence had definitely changed the mood. This was *ABC*! While the French and British had always had well-recognized media on-site, this was a first for us Americans.

Prior to arrival, we had all thought how exciting it would be to have ABC along with us. After months of being introduced by friends and family as the "crazy friend" and having to explain to disbelieving ears our plans to run 150 miles through the Sahara Desert, it would be an exciting sense of vindication to get our proverbial fifteen minutes of fame. Even in today's digital age, with Websites dedicated to everything from ultra-running to poodle hairstyles, there is no denying that it would mean something special for our event to be featured on ABC. Finally, we thought, everyone back home would get to understand a small piece of the insanity that had consumed us for months. They would experience it alongside us; they would understand.

That had at least been the thinking until the camera showed up.

Here we were on parched dirt in Northern Africa, awaiting the most grueling physical feat of our lives. We had trained, but we were in the final stage of our preparation: commiserating with one another in hopes of settling our nerves prior to the start. As we spoke with some race veterans, we realized in waves just how difficult our journey would be. We would be hot. We would ache. We would suffer.

And we now realized that there would be a camera obsessively documenting our every struggle. At those moments when we felt like crying, felt like being alone, felt like having a private conversation, we might very well have all of America watching us. We had all seen so-called "reality" television shows in which the participants crack, trying to avoid the camera but all the while being documented in the name of boosting ratings. We wanted the attention but were worried about reaching an ABC saturation point.

Many of us felt bittersweet about the crew. Clarissa, Matt, and Bruno seemed nice, but would we want them around when our feet had blistered, we were dehydrated, we were vomiting, or we were delirious?

My own concerns were alleviated that night when, during dinner, they just so happened to sit at a table beside me. Their proximity gave me an excuse to explore these animals, to conduct a little research and learn whether or not they would be pleasant company once I had turned miserable. After finishing my ration of pasta and a single French cheese chunk (Andrea had been right about the portion control), I slid over and asked them what their initial take was on this event.

"We're just blown away, honestly," Bruno responded, leaning forward with wide eyes and obvious enthusiasm. "We've been a lot of places before—Afghanistan, Iraq, you name it—and we've seen nothing like you people." It was genuine flattery and awe.

"Yeah, I guess that the food they're serving you now is a little better than what you'll be eating out of your backpack in a few days, so I imagine that the experience will change a little," Clarissa said, again smiling in what was to become her trademark greeting throughout the race.

"We're really just looking forward to watching how you guys fare," Matt offered. He was the quietest of the three, only occasionally interjecting his comments.

My tent mate Brendan slid over from our table to join the conversation. For the next half hour, we were surprised at the number of questions that ABC had for us. Everything about this event was new to them; everything was fascinating. Their expressions and questions were the same that we had received back home: intensely interested probes that were layered in partial disbelief.

"I mean, are you nervous?"

"How do you think you'll feel?"

"Do you think your feet will hurt?"

"What in God's name possessed you guys to want to do this race?"

They did not know it all; they were not arrogant; they seemed to have no preconceptions about the story that they were going to tell. Rather, they were researchers who could not help but be fascinated with their subjects. It was calming and encouraging to realize that they were human. They were reacting just as our friends and family had for months, not like a journalistic stereotype of the brash, fast-talking producer who arrives at a scene with an agenda and a timeline. They had signed up for the full experience and would be learning and suffering alongside us.

Were this a scientific study, they would be criticized for being too close to their subjects. But, since I cared more about my own experience, I felt honored to have them along. It was clear that we would be teaching them through our actions, not taking stage directions. Whatever America saw, it would be genuine, and I no longer felt concerned that Clarissa, Matt, and Bruno would make us miserable with their giant black glass eye.

As Brendan and I returned to our tent, it struck us how quickly the temperature had dropped. Shivering as we shined our headlamps on the ground, we were tired from a day that had begun a world of comfort away. The winds had begun to pick up a little, and small bits of sand shot toward our faces.

We got back to our tent and shook our sleeping bags free of sand. Karen, Andrea, Georgia, Jeff, and Michelle had already buried themselves into their sacks, and we too settled down to try to sleep. Tomorrow would bring nothing exciting, just another day of learning to dance with the desert.

Fifteen minutes after lying down, it was obvious that no one had actually gotten to sleep. With the winds whipping and sands blowing ever more, someone vocalized the nervous anticipation that every one of us felt inside: "I can't believe that we've got to wait a whole other day before we get to run."

4
The Day Before

"I wish we could just start today. Waiting sucks."

It was Saturday, and everyone in camp had begun stirring just after sunrise. After a night of sandstorms and discomfort, all of us in Tent 77 were a bit crankier than we had been twenty-four hours earlier. Sleeping on compact dirt and pebbles has a way of doing that. I had only slept a few hours all night, and I was certain that everyone else had suffered equally.

I spent a few moments wiping the sand off of my face and then used my pinky finger to try to clean my ears. I had been warned that "sand will get everywhere, and you'll just stop caring after a while," but I decided to try to feel normal for as long as possible. My tent mates were having a few groggy conversations, and the sounds outside our tent had changed as well. Mostly, everything sounded subdued: conversations were somber, and even peoples' footsteps seemed slower. Our camp was very much stirring, but not yet fully alive.

I lay in my sleeping bag a while longer, hoping that perhaps I could drift back to sleep. But I remained uncomfortably wide awake—and further aggravated by my level of consciousness.

Exhausted, I nonetheless decided that I should be the one to provide remedy for the hitch in everyone's giddy up. Clearing my throat and mustering as much twang as I could, I dug deep and channeled Brad Paisley: "Well, I love her…" I sang, pausing for several seconds before continuing, "But I love to fish."

A few chuckles came in from surrounding tents. Someone groaned, "Oh my God."

"I spend all day out on this lake, and hell is all I catch. Today she met me at the door, said I would have to choose. If I hit that fishin' hole today, she'd be packin' all her things, and she'd, be gone by noon…" I trailed off and could hear Brad's wailing guitar trail off behind me. It was time to cap it off: "Well, I'm gonna miss her," I sang, garnering a few more laughs and a few pleas to, "Oh, for heaven's sake, stop." I felt better, anyway, and whether or not others did, there did at least seem to be a bit more energy. At 6:30 a.m., we had all day before us—and our only planned activity was our group's mandatory race check-in meeting at noon. Motivation would be difficult during a day that had no purpose but to stand between us and the start of the race.

Wandering around the camp, I decided to check in on some other friends. In the clutter and disruption of our arrival the day before, I had not had the time to see where everyone had been put. The Dreamchasers group (the folks from the U.S., Canada, and Australia) had been assigned to ten tents in two rows. Starting at Tent 80, I slowly walked by, peeking my head in to see which faces I recognized.

Two tents from mine I found Andrew, a twenty-one-year-old college student from Tennessee. We had shared a hotel room in Ouarzazate for three nights before the race, so I had taken a special interest in him.

With the exception of a ten-mile "fun run" organized by a local fraternity, Andrew had never run a race before. That experience had ended with beer drinking, whereas our days would end with a specially formulated recovery drink in powdered form. In the few nights before being bused to the desert, we had talked about our respective training regiments. It certainly seemed that he had prepared well, having completed several training runs of more than thirty miles with a backpack weighing more than thirty pounds. Though he had never signed up for other races, he did not appear to have taken this event lightly, even taking the time to vacuum-seal his food for the week in order to save space.

By the time I had reached Andrew's age, I had run only two races: the 1997 and 1998 editions of The Big Sur International Marathon. I had trained for both, but I knew absolutely nothing about running. I neither drank nor ate anything throughout both races, and both years I spent a week afterward relearning how to walk. The thought of a thirty-mile training run with a heavy backpack would have been absurd to me. I marveled at Andrew's will and preparation. He had flown thousands of miles to conquer the world's toughest footrace, spending months preparing himself to do something that, at his age, I would have derided as being positively insane.

I was also impressed by Andrew's genuine, collected demeanor. He had not come to the desert on a macho bet or to conquer anything. His reasons were as simple, but determined, as any of the rest of ours: to finish the race and learn something more about himself in the process. He showed me a Frisbee that his friends had signed to wish him good luck, and he told similar stories of having been made fun of in a respectful, almost reverent way. I saw nothing of myself in him; in fact, it occurred to me that he made a much more enjoyable companion to us than I would have been at twenty-one.

"How're you holding up?" I asked, seeing his eyes through the mummy hole of his sleeping bag.

"Oh, man," he moaned. He looked up and offered a disgusted expression. "I slept horribly; this chest-cold-cough thingy kept me up all night."

I winced a little. For the past few days he had made casual references to a bug that he had picked up on the plane from New York to Casablanca. It had seemed to subside somewhat, but it was obvious that his first night in the desert had allowed the sickness to reassert itself.

"Sorry to hear that, Andrew," I offered. He knew that my greatest fear for this race was the unknown—that a force outside of me would somehow prevent me from finishing the race or performing as well as I had trained for. I was less scared of the heat and mileage than I was of spraining an ankle or popping a knee. Getting a chest cold certainly fell into that category, and I had nothing but sympathy to offer him: "Just try to rest as much as possible today, and hopefully the adrenaline will cure everything by morning."

"Thanks, man. I'm sure it'll be fine," he offered, yawning and still rubbing his eyes. I told him that I would see him at breakfast and then continued walking to inspect other tents.

I next found George and Leigh, two good friends who traveled around together to run the world's most grueling ultra-marathons. I had met them both at a running camp in Death Valley six months prior, and I remembered being simultaneously intimidated and impressed by them. I had traveled to Death Valley to learn how to run longer distances, and they were telling stories of their countless 100-mile finishes. Just this past February I had met up with them again—this time in Texas for the Rocky Raccoon fifty-mile race, our way of preparing for the Marathon Des Sables. They were just as mythical the second time around: capable, determined, accomplished, and unwavering. My first-ever fifty-mile run was "just another fifty" for George and Leigh.

An ex-Army man in his fifties, George had been recalled during our post-September 11 wars. I could imagine him in Afghanistan with kids half his age. I could imagine them whining from a long march, sore feet, or aching backs, and I had no doubt that George would have quietly plodded along. He does not look like an ultra-runner: shorter and stockier, determined but quiet. In both Death Valley and Texas, I had concluded that he was one of the tougher men alive, but he would never admit to it. Rather, he remained understated. It was as though he saw his role at these events as being to provide comfort and protection to his good friend Leigh. He came to cheer her, not so much to run himself.

Other than an equally accomplished running resume, Leigh

was a mirror opposite. She was in her forties and talked about her grown children, but she could easily pass for a twenty-something. Even this morning, after a night of sandstorms, she looked ready for a photo shoot. Wearing her running skirt and a stylish top, she had fashionable hair that belonged in a shampoo commercial. I could not be sure, but she even seemed to be wearing makeup. Had I not seen her 100-mile finisher belt buckles and heard George's stories of her triumphs, I would never have believed that she was a running machine.

"Well, Ted!" Leigh yelled, enthusiastically. "Did you come to visit us?" Just hearing her enthusiasm was enough to wake me.

"I did, in fact," I responded. "How is everything going for you two?"

"Oh, fine," George offered. I was confident that I would get the same understated response whether he had just won the lottery or been informed that he had contracted a life-threatening illness.

Leigh's reaction seemed more human, more in-line with my experience: "Oh, okay. Last night was sort of tough, huh?"

But just as I had started to think again about the night's sandstorms, Leigh quickly changed the direction of the conversation.

"I'm trying to decide which top to take," she said exuberantly. She had a few articles of clothing in her hands and was half pointing to the shirt she was wearing. Here we were, a day away from what was to be the most brutal week of my life, and Leigh was not just unfazed, but consumed by an entirely different line of thought. I couldn't help but laugh out loud. I noticed George roll his eyes.

"Leigh, I just can't help you," I chuckled. Her earnest eyes made me laugh even more.

"But I want to make sure I look good during the race," she pleaded. She was smiling but very much sincere, not wanting me to in any way diminish the importance of proper race fashion.

Her line of thinking was a luxury, I thought. Neither she nor George had any doubts that they would finish the race. Having completed so many ultra-marathons, this was just the next challenge.

They knew how their bodies would feel after seventy, eighty, or ninety miles. Sure, the Sahara had heat and unpredictable terrain, but Leigh had seen and done enough that she no longer had to worry herself with the details that consumed mere mortals.

I was a considerably faster runner than both of them, but I was much less certain about my destiny. Sure, if I finished I would finish faster than them. If I finished. I knew that there was a possibility that I would hit a wall. My mind kept fixating on the race's road book and the ominous dunes a mile away, but here Leigh was concerned with looking her cutest. It was certainly a refreshing break from my obsessions.

"You're hilarious, Leigh," I responded. We chatted a while longer about our anxieties and perspectives on the event. Eventually, I left them to pack and repack their backpacks, the last remaining entertainment prior to our group's noon check-in.

As I traveled around to the rest of our group's tents, I found that most of the folks I knew were in two other tents. Jay, our dad for the week, shared a tent with a number of Marathon Des Sables veterans: Toby, an Englishman with an exceptional, albeit at times disgusting, sense of humor; Terry, who was back after finishing the previous year; Ed, who had returned after a year off; and Mark, another Brit who was a world-class 10K runner and marathoner but who had been forced to withdraw from the MDS two years earlier. There was Laurie and "Trader Jeff," and of course "Bunny" (Marianne DeMarco), who had become somewhat of a blogging legend during the run up to the race. Her postings to various running forums had offered us a unique look into what happens to a person's psyche when her toenails begin to fall off during training. Her dry and outrageous sense of humor left us constantly waiting for what would come next.

We all shared a nervous anticipation, a desire to get started. But each of us was dealing with the day before a bit differently. The more neurotic among our group continued to pack and repack their backpacks, checking to make sure that they could locate the mandatory race items (a lighter, safety pins, compass, snake bite kit, disinfectant, knife, aluminum blanket, flashlight, batteries, sleeping bag, signaling mirror, whistle, and a minimum of 2,000 calories per day). With only a few hours until mandatory check-in with the race officials, obsessive personalities wanted to make sure, make sure, make sure, and make sure that they were in compliance with all of the rules.

The more relaxed of the group simply relaxed, lazily lying on their sleeping pads and awaiting the call to breakfast. A few left their tents to explore the bivouac, and a few more adventurous souls had decided to make the mile walk to Erg Chebbi, hoping to learn something about the feared dunes that would confront us the following morning.

That was my morning—a seemingly endless drift. I wandered from place to place, as though I could avoid emotions by visiting and observing others'. In this manner, I managed to pass the entire morning before arriving back to my tent shortly before noon. None of my tent mates was present, so I picked up my backpack and headed for check-in, hoping to beat the rush.

After speaking with race veterans, I had built up check-in as a grinding experience. I had expected the French race officials to scrutinize me for being an American. Though I had brought more than 3,200 calories per day and had a pack that weighed 7.5 pounds more than the required 14.3 pound minimum, I was prepared to need to justify every item that I was carrying.

"That's freeze-dried lasagna, 560 calories."

"Those are Pop-Tarts, 400 calories."

"That's one and a half ounces of macadamia nuts, 365 calories."

"That's an ounce of crushed potato chips, 150 calories."

"Knife? Yes, right here in the left-side pouch, underneath my Band-Aids and next to my lighter."

"Spare batteries are in the right-side pouch underneath four pair of spare socks."

"I not only have an EKG with the required trace form, but I also have a seventeen-page stress echocardiogram with a full review, performed by a cardiologist and with a complete release."

As I tramped across the dusty plain, I worried endlessly. I had trained for the better part of a year, flown thousands of miles, and spent thousands of dollars. And yet, all of my preparation could be ruled irrelevant at race check-in: If someone disapproved of my gear or a doctor disliked my EKG, I would end up playing less of a role in the 2008 Marathon Des Sables than the camel munching brunch outside the registration tent.

I walked into the race organization's tent, offered my name, and was given a tag with my bib number: 466. It was then that I noticed that the ABC crew had been following me, no doubt in hopes of capturing my impending arguments with the medical personnel. But all of my obsessions and preparations were for naught; I cleared the entire process in fewer than ten minutes. My bag was weighed, but never checked for compulsory items. The doctor asked me if I had trained and was satisfied when I mentioned my coach's name—Lisa Smith-Batchen, who had won the race in 1999.

And that was it. After months of gathering the lightest possible compulsory items that I thought would pass muster, I was cleared to run without a single challenge. I emerged from the tent, and ABC followed. No doubt there must have been some disappointment at the lack of any challenge from the race officials, but we spoke a while before they returned to the tent to capture other Americans' check-ins.

I went for a brief walk into a dusty clearing. With nothing but the food and clothing on my back, it was now official: I would step up to the starting line the following morning with the full approval of the race organization. I had flown thousands of miles, trained for months, and obsessed, and yet I had been unnecessarily prepared for a last-minute fight to convince them to allow me to run. I was relieved at the simplicity of the check-in process but also somewhat disappointed, as though I had been robbed of something into which I had invested so much emotional energy. Standing alone in the dust, staring at rock flats and sand dunes, I felt a sense of completeness and finality. For so long this experience had been a future event, but that moment served as the ideal time to reflect on my training runs, trips to my local sporting goods store to purchase clothes, and the pain that I had endured to get here.

It was peaceful. It was blissful. It felt right. I walked back to Tent 77, marveling at how far I had come and how much farther I would travel during the following week.

"Well, that sure was a piece of cake, huh?" I asked as I entered my tent.

There was a pause; something seemed amiss. I looked at Andrea, Jeff, and Michelle, and they just looked back.

"Not so much, actually. They're not going to let Karen run," Andrea said. "There's something wrong with her EKG and whatnot, and she's having to fight them right now to try to be allowed to run."

I had known Karen all of a day, but Andrea's words pained me. It was as though a piece of me had been stolen. None of us had to know Karen well, for we all knew that she was one of us: a slightly crazy runner who found satisfaction in punishing her body beyond sensibility. From the moment that we arrived at camp, our tent represented ourselves; it would not just be where we slept, but also where we derived our support. We were all emotionally invested in each others' success; failure of any sort would remind us of our own mortality.

"Geez, do we know what her chances are?" I asked.

"Not really," Jeff interjected. "She's arguing with them. They had to redo the test, but they're haggling over the results. She's 100% okay with them giving her an hour penalty for having to redo the EKG, but she just wants them to let her run." This was another of those terrifying, outside-of-oneself obstacles that I had discussed with Andrew during the past few days. Karen had trained and was ready. All she wanted—all any of us wanted—was to be allowed to fail or succeed on her own merits.

"What a nightmare," Jeff concluded.

"A total nightmare," Andrea agreed.

We sat in our tent, mostly in silence. We waited. My mood and perspective had been robbed from me. Only minutes before I had reflected and reached a blissful state. I now felt sick. We all needed each other; it was all that we had to hang onto for that week. I felt bad for Karen, and I felt a bit guilty as well. It could have been any of us, I guess, but we had been lucky enough not to have had our paperwork and supplies examined in detail.

So, we sat, with no breeze, as the temperature topped 100 degrees.

A few bodies shuffled outside our tent, but we just waited, contemplating how it would feel to be in Karen's situation. How would it feel to have traveled from Canada to the Northern Sahara? How would it feel to have spent thousands of dollars on an entry fee and thousands more on equipment? How would it feel to have neglected friends for months on end? How would it feel to have climbed mountains, completed day-long training runs, and to have braved the world's most brutal cold—and then have a doctor inform you that you were not healthy enough to compete?

What seemed like an eternity passed, with the heat seeming to stretch each minute into an hour. Mid-afternoon, Karen appeared at the tent, her face shiny from exhaustion and little beads of sweat. Her normal demeanor—that smile and those rosy cheeks—was missing. More than anything, she just seemed tired, broken, and defeated.

"How did it go? I mean, what's the story?" Jeff asked tentatively.

Georgia spoke at the same time: "Are they gonna let you run?" She had a more optimistic but simultaneously desperate tone; she needed to know.

"Well, whatever, yeah," Karen said, exasperated. It was not the tone that we had expected from someone who had been successful in convincing race officials that she should be allowed to compete. But she immediately changed moods and began speaking rapidly.

"I had to go over to the medical tent because they wouldn't accept my EKG, and they needed the trace thing, which my doctor wouldn't give me. So, I said, 'Whatever,' and I just told them to give me the penalty, but they said that they needed to redo the test as well. It was this whole ordeal that they made me go through, and this doctor finally got around to doing the test, and when he finished, they didn't want to approve me to run. There they were, talking in French, and I understand a lot of what they're saying, and I'm pleading with them that there's nothing wrong with me, but they don't want to hear any of it. So, they're talking in their committee, thinking about not letting me run. But finally they approved me, and I got the one-hour penalty. I don't know. I'm just so frustrated. And tired. That was so horrible; I shouldn't have had to go through that. I'm just mad at them for making it so difficult."

We sat there a little stunned. She had spoken so rapidly that we all were repeating the monologue in our heads to confirm that it was in fact good news.

"That's great," Jeff said. It was almost a question as he looked to Karen for confirmation.

"I guess, I guess," she said, giving the rest of us confidence to congratulate her.

"That's *great* news."

"All right, you're in! You're in!"

"Congratulations, Karen."

At that moment, the temperature seemed to drop just a bit, and a slight breeze picked up. Our moods improved noticeably, but we felt exhausted—emotionally drained. The previous night's sandstorm had been tumultuous, but this had been our first true crisis. We enjoyed our reprieve, even though we knew that it really was the precursor to the following morning's chaos.

It was late afternoon, meaning that we still had some time before a mandatory meeting with race officials. I decided to take a stroll.

Certain that he would be able to lighten my mood, I was planning on visiting Toby (the affable but raunchy Brit who traveled with the Americans). Yet, on my way, I became distracted by a conversation I overheard between Ed and Terry, two race veterans who had provided me incredible advice in the run up to the race. I heard one of them say "Elastoplast," the name of an ultra-sticky medical tape designed to adhere to one's body for a week or longer. Many competitors had pasted it on various parts of their bodies to reduce chaffing. I thought about the open sores that I had developed on my spine and waist while training and decided that it might be a good idea to take precautions.

"Hey, Terry!" I yelled. "Did I hear you say 'Elastoplast'?"

Terry looked my way. "Yeah. Do you need some?"

"Well, I was thinking about it. How exactly does it work?" I knew that I would develop sores without it, but I was concerned about trying something new before embarking on the longest run of my life.

"It stays on for an entire week," Ed promised. "So, once you get it on, don't expect to get it off. It's super painful to remove," he continued. Terry noted that it does exactly what it was designed to do—but, like Ed, cautioned me that it should not be removed until the end of the event.

"I've got the spray if you want it," Ed offered. He held out a two-ounce spray bottle of orange liquid. "You spray this on before putting on the Elastoplast. It makes it stick even more." It felt a little like an after-school special: Cool kids Ed and Terry were offering me "the stuff," and I needed to decide if I was going to run with the popular crowd.

Remembering how painful it had been to run with open sores around my waist, I decided to give it a try. I cut an eighteen-inch strip of Elastoplast and then asked Terry if he would mind placing it down my spine. The orange liquid felt cold on my back; I felt a tingle as the tape was laid on top. Terry smoothed it over and then told me not to bend my spine for a few minutes.

I then measured out a longer strip for my waist. After spraying myself, I attached one end of the tape to the front of my right hip. Then I strapped it around my lower back and over to the front of my left hip. I handed the little bottle back to Ed and the roll of Elastoplast back to Terry.

"What do I do now?" I asked. The after-school special was

continuing: I, the novice, had agreed to try "the stuff," and now I was waiting to see what would happen to me.

"Reach back and try to remove the tape from your spine," Terry suggested. Both he and Ed wore smiles. I tugged, but the tape remained in placc. "It's not going anywhere, right?" Ed asked, a smug satisfaction in his voice. They were right: I felt confident that, for better or worse, the Elastoplast would not be going anywhere.

Proud of my new accessory, I jogged back to my tent to model it for my tent mates.

"Very sexy," Georgia said sarcastically. All I could see were the two strips curving around my waist. I could tell by the chuckles that the white strips down my back looked ridiculous.

As I was getting ready to replace my shirt, a race official walked by and announced that it was approaching five o'clock, which meant that it was time for our mandatory meeting in the middle of the bivouac.

We rose and shuffled toward a worn Jeep with a platform atop it. Music was playing.

Patrick Bauer, race director, stood perched atop the Jeep with a translator. Hundreds of runners had begun to congregate around them, and he yelled in French that everyone should move closer; we understood when his companion repeated the same instruction in English.

"You excited?" Jay asked. He had a beaming, little boy's grin. I was impressed that he still seemed to find the experience magical after ten visits.

"Getting there," I responded. It was the truth. My moods have always changed radically throughout a day, and being out in the desert had only seemed to cxacerbate the process.

"Toby!" I yelled, seeing the man whom I had tried to visit before getting distracted by the world's stickiest tape.

He smiled and nodded, giving me a pat on the back. He looked toward the Jeep and motioned with his head. A mischievous smile curled up. "Naughty Patrick" was all he said, his thick British accent making it that much funnier.

"What? The gal?" Something in my response must have set off an alarm of naïveté.

"Are you kidding me?" he asked. "She's not here just to translate. Are you kidding me? Listen." He paused, tilting his head lower in such a way as to suggest that what he was about to say could not possibly be refuted. "I've done this five years running, and why do you figure he's always got the same translator? Uh?"

I finally understood but decided that playing dumb would be funnier.

"Toby, maybe she's really efficient at her job, and they have good conversations."

He let forth a loud set of chuckles. "Right, bloody conversation. That's it. Bloody conversation!" He laughed some more, and I had started to feel better. Terry joined the conversation.

"You know, after last year, I'm convinced that she really runs the show around here."

"Oh, no doubt," Toby responded. "She's definitely in charge."

The music got louder, and I noticed two camera crews in our vicinity. One was ABC, which would serve as a bit of incentive to behave. The other was from Japan. They were following a Japanese pop star who had decided to embark on a different type of journey. As we had been loading our gear onto the buses back in Ouarzazate, we had wondered to one another how long the camera crew would tape his every movement. Thirty-six hours later, they were still following his every move.

"I saw them follow him to the bathroom earlier today," Terry said. It was very matter-of-fact, but a few of us could not help but chuckle. Toby laughed the most and was obviously primed for commentary.

"Look, I can't possibly imagine what they'd want that footage for, but they'd better get it now. 'Cause I can tell you that everyone's innards are going to change the bathroom experience very quickly." His tone and emphasis were hilarious. We had all either lived through what he was referring to or heard the stories of how runners' bowels can morph after days of eating gels, nuts, and freeze-dried food. "So, whatever shots they need for their footage, trust me: it's best to get 'em now."

The speakers up front thundered in French, and the translation told us that we were set to begin.

"Welcome, everyone, to the twenty-third edition of the Marathon Des Sables." The cheering was staggered into two groups: those who understood French, and those who waited for the English.

"We have broken some records this year! This year's race has 802 competitors, which is more than ever before in the history of the Marathon Des Sables." More cheering. I thought about friends back home who were shocked to learn that more than a dozen idiots would ever want to do this.

"But that isn't the only record that we've broken…" Her voice trailed off after stressing "we've." Both Patrick and his compatriot had large smiles. "This year's race also has the largest distance ever—more than 245 kilometers!" A collective groan rose from the crowd. It was Patrick's job to give us hell and ours to give him grief.

"There are competitors from thirty-two countries!" He proceeded to introduce the various national contingents, beginning of course with the Moroccans. It was not only the respectful thing to introduce the competitors from our host country, but he was also paying homage to the fact that two Moroccan brothers, Lahcen and Mohamad Ahansal, had won every year's race for more than a decade. With each country's introduction there was light clapping throughout but robust cheering from one section of the bivouac. Most countries had only a handful of competitors, which made it humorous to hear them try to cheer loudly enough so that all 802 of us could hear them.

The French and English each boasted a third of the runners, and their introductions were loudest. Though outnumbered, the Spanish and Italians were the most enthusiastic. We Americans cheered when introduced, and I was pleasantly surprised that we were not booed. With everything I had been told about other countries' perceptions of Americans, it was clear that we were all here for a common reason. Running would be our spiritual bond. For this week, a competitor's nationality would take a backseat to the prerequisite that mattered most: that we all share the same passions and insanities.

Once all of the countries had been introduced, Patrick informed us that this year's oldest competitor was a seventy-one-year-old Japanese woman; the youngest was an eighteen-year-old Italian running with his father. All of us, young and old, looked around at one another and shook our heads. We took comfort in being normal—at least with respect to age.

The excitement died down some as Patrick launched into the race specifics and then the rules of the race. He offered a laundry list of penalties—littering, failing to cross a checkpoint, taking extra water, taking an IV or other medical treatment, and so on. Finally, he cautioned against the unauthorized use of a flare gun, which we had all been given as a mandatory item during that day's check in. He invited a man to join him atop the Jeep.

"We are going to have a demonstration of the flare gun so that you know how to use it."

The man held the twelve-inch cylinder in his hand, pointing it outward. "It is very simple. First, point it away from yourself . . ."

"No," Toby yelled to the American group. "You point it at Jay's crotch!" Everyone around us erupted in laughter. Were it not for what had happened in 2006, it would have been an entirely inappropriate comment. But, given that year's events, it was actually a reasonable warning. That year, Marc, another Brit, had suddenly collapsed while running through dunes during the second stage. Jay just so happened to have been behind him, and he stopped to help. Marc understood enough to know that something was seriously wrong and that he could not continue the race. But he was evidently disoriented enough that when he and Jay went to fire the flare to signal for assistance, the flare was pointing in the wrong direction. Instead of reaching for the sky, the flare shot directly into Jay's shorts. Luckily there was no lasting negative fallout, so we could all laugh at the story now. But, even while laughing, I was convinced that Toby had in part brought it up to caution us. As funny as the story had been, it was a sober reminder that serious things could go wrong out in the desert.

"And you grip the bottom of the flare. You don't have to remove the cap on the top. All you do is turn the bottom of the flare a few times, and it will go off. Like this..."

Moments later, a mini rocket launched into the air. It was like a firework at a state fair, shooting thousands of feet high. When the race volunteers had handed me my flare, I had thought that it would function much like a roadside flare. I had assumed that it would burn bright red and send up smoke, serving as a signal for the race organization to send help. I had no idea that I would be running with something in my backpack that could literally kill someone.

The bright red light continued to burn as a little white parachute emerged. The light floated slowly downward.

"Uh, we are sorry," the translator said. "That was not the way to shoot off a flare. It is in fact very important that you do take off the cap before you shoot it off."

Nervous laughter trickled throughout. It had appeared that everything had gone just fine without having removed the cap, but each of us thought that it would be just our luck to do something wrong and end up with a fiery projectile in our private region.

"So, you first *remove the cap*," she emphasized as the man proceeded to launch another flare into the heavens.

With a few more announcements and a few more cheers, we were sent on our way and reminded that our final catered meal would be served in about an hour.

We started to scatter, but Clarissa and Bruno of ABC ran up and began frantically asking if we could all hang around. Following an hour of introductions, discussions of penalties, and botched flare demonstrations, most of us wanted a little alone time before heading to dinner.

"It's important," she emphasized. "Please, guys. I know that you're tired now, but we really want to get a 'before' shot now before the race begins. It'll only take a few minutes. We promise."

We agreed and walked across the bivouac and beyond the tents. Two clusters of Moroccan flags were to one side and the ominous Erg Chebbi beyond. To another side was a long, scraggly plain with sand and small bushes. Far into the hazy distance was a mountain. Just past six o'clock, the sun was low on the horizon. The cloud cover had started to get its color—oranges, pinks, and a touch of purple. As forty of us walked with ABC's camera crew beyond the tents, we quickly transitioned from peeved to serene. The desert, despite its unforgiving nature, really was beautiful.

Clarissa assembled us as a group, like a team photo, and had the camera capture a minute of tape. She then asked us to link arms and form a tight circle, looking inward. Matt, who would be behind the camera all week, stood in the middle of us, rotating at different speeds to get each of us. "As I pass by you, let everyone know where you're from."

"Alaska."

"Los Angeles."

"Atlanta."

"Colorado."

"New York."

The list went on and on. It provided incredible perspective. We had come from all over the United States to a little spot in the middle of Morocco. Looking around the circle at everyone's faces, I was happy and proud to be with such a good group of people. I realized already how much I was enjoying myself. Looking around the circle, participating in ABC's cheesy made-for-TV moment, I got something more: this race clearly was not only about the running, but also, the people with whom you run.

Those two shots only took ten minutes, at which point Clarissa dismissed all but five of us. She explained that while they would be taping everyone throughout the week, they would be focusing on a few of us so that they could profile individual characters. I was to be one of the five, and Clarissa asked me if I would go first.

She instructed me to walk ten feet into the distance, face the camera, and stay as still as possible. It was called a "still portrait," and it made me feel as though I was posing for a Wheaties box and that the American flag would be inserted into the background by the time the image was done. She then asked a few simple questions, and I was done. It was casual, and I still had somewhat of a magical feeling from the circle experience and the gorgeous landscape.

I walked back behind the camera and struck up a conversation with a few of the folks who had chosen to linger and watch ABC tape. A few people played with their butane lighters, which the race officials had given all of us that day as a mandatory item to carry. We watched as Clarissa Ward of ABC instructed Chloe on what to do. Chloe, with her deep tan and bleached blond hair, was radiating with the tan desert and the colors in the background.

"Clarissa!" I interrupted. She turned around abruptly, and everyone wondered why I was disturbing the taping. "I just wanted to ask if you guys are trying to include the naked guys rubbing themselves in the background of Chloe's shot."

A look of shock on her face, Clarissa swung back around. Everyone suddenly realized that, a few hundred meters in the distance were two men, independent from one another, standing completely naked in the desert. They poured water over the tops of their heads and rubbed their bodies with a washcloth.

"Oh my gosh!" Clarissa exclaimed. "Matt, they're not in the shot, are they?!" Everyone was laughing, and we all paused for Matt's evaluation.

"No, I think that you're okay. I've got everything focused in on the foreground, but that's good to know. I won't be panning out to get a shot of the landscape."

The laughter died down, and the taping continued. It was certainly ridiculous to see two naked men attempting to shower in the middle of the Sahara, but it served as a sober reminder of what we were to endure. Those two men, during the day when they had access to extra water, were trying to feel as normal as possible for as long as possible. It also was a harbinger of the behavior to come: when hungry, tired, dirty, and miserable, people lose their inhibitions and focus less on maintaining decorum.

Following a few more chuckles, a few of us walked back to our tents to make a few last-minute adjustments and grab our headlamps.

By nightfall the wind picked up again. As we walked to dinner, we covered our mouths and eyes to prevent sand from getting in. It was to be our last cooked meal, and though many of us had made fun of the food that the caterers had fed us during our first two days in the desert, we looked somberly at our soup, steaming pasta, stale bread, and cheese wedge.

It would have been nice to sit and talk, to enjoy the moment with one another and speculate on how the week would go. Instead, our energies were consumed by covering our food—and then eating rapidly so as to prevent the desert from stealing our last precious morsels.

Back at the tent after dark, we had learned something from the previous night. A few of us had chanced upon the Moroccans' tent, taking note of the way they had buried the sides of their tent in sand and rocks. It was ingenious, really. They had lowered a beam holding up the open sides of the tent so that the open tent flaps could reach the ground. Then, they had secured all but a very small opening to allow someone to exit in the middle of the night. We attempted to duplicate their efforts, using sticks and rocks to stir up enough dirt to cover the edges, hoping for a better night's sleep.

We listened to the wind howl and tried to get comfortable, but the ground was hard and our nerves were soft. As with the previous night, no one fell asleep quickly. Someone temporarily broke the silence by saying, "I can't believe that we've got to run tomorrow. I can't believe this thing is starting."

5
No Heart

"You've got blockage in one area, thickening in another. The most likely cause is a birth defect in your heart," my doctor said.

I simply stared at him. I had only had one prior experience with this physician, but he had shown himself to be of questionable competence the first time around. This gave me confidence; I knew that I didn't have a heart problem. The only question now was whether or not he would be signing my release form so that I could travel to Morocco in three weeks. Without an EKG and a doctor's release, I would not be allowed to compete.

He quickly gave me my answer: "This is bad. *Really bad.* There's not a doctor around who cares about keeping his license who would sign this form."

Though I knew from prior experience that his pigheadedness would prevent him from signing my release form, I thought that I needed to try.

"Well, Doc, I certainly don't want to try to teach you medicine, but I find it unlikely that I have any sort of heart problem. Given what I put my heart through on a daily basis, I can't imagine that I'm near keeling over. For example, I not only ran, but also won a fifty-mile race last month. Doesn't that sort of prove that I'm healthy?"

"Hey, the read-out doesn't lie," he said, thrusting the pink EKG trace out in front of my nose. "How would you explain this?" he asked, condescension and disbelief coating his words.

I was offended, but I tried not to further upset him. Yet, I did feel that I needed to make a point: "The rest of my family members are in medicine, not me. I see a piece of pink paper with peaks and valleys; do you really expect me to be able to interpret it?"

Less than half an hour before, his nurse had placed little pads all over my chest. As she avoided the sticky parts with her long fingernails, I had asked her how frequently she and her boss performed these tests. "Almost never" was her response. I was nervous at the time: *What if she makes an error?* I had thought. *Or what if the doctor's inexperience causes him to inaccurately interpret the results?* I put these thoughts out of my head, however, because I had heard time and time again from fellow competitors that getting a doctor's clearance was merely a formality. *These are simply the things that are required in today's litigious society.*

"I'm just saying," the doctor said, "that no doctor who wants to keep his license would sign off on this EKG. It's bad."

"You mentioned that," I mumbled. My tone was tempered. He had defeated me. I knew that I would not be walking out of his office with a race clearance.

"You know, a study was done with 500,000 people," he said. That number seemed a bit suspect, but he sure spoke with confidence—just like he had when he had told me that my leg was broken a few months back. "The study divided people into three groups: those who did no exercise, those who walked thirty minutes a few times per week, and those who exercised strenuously, like you. The study showed that the walking group reduced its risk of heart attack by 30% while the strenuous group increased its risk by 300%. That's why you see all those marathon runners having heart attacks out on the course."

I wanted to scream at him. Here I was being told by a man who was easily seventy-five pounds overweight that people just like me are dropping like flies. I thought about reminding him that he had misdiagnosed me with a broken leg six months earlier. But I realized that it was my fault for having returned to him for a subsequent medical opinion, so I decided to play along with his story instead of force a confrontation.

"Uh, yes, it happens," I said. "But, I've been to a lot of races, and this isn't exactly an epidemic."

"Anyway, you've got to get in and see a cardiologist. He'll want to run some other tests, and perhaps he'll conclude that you're able to run. But with just this EKG, there's no way."

"Okay."

"Lots of people who think they're healthy can have heart attacks."

"Okay."

"I'll work with the girls to get your insurance authorization, and then we'll call you."

"Okay, thanks, Doc," I said feebly. I mustered what sounded like a little sincerity and shook his hand.

As I walked out of the office, I had a myriad of emotions. I was angry at the doctor who, in two visits, had been so unaccommodating. And yet, as upset as I was at him, I was angrier with myself for having returned to his office after a poor first experience.

Panic began to set in as I realized that I would now need to find some other way to get clearance for this race. I was set to leave for Morocco in eighteen days, and with a week of upcoming travel for work, I didn't have much time to resolve the matter.

And, though I firmly believed that there was nothing wrong with my heart, a piece of me did wonder. What if something were actually wrong? What if I had lived thirty years and forty-nine weeks with a heart that was just waiting to explode? It seemed ridiculous, but I had read sad tales of others who had seemed perfectly healthy, only to drop dead of a heart attack, stroke, or aneurism of some sort.

What if?

As soon as I was in my car, I called my father. A practicing anesthesiologist for most of my lifetime, he could hopefully provide me some insight. I read him the numbers atop the EKG printout, and he said that nothing sounded particularly abnormal to him.

"Listen, dude," he said, using a mutual nickname that we had both started using before the word had become dorky. "I've seen a lot of EKGs, and while I can't give you a firm diagnosis without observing you, I'd suspect that everything is fine. You just need to see a cardiologist, and I'm sure this will be all cleared up quickly. Don't freak out. Just see the cardiologist."

I felt a little better. Throughout my life, my dad has always exhibited medical paranoia when it comes to his children. Countless times he had reminded me that Tylenol and alcohol should not be mixed. For the past fifteen years, every phone call concluded with a reminder to wear my seatbelt. So I felt better. If Mr. Paranoia was calm, I could stop worrying myself.

And stop worrying I did—until I arrived at the office. That nagging *What if?* kept ringing in the back of my mind. I decided to scan the EKG and send it to Bill, a Canadian doctor and fellow runner I had met during our preparation to run the Marathon Des Sables. I had an opinion from a Texas doctor (my father), where hearts are continuously under attack from the world's best barbeque. I figured that Canadian hearts were mostly the same as American ones. It was worth the risk.

Bill's evaluation was mostly the same as (though much more detailed than) my father's. "Honestly, Ted, I can't understand why he's concerned. While there could be something wrong, everything looks fairly normal for an athlete." He had typed out in great detail all of the potential problems but offered the same conclusion: "Just see the cardiologist, and this will get cleared up."

My panic subsided—or most of it, at least. There was nothing wrong with my heart. That much was settled. However, I still had the matter of getting cleared to run during one of the eleven business days during which I would be in town prior to my departure.

It was difficult to concentrate as I waited for the nurse's call. My mind began drifting, as often is the case, to the societal and political ramifications behind the chaos.

With both parents as doctors, I've seen and heard a great deal about the impact that HMOs have had on the declining quality of our health care over the past twenty years. No longer can I get the tests my doctor recommends—unless the insurance company approves them. It was government intervention in the 1970s that led to our current system of health care—one where individuals are separated from the costs of the services they receive—and now we're hearing calls for the government to "fix" things by nationalizing medicine.

As silly as it may sound, these were the musings of a man who had just been told that he had a heart defect and might not be able to participate in an event with two years of preparation behind him. Most people would likely be fixated on a potential health problem, but I drifted down the path of examining the idiocy of our politicians—those with so little understanding of economics that they would propose legislation that would not only wreck the world's best health care system, but also bankrupt our society. Brilliant.

After a few hours, I had received my HMO blessing and immediately called the approved doctor. Monica, the cardiologist's assistant, had already spoken with my doctor's assistant and was ready to spring into action.

"Okay, Mr. Archer. Dr. Gold wants to order full blood work, a stress EKG, a chest X-ray, and another cholesterol test."

"Another?" I asked, unaware that I had ever had a cholesterol test and shocked at the list of tests that I was to endure.

"Yes, he felt that, given your recent high cholesterol test, family history of heart attacks, and your high risk of a heart attack now, that you should have a full workup."

"Uh, okay, Monica. I certainly don't want to step on Dr. Gold's medical toes, but I think that there has been a misunderstanding. I didn't have a high cholesterol test, and I don't have a family history of heart attacks."

"Really?"

"Really."

My head started spinning. I felt as though I were back in

elementary school, sitting in a circle with Mrs. Nash and a group of my classmates playing a game of "telephone." Just as Mrs. Nash's message had become grossly distorted by the time each of us students had whispered it to the next, Dr. Gold had somehow received a warped medical history that more closely represented a 400-pound, seventy-four-year-old man than a guy who can run back-to-back-to-back-to-back-to-back-to-back-to-back-to-back six-minute miles. Try as I might, I could not understand how my doctor's office could have transmitted that information.

"Ted, can you hold on just a moment?" Monica asked.

"Sure," I said, assuming that she had another call to answer. It was several minutes before she returned.

"Okay, I've spoken with Dr. Gold, and now that he understands what is going on, he'd like to do the stress EKG and go from there."

Relieved, I thanked her. Everything seemed to be falling into place. Dr. Gold was a reputable guy who not only knew the human heart, but also had experience working with a number of athletes. If my heart were abnormal because of my fitness level—but still 100% healthy—he would be the perfect guy to make that judgment. My thoughts began drifting back to Morocco—back to the images of dust-coated runners, mile-high sand dunes, oppressive heat, and the inter-lingual friendships that would be formed as we suffered together through the world's toughest footrace.

"So, how soon do you want to come in to get this done?" Monica asked.

"Immediately," I responded without hesitation.

"Okay, well, the soonest I can get you in is April 1. Will that work?"

If I had actually been at risk for a heart attack, I surely would have died that instant. April first was to be the third day of the race—and about two weeks too late for me to participate. Being placed on the waiting list was little consolation. Panic again ensued as a flurry of thoughts swirled around my head. I needed to find another doctor, outside of my insurance network, and just get this procedure taken care of.

For the ensuing two days, I asked family and friends if they knew doctors in the area, at Stanford, in Sacramento, or even in Idaho and Arizona. I was prepared to travel anywhere, so long as the doctor in question was a cardiologist and was willing to see me immediately. In fact, I even Googled "Doctors in Tijuana," thinking that perhaps I would be reduced to heading south of the border and exchanging greenbacks for a less-than-reputable medical consultation.

When the phone rang Thursday afternoon, I had not yet finalized my fallback plan.

"Ted, this is Monica from Dr. Gold's office. We've had a cancellation for tomorrow morning if you'd like to come in." I enthusiastically accepted.

When I arrived the following morning, McDonald's bag and coffee in hand, Monica scolded me for drinking coffee. She was nice about it, but my already fragile mind-set began to crumble again: *What if I've screwed up the test results because I had a cup of coffee with breakfast?*

I walked back into the office with the nurse who had been tasked with readying me for my stress EKG. After taking my pulse and blood pressure, she pulled out a razor and asked me to remove my shirt. Unlike Tuesday's EKG, this version required some spotty chest shaving. I could not help but think about Brad Paisley's song, "I'm Still a Guy," and the number of times I had told my girlfriend, "I don't do pedicures and manicures and hair coloring and all that stuff; I'm still a guy."

I mentioned the exchange to the nurse, noting that she was setting me up for a little well-deserved ridicule when my girlfriend found out that I had shaved my chest.

"Oh, I totally understand," the nurse said. "I went out on a first date with this guy recently, and he actually took pride in telling me that he's a *metrosexual*. Let's just say that was also our last date."

During nerve-wracking times, humor is by far the best medicine. I was glad for both of us and told her, "Yeah, you definitely don't seem like you deserve that. No woman should have to date a *metrosexual*."

After she had attached a dozen or so wires to my chest and

strapped a belt with a plastic monitoring box to my waist, she looked up nervously and said, "So, we're, uh, not yet ready for the test, but we sort of need this room. Would you mind waiting in the lobby until we're ready?" I looked down at my bare chest, the cords seemingly coming out of each rib.

"Sure, why not? I mean, you've covered the shaved parts with those pads, so nobody will see what you've done to me."

I took a seat in the lobby, where a feeble man with a walker grinned and said, "Nice get-up."

"Shoot," I responded, "this is next fall's hottest fashion trend. You're getting a preview today."

The test itself was fascinating. Not only was I asked to run on an inclined treadmill with cords flopping around, but I could see two giant machines with images of my heart, beats per minute, a cardio trace, and more. As my heart rate climbed, I treated it like a video game: *How high will it go?* The machine indicated a target heart rate of 160, which I reached after about ten minutes. My legs began to burn at an incline of 20% and 6.5 miles per hour.

During my entire training schedule for this race, my coach had encouraged me not to tire myself out during strenuous uphill sections. Instead, she advised, I should walk briskly and use the opportunity to recover so that I would feel better when I resumed running. Though it seemed absurd to me at first, she had slowly broken me down. The pain required to run uphill at a 20% incline was rapidly becoming uncomfortable. After sixteen minutes, I presumed that they had plenty of data and elected to stop.

As I waited in Dr. Gold's office to discuss the results of the test, I couldn't help but chuckle. I would have my results in moments, and this whole scare would be over. My form would be signed, and I would be cleared to fly to Africa and punish my body in ways that no sane person ever contemplates. Of course, if Dr. Gold refused to clear me, the frantic process would begin anew later that morning.

"So, you're going to run 150 miles through the desert, huh?" Dr. Gold asked, a simultaneous sense of wonder and derision in his voice. He smiled and shook his head, "That's just crazy."

"I've been called worse," I said.

"Oh, don't misunderstand me; I'm sure you have," he shot back, his lips curled into a wry smile. Now *this* was my kind of doctor. "I've reviewed the test results, and you're absolutely, 100%, positively healthy. As many reasons as I could give you not to run that race, your heart isn't one of them."

"Excellent." I would have a signed form *that day*! This entire ordeal was done. My panicked calls to my father, e-mails to friends and family to find other doctors, and even my plans to head to the land of Tequila for medical advice—all could come to an end.

"So, this race form wanted a regular EKG," the good doctor said while reviewing the documentation I had handed him. "Out of curiosity, why did we do *this* test?"

I recounted the tale of my primary care physician, the discussion of blockage, the purported thickening of the heart wall, and the likely birth defect. As I spun my tale, Dr. Gold's eyes widened and disbelief coated his face.

"Has your doctor *ever* seen a heart before?"

6
The First Stage

I can only describe that Saturday night in the Moroccan wilderness as the longest of my life.

We had thought that a few pounds of sand and a cadre of fist-sized rocks would be adequate to prevent nature from penetrating our fortress, but we were sorely disappointed.

I awoke in total darkness to a mouthful of sand. The sides of the tent flapped incessantly in the wind. *Thwap! Thwap! Thwap-thwap-thwap-thwap-thwap!* I could see nothing as I opened my eyes, but sand instantly stung and forced me to close them. Blind, I grasped around until I could feel my glasses. Race veterans had stressed the importance of having foam-lined glasses with light-adjusting lenses so that I would be able to see in a sandstorm. As I slipped them on, I appreciated having spent the $135.

I slipped on my flip-flops and walked out into the night. The cloud cover meant no moon or stars, just an eerie white glow overhead. I turned on my headlamp and began fidgeting with the sides of our tent, taking time to repack the sides into the dirt and rocks that we had readied the night before. As the night wore on, I heard three other tent mates arise to do the same thing. None of us succeeded.

B1
K0,9
K1,2
187°
K3,3
K4
140°
154°
N
W
E
S
Oued
Rheris
K8,5
Mekta
SFA
154°
CP1
K12
206°
195°
K19,8
CP2
174°
189°
180°
K23,3
B2

It was much more than the sandstorms that made the night interminable. I would have thought that one night's experience sleeping on the compact, rocky ground would have made it easier to sleep, but I noticed rocks that I had not noticed the night before. But, without question, the most unsteadying thing was the endless flow of the thoughts streaming through my head. The night was a buffer, an impediment to reaching the starting line. Mindless chatter, silly mental repacking, and replays of the previous months' training all swirled throughout my mind. I would drift briefly into a slumber, only to jolt myself awake in a panic that perhaps I had missed the starting gun.

The sun rose, and the slits of sandy light served as a warning that the Berbers would soon come topple our tent, leaving us exposed to the elements. People stirred early. A few whispered; others tore open food; yet others fired up compact stoves so that they could heat water. I saw little sense in getting out of my sleeping bag before it was necessary—especially since the night's sandstorm had not taken its cue from the previous morning. No, the wind raged on.

In due course, our tent was felled. With sun on my skin, I inched out of my bag and tried to ignore my shivers. Summoning Mr. Paisley had taken me a bit longer than on our first morning in the desert, but I figured that was to be expected given the conditions.

"Every time you take a sip," I sang, pausing. Something about the twang and ridiculousness of Brad's lyrics had me convinced that I would lean on him throughout this event.

"In this smoky atmosphere…press that bottle to your lips…and I wish I was your beer."

A few members of my tent wished me good morning. Someone across the way moaned, "Here we go again."

"In the small there of your back…your jeans are playing peek-a-boo…I'd like to see the other half…of your butterfly tattoo." A few more chuckles and a little more disbelief surfaced, but I needed to continue. I knew what was coming but could not stand the thought that it might not be spoken aloud.

I picked up the tempo and belted, "Hey, that gives me an idea: Let's get out of this bar, drive out into the country, and find a place to park! 'Cause I'd like to see you…out in the moonlight… I'd like to kiss you, way back in the sticks…I'd like to walk you… through a field of wildflowers…I'd like to check you for *ticks*!" I emphasized the punch line; only under such dire conditions could it be considered somewhat touching. I heard a few women laugh. Not far off I could hear someone wonder if that was how I wooed gals back home. *If only they knew.*

My attempt to brighten the mood was really an attempt to wake myself. It was the morning that the race would begin, and I had less energy than at any time during the past week. The day's stage, scheduled to start at 9 a.m., was nearly twenty miles and started with an eight-mile journey through Erg Chebbi, North Africa's largest dunes. A mile away, we had stared at them for two days. In the distance, they appeared somewhat placid, almost comforting. I knew that I would need all the energy I could get.

"Are you guys excited?" Karen asked matter-of-factly. She was shuffling through her pack, looking for something.

"I will be, I think," Andrea trailed off. She was distracted, also rifling through her bag. "I just don't know where I put my…ah-hah! My spoon for breakfast. I thought I had lost it."

"Hopefully this sand will die down before we hit the dunes, eh?"

"Yeah," Jeff chimed in. "This would not be fun in those dunes."

I was thinking less about the dunes or the sandstorm—which continued to pick up speed and make everything uncomfortable—and more about my decision the previous day to throw away a pair of long john's. After having spent the first night in the desert, I had decided that I would likely be warm enough throughout the event and would rather not carry the pound of extra weight. As I squatted and tried to pack my sleeping bag, I shivered. I could generously claim 6% body fat, and I had little to protect me from the chill.

"I just want the heat to kick in," I chattered. Others seemed to have been smarter about their clothing selections, but I knew that no one would claim to be comfortable. I pulled my buff out of my bag and slid it over my head. A long string of stretchable nylon, it could be bent and folded into various positions to protect oneself from the sun, sand, and wind. I pulled it such that it covered my neck, face, and the back of my head. Only my forehead and eyes remained uncovered, and the latter were protected by my glasses. My hope was that I could retain a little heat that way.

"You won't be saying that in a few hours," Andrea laughed. "You'll be asking for this weather to return, so enjoy it while you can." She was right in a way. The race had not yet started, but I had already begun to whine.

"After training in Canada all winter, this isn't so bad. It's a lot warmer than back home," Andrea noted. She was not trying to rub anything in, but my hometown of San Jose, California, was no place to prepare for inclement weather.

The race organizers had begun gathering in the middle of the bivouac. A large truck filled with water bottles stopped and was being unloaded. Jay, the American rep for the event, had warned us that these morning water distributions were mandatory. Failure to present our water rationing card and get checked by race personnel would mean a time penalty. Despite my pleasant check-in process the day before, I still viewed the French skeptically and worried that they would jump on any opportunity to penalize an American competitor.

"I'm going to go grab water before the line gets long," I announced to my tent mates. "Anyone want to give me your cards, and I'll grab your water?" While the morning checkpoints were mandatory, we had learned that it was the card that was required—not the competitor. Everyone handed me their cards, and Michelle offered to go with me to help carry the bottles.

"Don't drink my water," Georgia warned, a joke in reference to my insatiable thirst.

The water distribution process was different this morning than it had been during our first two days in the desert. Previously, the race officials had just offered us bottles whenever we wanted them.

Now they were limiting the amount of water that each of us could take. One card, one bottle. Michelle and I handed over our tent's water rationing cards—three-by-two-inch white plastic with red squares denoting each checkpoint—and watched as the volunteers wrote our respective numbers on the bottle caps and sides. We recalled the previous day's warning about littering: any competitor who failed to deposit his bottle in a trashcan would receive a time penalty.

Michelle and I cradled the many bottles and returned to distribute them to our group.

Brendan had started eating, and Jeff thanked us with his mouthful of morning mush. There were still more than ninety minutes until the start, but I figured that I would eat the first half of my breakfast.

I had packed the same breakfast for all seven days: a package of Pop-Tarts and freeze-dried blueberry granola with milk, made by a company called Mountain House. I had sampled many of their dinners to decide which meals to bring, but I had never eaten their breakfasts. This would be, therefore, a critical test. If I did not like the granola, I would suffer for the duration of the event.

I added four ounces of water to the Ziploc bag and stirred. The powdery chunks turned into a blue-tinted, crunchy mush. I took a bite and was relieved; it was considerably better than I had expected. In fact, after finishing the bag, I turned it inside-out and licked the remaining contents.

"That's disgusting," Andrea laughed. I was a bit disappointed that she had caught me. I had justified in my mind that I needed the calories, but the truth was that I *really* liked it. However, the spoonfuls had been better than the lickings once the whipping sand had stuck to the bag.

I ate it anyway.

Ordinarily I would have thought that the morning of such an event would be filled with chatter, laughter, and excitement. But the strong winds had everyone struggling for security. People packed their bags and covered up any way they could.

A little more than an hour before the race was scheduled to start, I found myself sitting on the ground. Countless other runners in every direction were doing the same. I leaned against my pack with the wind at my back. I pulled my buff over my face and tucked my arms into my short-sleeved shirt. I shivered but tried not to think about anything. The wind and sand blew violently at my back, but I just sat, head down, and did what would become a pattern for me throughout the race: I passed time while thinking about absolutely nothing.

I returned to consciousness and noticed that the wind had subsided somewhat. I looked at my watch: 8:25. I was surprised that no one had yet headed to the starting line, where we were supposed to assemble in five minutes. I jumped up, grabbed my bag, and joined a few other Americans who were talking nearby. Thankfully the wind had become a frail, dying memory of its once powerful self.

"'Bout ready to do this?" Terry asked. Terry had run the race in 2007 and had offered me countless tips over the past six months. I liked him not just because of his stories, but also for the incredible energy that he radiated every time we talked. Whether we discussed running, sports, or politics, I felt alive around him.

"Yeah, let's do it," I responded. Still cold, I tried to shake the shivers.

"How do you feel?" Terry asked. He looked great—a smile and a look of confidence.

"We'll see, man; we'll see. I slept horribly, but we've just got to go on adrenaline, right?" I was trying not to bring down the mood, and I was trying to ready myself for the craziest thing I would ever do. Feeling a sudden rush of energy, I let a scream loose. It was invigorating.

About twenty of us from the American and Canadian group grabbed our things and started walking the few hundred yards to the starting line. I reached into my pocket and pulled out the second half of my breakfast—s'mores-flavored Pop-Tarts. Unlike most of my fellow runners, I had always enjoyed a large breakfast immediately prior to running. I would have preferred a four-egg omelet but settled for the 900 calories in the prepackaged way that I could get it.

Directly in our path, between the many Moroccan flags that we had seen during ABC's naked moment, was a ten-foot tall picture of Morocco's king. No doubt the race organization had decided that it would bode well for future visits if they honored the man who held their entry in his hands.

As I looked at his highness and his country's colors, I remembered a conversation I had with my boss a few months earlier. One morning he informed me that the Dakar Rally, a famous African car race, had been cancelled because of Al Qaeda activity in neighboring Algeria and Mauritania. "You'll be fine for your race, though," he informed me. "Morocco isn't Algeria; the king wouldn't put up with any of that."

I stared at the mural. I knew nothing of the man but was happy to be in his country.

Beyond the king was the starting line. It was a collection of inflatable white structures ranging from four to more than ten feet high. The highest were two cylinders that stood about thirty feet apart at the starting line. They were plastered with the colorful banners of sponsors: Kia Motors, Eurosport, New Balance. From each of these cylinders, smaller inflatable tubes shot away from the starting line, forming a conical entrance that would funnel the runners through the two cylinders. Off to one side was Patrick's Jeep, and he was climbing aboard.

"Quickly, quickly, quickly! Please get to the starting line and get close. We want to start at 9 a.m., but we have many announcements to make."

I looked back toward where our camp had been and saw hundreds of runners still trickling in.

Aerosmith played overhead. I grinned as I saw French and Japanese athletes singing along. I had come to North Africa, only to be haunted by Steven Tyler. Back at my office, our software engineers used *Aerosmith's Greatest Hits* as their test album. Even good music grows old.

"Good morning, runners!" the translator thundered overhead. Cheers followed. I had worked my way up to within five feet of the starting line, wedged between the elite Moroccan runners and the speakers. French may be a beautiful language, but that loud it was torture. Patrick droned on and on about the number of competitors, the details of the day's stage, and the location of the checkpoints. His faithful companion dutifully translated, and I listened whenever my mind had not drifted to a hollow place.

"We have three birthdays today!" she thundered, and I jolted back to attention. Race veterans had bemoaned the lengthy morning announcements; I thought they had been joking about the birthdays. Music started playing overhead, and hundreds of people who cannot speak English proceeded to sing "Happy Birthday." Other than the repetition of the words "happy birthday" in place of where we Americans would insert "dear Sally," it could have passed for being sung at a neighborhood Chili's restaurant.

A few more announcements followed, and then the music returned: AC/DC's "You Shook Me All Night Long." Last year's starting song was "Highway to Hell," but I realized that this was our countdown.

"Two minutes until starting!"

AC/DC thundered in my ear; my heart hit 100 beats per minute. I sipped some final water before tossing my bottle aside. Scanning the faces in the crowd, I recognized no one. The rest of the Americans and Canadians had remained farther back, and I was suddenly suspended between excitement and loneliness. Competitors closed in around me, stealing the remaining air. I dodged elbows.

"Thirty seconds!"

The music got louder, and my pulse got faster.

"Ten, nine, eight, seven, six, five, four, three, two, one!" The music continued to play, and we shuffled through the start. Cheers erupted behind me, but I focused intently on the event. My joking, my singing, my thinking—it all stopped immediately. During every long run I had ever done, I had learned to switch off my mind and go into autopilot. Part of it was an effort to conserve energy—unlike the Brit to my left waving a Union Jack and a set of ski poles—but part of it was a need to numb the mind.

My objective was to be one of the first fifty or so runners to reach the dunes. Having practiced running through sand dunes in Death Valley, California, I figured that only the top few runners would actually be capable of running. The rest of us would be relegated to a brisk walk—at least on the uphill sections. Other than the obvious difficulty of running in soft sand, there were two problems with dunes: 1) the more feet that had run over an area, the softer it would become, and 2) oftentimes there was only one efficient path through a particular area. This meant that being efficient often meant staying in a line with the other runners, preferably before too many had trampled the terrain.

I forced my breathing into a rhythm, inhaling for three steps and then quickly exhaling on the fourth. Able to open up my stride over the compact dirt, I made my way toward the front of the pack, reaching the base of the dunes in six-and-a-half minutes, less than 100 yards behind Mohamad Ahansal, the favorite. *How long can eight miles of dunes take?* I reasoned with myself that it would be in my best interest to stay ahead so as to benefit from the compact sand.

My first step sunk in six inches. My brisk pace immediately slowed to a pained trot. A full step forward routinely gave way to half a step back. Fewer than eight minutes into the race, my forehead was covered in sweat, and I could feel my hamstring, quadriceps, and calf muscles tightening as I pushed upward. They were rolling hills, ever so slightly edging upward. The few flat and downhill sections were critical to my psychological well-being.

The race organization's helicopter zoomed immediately overhead, too close to the ground to be safe but far enough not to blow the sand.

I had settled into a group of runners of similar ability. A small group of elite runners had pulled away, and the rest of us seemed content with the notion that if we were all together after ten minutes, we must be about the same speed. When one runner began walking an uphill, it gave the rest of us permission; when he started running a flat section, we scampered to keep up.

The monotony would have been monotonous had it not been so painful. After cresting each dune, a new ridge of taller dunes would appear in the distance. With each minute, the line of runners thinned, and I began to worry that the unvarying terrain would disorient me. I remembered Terry's promise that "You won't need a compass for the entire race. You'll be able to follow other people's footsteps." I could see three men in front of me—ten, twenty, and fifty yards away—and three more behind me at similar distances. I was determined to stay close enough to their footprints, and I decided to follow #320, who I would later learn was a Frenchman. No doubt he would follow the footprints of the men in front of him, I would follow his, and the men behind me would follow mine.

This worked well enough, and we climbed higher and higher dunes. The smaller, twenty-foot dunes gave way to fifty-, seventy-, and 100-foot monsters. With each cresting, I fully expected to look into the distance and see the horizon. But inevitably I was disappointed as the dunes continued their upward slant.

Almost an hour into the event, I had consumed nearly all of my water. I had sewn two half-liter bottles into the front of my backpack. Short straws bounced in front of me so that I could drink whenever I wanted. During my training runs back home, I had consumed an average of one twenty-four-ounce bottle per hour. Without knowing how far away the checkpoint was, I had nearly doubled that rate. I would need to slow down my drinking.

Ahead of me, #320 stopped at the crest of a tall dune and put his hands on his hips. He was taking in the view. He had reached the summit and could see the valley below.

I struggled with my last few steps to the top of the dune and noticed that two other runners had paused a few steps below him. The view was not what I had expected, however. We had indeed reached a critical summit with a valley below. We could see for at least a mile, perhaps two, but there was nothing but sand. There was no checkpoint, no salt flat, no bushes, and no valley. More disconcerting, we could see neither runners nor footprints.

An hour into the Marathon Des Sables, I was lost.

I looked in every direction, praying that I could pick up a trail. As five others climbed up behind me, the arguments began. One of the men, an Australian, spoke English, but he quickly told me that he had never run the MDS before and therefore had no ideas. One man spoke Spanish, but I struggled to understand his Castilian accent. From what I could tell, a few spoke French, one spoke Italian, and one spoke Portuguese. I communicated with the Spaniard, who relayed a message in broken Italian, who in turn relayed a message to the French contingent. The argument proceeded in this fashion, with voices rising and falling as someone wanted to get an international word in edgewise.

I stopped and shook my head. I was back in Mrs. Nash's class at St. Alban's Elementary School, once again playing the game of "telephone." It was a simple game to show us how quickly a message's meaning could be lost as it passed from one person to another. She whispered a message to one student, whose job it was to whisper the same message to another, and so on. We did our best, but inevitably the message had lost all of its meaning after being passed along a few times. I looked at the Aussie, the Italian, the Portuguese, the Spaniard, and the French. Then I laughed. We were the proverbial blind leading the blind, except that we were more dangerous because we each assumed that we could in some way communicate with the others.

"Forget this," the Australian yelled. He rose to his feet and started sliding down the dune. I looked around, nervous. Being lost was worrisome; being lost alone would be terrifying. Another man rose to his feet, shrugged his shoulders, and headed down the hill. Almost on impulse, I followed, convinced that the others would follow, scared like I was to get separated from the group. They did. None of us had any idea where we were, but at least we were together.

Nine lost people should be easier to find than one, I assured myself.

A few minutes later, we reached the bottom of the sand valley, which opened up more than we had expected. I could see a small, abandoned hut a few hundred yards to my left. Three more sat to my right.

I brought out my race book, remembering that the childlike drawings of each day's stage often identified when we would come into a town or see a ruin. I prayed that the drawing of Erg Chebbi would show a few scattered buildings just to the left or right of the prescribed course. Nothing.

Fifteen minutes following our mountaintop dispute, the dunes turned almost white. Instead of the towering golden peaks, we were running over rolling sand hills with spotty shrubs. Still no sign of others or their footprints, I began to seriously worry. I had but a sip of water remaining, and though I knew from experience that I could persevere for hours, this was precisely the sort of thing that my friends and family back home had assumed would happen. At the time, I had thought that they were unnecessarily concerned. Now, lost after seventy-five minutes of the event, their concerns made such perfect sense.

At that moment I saw the helicopter emerge from a ridge to the left. We had been headed in a different direction but immediately turned toward the copter. I assumed—or, rather, I hoped—that it had flown over the checkpoint before heading back into the dunes. I prayed as I ran faster, still unwilling to lose sight of my companions. Within moments the helicopter had flown by, but we continued to run toward where it had come from.

Ten minutes later we were climbing again. I paused on the way up and looked back into the valley. I could see the four little huts but not another runner outside of our group of nine. My water gone, I held my breath as I reached the dune's summit.

As I crested the dune, the colors changed. In the distance, there were deeper browns and rough color palates. A mile or two of dunes remained, but I could clearly see the checkpoint just beyond a series of smaller dunes. Relieved, I opened my second gel pouch and ate its contents. They tasted horrible, but they were quite effective at providing a boost of energy.

The volunteers at the checkpoint were animated but efficient.

As I approached, I heard my name and number being repeated: "quatre-cent-soixante-six." As I ran through, I pulled my water rationing card out of the left side of my backpack and grabbed my allotted water bottle from the volunteer.

When I had sewn the bottles into the front of my pack, I had done so with the belief that this would reduce the time that I would have to spend at each of the checkpoints. I had heard that many runners spent several minutes at each—not because they want to rest, but rather, because they are unprepared to continue. So, I had been determined to be as efficient as possible, hoping to spend a mere thirty seconds at each checkpoint. In practice, however, the process was more awkward than I had expected.

Unscrewing the bottles was disorienting. I looked down, trying to focus on the tops of the bottles, but they were too close for me to get an adequate perspective. Once I had loosened the tops, it was time to empty a bag of energy mix into one of them. I reached into my pocket and pulled out a Ziploc bag full of white powder, bit the corner, and then tried to empty the mix into the bottle's small opening. All the while, I was running and trying to watch my footing.

As I departed the first checkpoint, I looked at my watch: I had wasted three minutes and had been running for a total of 1:39.

After the dunes, the stage became rocky. At first, there were occasional pebbles that I could easily avoid. But the rocks multiplied and grew larger, to the point that I could no longer avoid them. In an effort to navigate them, I started prancing. I tried, unsuccessfully, to jump from place to place and find flat ground to place each foot.

It then opened up to an enormous salt flat—endless, packed sand with crusty white ridges. I was making good time now that I no longer had to fight the dunes.

By the second checkpoint, I had perfected my transition strategy, shedding a minute from the previous experience. But, nearly two-and-a-half hours into the race, I was tired. My legs ached, and I was psychologically wounded from the morning's ordeal. I was pleased that fewer than five miles remained. I could run briskly until I got to the final section of the day: another set of dunes.

My plan was immediately thwarted as I entered what the road book called "wadi." Relatively flat ground with occasional shrubs, wadi looked passive. But it was unpredictable. As I prepared myself to sink into the ground, I would hit compact, hardened terrain; when I tried to push off, I would sink into soft sand. During this short stretch, more than a dozen runners passed me. Though they had kept relatively close over the past hour, not a single runner had passed me since the dunes. It was demoralizing to watch one person after another stride by as I was fighting my footing. The wadi took pleasure in humiliating me.

The final dunes approached, which meant that only 1.5 miles remained until the day's finish line. I looked behind me and saw another runner 100 yards back but no one behind him. As I reached the base of the dunes, I saw a Jeep and two volunteers.

"Three miles more, that is all!" one of them yelled in a thick French accent. I turned quickly to correct her.

"You mean three kilometers, right?" After three hours in sand and rock, this was important.

"No, three miles—just under five kilometers," she said. My neck tensed; she had done the conversion correctly. Either she was mistaken, or the road book was wrong. As I looked up the dunes and could not see the finish line, I decided that it must be the latter. Deflated, I decided that I had only one task: I would not allow the runner behind me to pass. I would walk if he did but would sprint if necessary. The time difference and ranking would not matter, but I could not endure being passed by yet another competitor. In my weakest moment, I was making a stand.

I walked the uphill sections of the dunes but noticed that he was running them. I sprinted downhill and then realized that this more than compensated for his extra effort on the way up. Evidently I had something going for me on the downhill sections. He remained a hundred yards away, and I plodded along. Unlike in the first section of dunes, I could see footprints the entire way.

Following twenty minutes of using willpower to override my desire to stop, I reached the summit of a dune and could see miles into a valley. Below, a few football fields away, I could see the inflatable white structures that had been at the starting line. Just beyond was the bivouac—more than 100 black tents arranged in a horseshoe pattern.

I broke into a sprint. Though the ground was sandy and soft, I ran as much as possible. I could see the finish. Following more than three and a half hours and nearly twenty miles of running, I would be done. Exhausted, I turned around but could not see my threat. He would not catch me. I slowed and took a leisurely jog across the finish, where a five-foot-two-inch French woman called out to congratulate me: "Goot job, See-o-door," she said, her way of praising the American named Theodore.

I limped around and took stock of my body. I could feel some rubbing on both my back and feet. Determined to get out of the sun, I grabbed my day's final water ration and proceeded to the tent. It was 1:30 in the afternoon, the hottest part of the day. I worried about how my body would feel as it tightened.

But a funny thing happened: ten minutes after finishing the day's stage, I was once again energized. I had slipped into flip-flops and drank a recovery drink. Lying down, I found myself restless. I did not want to be there. I needed something else. I needed to be back in the race. I decided that I would return to the finish line and search for a shaded area to sit and cheer on my fellow runners.

There was no natural shade in the desert, but the finish line's giant inflatable structures served as a perfect barrier between me and the sun. I slid around the side and looked at a race organizer. The small French woman said hello again—"See-o-door"—and I asked for permission to sit on a wooden box just below a giant canopy. She agreed, and I sat and felt the gentle breeze against my face. It was the most comfortable I had been in days. How much we take for granted life's simple pleasures, such as a chair. Three days without any human comforts, and I was appreciating the impact that a comfortable position could have.

The runners drifted in. The gaunt man with an aching back winced, and I could see him back at home holding his children.

Life was good but predictable. The day-to-day tasks of going to the store and driving to soccer had turned family into monotony, and he yearned for something that he could hold onto when bored. He smiled as he staggered across; he had found it.

A French woman ran in but was clearly running away. As she crossed the finish line—that moment when she should have exalted in having conquered the most difficult opening in the history of the event—she still harbored resentment toward him. Had it been her weight? Her personality? Her career? She had been unwilling to accept that it had been his insecurities and infidelities—not something that she lacked. *I will show him.* Today had been a first step. Maybe, just maybe, the sand and the grime and the pain could cause her to stop hurting. Maybe, just maybe, her tent mates could stoke the embers that had so long ago hardened into coal.

A couple threw their arms into the air. They had bonded for thirty-one years, and this was only their most recent journey. He smiled at her, and she loved him back. The kids had graduated college, and they were using every last minute of the time they had left on God's brown earth to extract meaning.

I cheered friends and strangers, and though every emotion was different, we were all the same.

After a few hours, I headed back to the tent. I had seen Jeff and Brendan finish within moments of my arrival. Jay, Mike, Laurie, Michelle, and more trickled in. I returned to talk with them about their days. We chatted about the dunes, my getting lost, the heat, and our pride. The hardest parts were yet to come, but there was satisfaction nonetheless in having conquered the first stage.

By five o'clock everyone in my tent had returned, and we shared our stories. A few had taken more than twice as long to complete the stage, but in most respects we had experienced the same thing. It was a striking contrast to team sports, which I had played all my life. Teammates on the same field always had different stories, different experiences. Someone had scored, someone had sent an errant pass, and someone had stopped the other team's hero. But, as I listened to Andrea talk about her day, I walked alongside her.

She very well could have been telling my story.

Most Americans had returned, but we realized by early evening that Andrew had not. The youngest in our group, the twenty-one-year-old also had one of the heavier backpacks. I stopped by to talk to Jay and Terry, and we decided to investigate. The time cutoff for the stage had passed. We walked across the bivouac toward the finish line, hoping to speak to someone at the registration tent to learn if he had abandoned the stage, gone to medical, or was still struggling out on the course.

Trying to get an answer out of the race organizers was difficult. Aside from the fact that they spoke limited English (and we no French), they seemed to process information in a myriad of places. It took time to transfer information regarding penalties and withdrawals from checkpoint to checkpoint. We wandered from the registration tent, to the finish line, and then to the medical tent.

"He's at medical," Jay announced.

"What does that mean?" I asked. The race had two sets of medical tents—a preliminary check-in where anyone could go and a secondary set that was closed to anyone but the very sick. "Is he in there?" I asked, pointing to the check-in tent.

"No, he's back in the off-limits medical area."

"That's not good," Terry broke in. "You've got to be in pretty bad shape for them to take you back there."

"Well, not necessarily," Jay explained. "They might just have wanted to check him out and get him out of the heat."

Terry nodded and said, "Yeah, that's true. Hopefully that's the case."

"Uh, okay," I abruptly said. "Can't we figure out which of those options it is?" I was not mad, but a little impatient. I was not sure what I hoped to do or learn, but I very much wanted to know.

"Probably not. They don't usually let people back there." Jay was thinking. "You know what? Let me see what I can go find out."

Terry and I decided to wander over to the registration tent to check our day's rankings. The race officials typically posted results after a few hours' delay. I had finished twenty-ninth for the day.

"Twenty-ninth! That's really great, Ted!" Terry was not so much surprised, but genuinely excited.

"Yeah, wow," I responded. "That's pretty good." I was definitely surprised. I thought about the thirteen runners who had passed me in the wadi before the final set of dunes and realized that I must have emerged from Erg Chebbi in sixteenth place. Evidently getting lost had not been such a bad thing.

Jay returned from behind the medical tents and called out to us.

"He's all right, but he's not so good," he said. Both Terry and I looked at him, confused.

"What I mean is that he's going to be okay, but they're not sure if he can continue. Evidently, his feet are really bad, and he's really sore. They're going to keep him for a while longer and make a decision either tonight or tomorrow as to whether he can continue."

Back at the tent, I talked with my group about Andrew's situation. Just as we had worried about Karen's plight the day before, we felt as though a piece of us was at risk of being taken from us. When Andrew returned to his tent, he moved slowly. His face was white, and he just shook his head at me.

"Not good, man, not good. Rough day. We'll see, but tomorrow's not looking good."

"You don't have to decide tonight, Andrew," I counseled as I walked him back to his tent. "Eat a good meal, and tomorrow we'll cut down your pack's weight. Eat a good meal and get a good night's sleep."

I walked back to Tent 77 just in time to hear Karen talking about husbands—and why not to get one. Andrea chuckled along, paying homage to her boyfriend while simultaneously encouraging Karen's analysis. Jeff chided her a bit, and Georgia added a few kind words for our sex, noting that her Monte was a great man and father. Brendan, quiet most of the time, felt compelled to join in and playfully defend himself. Michelle and I, on opposite sides of the tent, sat quietly. Perhaps it was that neither of us had been married. Perhaps it was that both of us were in long-term relationships that were likely headed in that direction. Perhaps we were just feeling the effects of a long day. Or perhaps we had learned enough to know that there are some discussions that can never be won.

The night was dark and cold. The cloud cover returned, but thankfully there was no wind. I rolled over and then back again, my mind consumed by the rhythmic pounding of my feet against the rocky plain. California seemed so far away; I was uncertain if I even wanted to return. But that was a decision for another time. More than 130 miles remained.

7
Hometown Dunes

Leg over leg, swishing tufts of yellow dust puffed upward. It was not accustomed to human activity, and Bunny's legs were pound, pound, pounding away. She sank to the knee with each step. Her shoes temporarily locked into the earth, and she nearly fell forward before the mountain released her. The wheel of her body spun along, and her fists pumped forward. She ran with incredible speed, much faster than most of us had dared to travel. She was a machine—albeit one that rocked forward far enough with each step that her forehead nearly scraped the sand. She had traveled halfway down Death Valley's tallest sand dune, and we were all amazed that she had not fallen over.

She fell.

It was a majestic tumble. There was no warning, no loss of balance, and no yell. She just planted forward, her face colliding directly with the dune, and her body immersing itself. The good news was that the sand was soft enough that injury was unlikely. The better news was that everyone—including Bunny—erupted in laughter.

There really is only one proper way to recover from a face-forward tumble into a sand dune: bow. And bow she did. Her hands extended outward, then one crossed her chest. Glasses tilted, her two-tone face was plastered in a giant grin as she dropped forward to acknowledge her greatness. We clapped and cheered—and then clapped some more as she returned upright and offered a proper curtsy.

"You rock, Bunny! That was awesome!" someone yelled.

"Oh my gosh…are you okay?! Really? Are you okay?" The phrases were choked laughter.

"You go, Bunny! Someone had to do it," Lisa offered.

Lisa was the woman in charge of the running camp in Death Valley. She had won the Marathon Des Sables in 1999, twice won the 135-mile Badwater ultra marathon through Death Valley, and won countless other running races and triathlons. Twenty of us had traveled hundreds or thousands of miles to spend five days in the desert learning how to cope with the heat, terrain, sand, and anxiety. Lisa, along with her husband Jay (the official Marathon Des Sables rep for our region) and a friend named Mike, took us under their collective wing for the week. It was slightly more than five months until our event would begin. I had never thought of myself as a runner, so this was to be my crash course in official running.

There we were in the heat, a few days into our camp, circling up and down the dunes. We were a trail of ants, slowly trekking upward in a single line, only to fly downhill as soon as we had reached the top. I had expected more structure, more intensity, more discussion about conquering demons. Instead, I got frivolity, laughter, and fun. In the course of enjoying running instead of approaching it as a chore, something funny happened: I realized that my body did not hurt nearly as much as it ordinarily would have after the distances that we ran on any given day.

Bunny tried hopelessly to dust herself off, spitting a bit to purge her mouth of sand. I turned toward Lisa, one of the ants on the hill, and she was just enjoying us. It was teaching through experiencing, and it worked. Here was a woman who had run and won some of the world's most grueling events. Were she a professional basketball player or a quarterback, she would have demanded ten times the fee to spend an hour giving a half-hearted talk to a group of aspiring athletes. Following her speech, we would have learned that she had been arrested for driving under the influence of alcohol and waving a gun at a police officer. Then, her press agent would report that she was a victim of her upbringing. An absurd comparison, perhaps, but the contrast was shocking: she was so darn decent.

That week was valuable preparation for the Marathon Des Sables, but the real value came from the conversations and laughter along the way.

"Wait a minute, Ted," Bill disbelievingly asked one night before dinner. "What do you mean by 'underwear'?" I had made a comment about how difficult I thought it would be to get one's backpack to a sufficiently light weight. I had mentioned that I would inevitably need a fresh pair of underwear for each day.

"Uh, underwear. You know, the stuff that you wear under your shorts?" My tone was half confidence, half worry; I knew that I was in trouble.

"You wear underwear when you run? What do you mean—like the liners in running shorts?"

"No, I mean underwear. I'm a soccer player," I said, my standard excuse each time someone caught me not knowing something about running. "I've always worn a good ol' pair of cotton briefs and a pair of soccer shorts when I play, so why would running be any different?"

Bill laughed hysterically, and a few others within earshot just looked on in disbelief.

"What about the chaffing?" he choked out. "Doesn't that get incredibly uncomfortable?"

I was uncertain how to respond. The looks on the others' faces had me convinced that my way of doing things clearly was not the right way. I have always been of the opinion that everyone has his own method, but I also figured that preparing to run six marathons through the Sahara warranted an examination of even one's most natural assumptions.

"I don't really know," I responded, somewhat questioningly. "I guess that it's gotten a little uncomfortable after longer runs, like the marathons I've run—" Bill cut me off.

"*Whoa!* You've worn cotton briefs—Jockeys—during a whole marathon?!!"

I explained that I had, and everyone enjoyed laughing at my expense. I was the fastest runner at the camp and likely the best natural athlete, but I was absolutely clueless. Within hours of arriving in Death Valley, I marveled at my own ignorance. It was somewhat fun to learn just how much I did not know, but it was definitely humbling each time someone pointed out how inefficient I was being.

A few of the other runners jumped in to nurture me, and I learned that the sport of running has evolved. They spoke of "fibers" and "weaving" and "compression" and "seamless" and "technical fabrics." None of it made any sense, but it seemed logical enough that I should look into alternatives for the trip to Morocco.

In time, the discussion turned from clothing to eating. Evidently, there is a whole industry of food science built around the ultra athlete. I imagined chalky powders and inedible bricks, and I desperately wanted a burrito.

"You've really got to start eating better," Lisa interjected one night at dinner. I was talking aloud about my desire for a burrito, cheeseburger, and Coke—while sipping my second beer.

"What are you talking about?" I playfully asked. I knew that my diet was abysmal, but I liked bad food. "The burrito is the perfect food. It has vegetables, legumes, meat, cheese, and rice. It's got it all." I smiled at her, and she shook her head.

At another table, Lisa's husband Jay ordered a vegetarian entrée. "I only eat meat in the few weeks leading up to the Marathon Des Sables. Otherwise, I'm vegetarian."

As a group, ultra runners are obsessed with their diets. They stuff their faces with six thousand calories a day, but certain foods have earned the right to sit atop the food pedestal. Dieters talk of low-carb, low-fat, low-cal, and the fashionable pill. Pregnant women talk of ice cream and pickles, but ultra runners share tips about the foods that give them energy without diarrhea. To call their conversations about food unnatural would be an understatement. I heard more talk of stomach problems, vomiting, bladder control, and other physical ailments, not because people sought to be disgusting, but because they were obsessed with finding foods that helped them to run better.

Throughout camp, we ran through sand, rocks, and prickly thorn bushes. We ran ten miles from the middle of nowhere to a small roadside diner at an outpost called Panamint Springs that offered $10 milkshakes. Sitting on the patio waiting for the other runners to arrive, I drank two. The air was dry and hot, but because of the shade, a slight breeze, and sixty ounces of half-frozen liquid, I shivered a bit. I removed my socks and threw my deep-brown legs onto the railing. Bill and I spoke of his wife back home—"the perfect woman who is far too good for me"—and then made fun of one another.

"Those man-pris are totally awesome," I commented, jabbing him for his calf-length Capri pants.

"Where can I get one of those hats?" he asked, referring to my multicolored, hand-woven Peruvian hat made of all-natural plant fibers.

We sat in the shade drinking milkshakes, making jokes, and waiting for friends to join us. We were in the middle of nowhere to do something that hurt immensely but brought out a smile. That, I think, is what life should be all about.

It takes being stranded in the desert to realize just how completely cell phones and e-mail have tethered us. Countless clichés allude to the way that modern life allows us to immediately connect to anyone and yet somehow prevents us from really connecting at all. Experiencing Joe spit out his Perpetuem energy drink and proclaim that it was bile-flavored was considerably more enjoyable than watching it on YouTube. Seeing the flecks of spit fall off Bunny's tongue as she walked up the steps to milkshake paradise told the entire story. There was something about the meaning behind the broken conversation born out of extreme exhaustion. It bound us together.

It was during this Death Valley trip that I met Terry. I overheard him talking about his dream to start a school that teaches kids through athletics. P.E. classes teach sports, but Terry focused on the passions that can only be roused by pushing oneself to the point where pain yields to illumination. His perspective was shockingly different from everything I had experienced playing high school and college sports. They taught competition—an element necessary if one ever hopes to receive the higher benefits of athletics—but somehow failed to create meaning. Nowadays, youth sports often emphasize collaboration and participation, shedding any hint of competition from the sport. Terry (and all of us there) talked about competing against oneself and striving to be the very best. It takes an incredible man to openly discuss when he has failed to reach his potential, but only he can ever experience the full satisfaction of achieving that perfect moment.

Death Valley is also where I met George and Leigh. George was his rock-solid self: consistent, calm, and never uttering a complaint. Each night, Leigh recovered beautifully from our day's run, sporting a different belt buckle that bragged of having finished a 100-mile race. She oozed modesty and spoke in tones so kind that I was warmed by her presence. But those belt buckles brought intimidation: 100 miles is a long distance to run in a single event. "No, you just don't understand," she would say. "It's only a hundred miles." Only.

Death Valley is where I met Georgia and her husband Monte. He was debating whether or not he would run the Marathon Des Sables, but she was determined. "C'mon, Ted," she would chide me as we sat outside on yoga mats, learning how to stretch properly for ultra running events. I writhed in pain at each position, and she took a special satisfaction in poking fun: "That's it? C'mon, c'mon. You can do more. A little further. A little longer. C'mon, Ted. Stop whining." I whined. That is when I learned that Georgia was not only a massage therapist up in Alaska, but also a yoga instructor.

Death Valley is where I met Andrea. Cue sarcasm, and cue dry wit. She would launch into one quick tale after another to illustrate a point. She would insult and deride but do so in a paradoxically inviting way and direct just as much of it at herself. If there was ever any doubt about her heart, we talked about her work for charities to help disabled people. We talked about her paraplegic friends and her endless patience. Her dry humor was her charm.

Death Valley is where I met Steve—and shared a room with him, in fact. A sixty-year-old cardiologist, Steve and I had the same build. He spoke of his children, and I wondered what I would have thought as a teenager had my father decided that it was time to begin running fifty- and 100-mile races. He approached training and running in a very methodical way. I moaned when longer runs were scheduled; Steve just matter-of-factly put on his shoes and said, "Well, it's time to run." Emotionless, he was utterly charming. The simplicity and insanity of embracing pain with a smile was refreshing.

And Death Valley is where I met Jay and Lisa—husband and wife, business partners, and all-around smiley people. Jay had the face of a seventeen-year-old, wire-rimmed John Lennon glasses and a mullet taken from *Backcountry Monthly Magazine*. He repeatedly mentioned that he only grew his hair like that for sun protection during the race; though I was inclined to believe him, I could not help but make references to moonshine and coonskin caps. Lisa found excitement and passion in everything. She dismissed negatives—including poor running or mild injuries—and found the positive in all that we did. She had won races around the world. We should have been in awe of her. And yet, she continuously expressed her joy and excitement at our moderate successes.

Everyone was a character from different parts of North America and with different careers and different stories. Everyone shared a passion to excel and, interestingly enough, a desire to coordinate with others in an attempt to learn how to perform even better. Perhaps it is the sign of a shallow life for me to say that never before had I met a group of people who were completely committed to enjoying and helping one another. But, nonetheless, that is what I discovered.

In business or in life, there always seems to be a plan or reason. For five days we ran at different paces but discussed strategy at night. We shared pointers and ideas, and all that anyone wanted to know of another was, *Are you getting what you need to do your best?* We drank Perpetuem, drank milkshakes, and drank beer, but mostly we drank of life.

As we parted, watching coverage on the news of the Southern California wildfires, we were impacted in two ways. The first, of course, was a sense of sadness for the people who had lost their homes. The second, more unexpected realization was that we were returning to life as normal. For five days we had traded cell phones, our bosses, e-mail, and life in general for a sense of peace and camaraderie that does not make sense in print.

I longed for March, when we would all meet up in Ouarzazate, Morocco, and learn how to do it all over again.

8
The Second Stage

"How are you feeling?" I asked. Andrew was still inside his sleeping bag.

"Uh, are you talking to me?" He shifted around and poked his head out of the mummy hole.

"Yeah, it's Ted. Feeling any better this morning?"

He sat up and squinted. He looked tired but was trying to focus, as though he had something important to accomplish. "I don't know, pretty crummy," he moaned.

"Pretty crummy? Of course you feel crummy," I said, trying to make a joke. "You've slept out in the desert on horribly hard and rocky ground for three nights now. Did you expect to feel rested?"

He chuckled, but it was just as much a cough as it was laughter. I wanted to avoid calling attention to the fact that the virus he picked up on the airplane had not seemed to subside. He knew that, of course, so I just tried to refocus his attention toward succeeding.

He said, "I don't know if I can go today. I feel really bad." He did not look particularly good.

"I hear you, man. I'm really sorry to hear that. Listen," I paused. I was choosing my words carefully; I did not really know what I was talking about, but my goal was to get him to continue running. I guess that I would have hoped for the same if the roles had been reversed.

"Listen, Andrew, nobody but you can know how bad you feel and whether you can't continue. But I'd just say this: Don't quit because of the psychological. This event is brutal. It's playing tricks on all of us. We're all feeling bad—somewhere—physically. So it becomes more of a mind game. If you *really can't go*," I emphasized, "then you can't go. But don't even think of quitting if there is a chance that you can make it. What's the harm in trying today and, if it doesn't work, just dropping out mid-stage? Unless you absolutely cannot physically go, go until you can't go anymore—or until they force you to stop."

My inspirational speech had not rallied him the way I had hoped. When I awoke that morning and walked toward his tent, I imagined my words stirring a battle cry. But, though he seemed somewhat comforted, he was in no way altered.

"Well, I guess that maybe I could give it a try..." he trailed off. He was distracted. Then he found more confidence: "But if I'm going to have any chance of making it, I'm gonna have to get rid of a lot of weight from my pack."

"I'll help, if you want it," I offered. I liked that the conversation had turned away from quitting and toward a prospective solution.

"Naw, that's all right. I think that I'll eat something and start playing around with the pack a bit and then see how I feel." He seemed headed in the right direction but was in no way the defiant warrior that I had hoped to resurrect. "How are you feeling?" he asked.

Had I been honest, I would have told him that I hurt all over and that my head was in a fog. Had I been honest, I would have told him that my body wanted nothing to do with running that day. But I figured that would have served no purpose but to bring him down.

"I'm tired, man, but everything will be good once the adrenaline is pumping," I responded.

I walked back to my tent, hoping for a little bit of a pick-me-up.

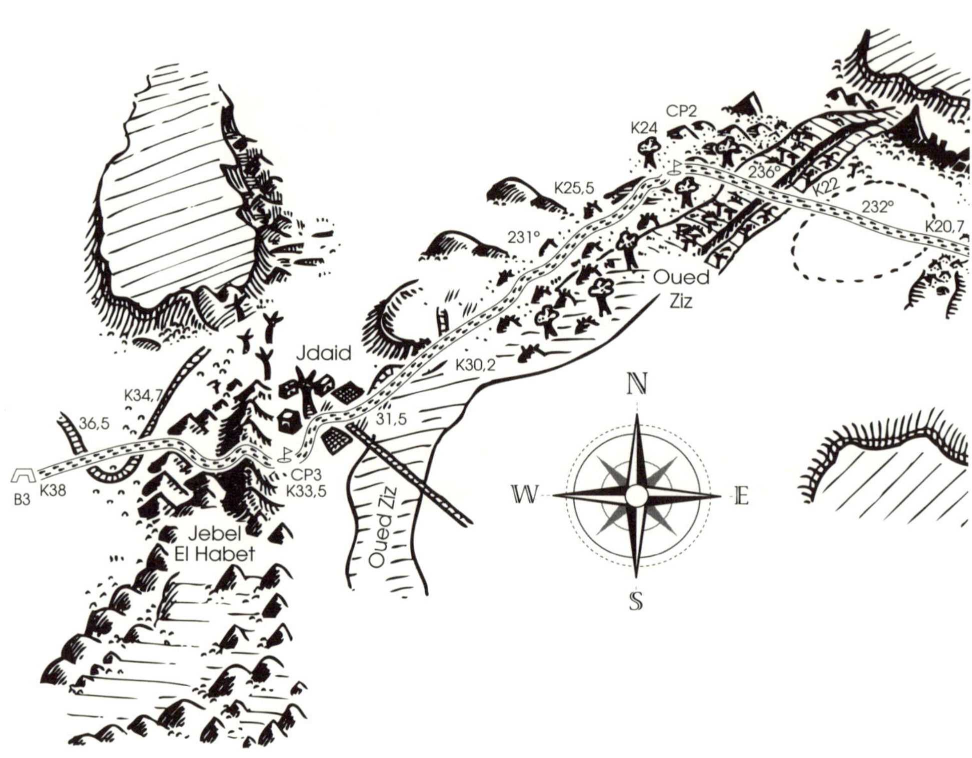

The conversation with Andrew had been emotionally draining, and I was feeling physically weak. In a fit of early-morning disorientation, Andrea did not disappoint. She searched for words but made little sense. She spoke in incoherent word jumbles.

"Okay, it just put it down somewhere. Okay, where it is? Do you guys know is it?" She looked at us and seemed to know that she had made no sense. Her hair was tousled, her eyes half-closed.

"What are you looking for, eh?" Karen asked. She was smiling but was trying not to laugh.

Andrea stared blankly, her eyes inquisitive and her cheekbones seeming to be interested in solving some dilemma. She tilted her

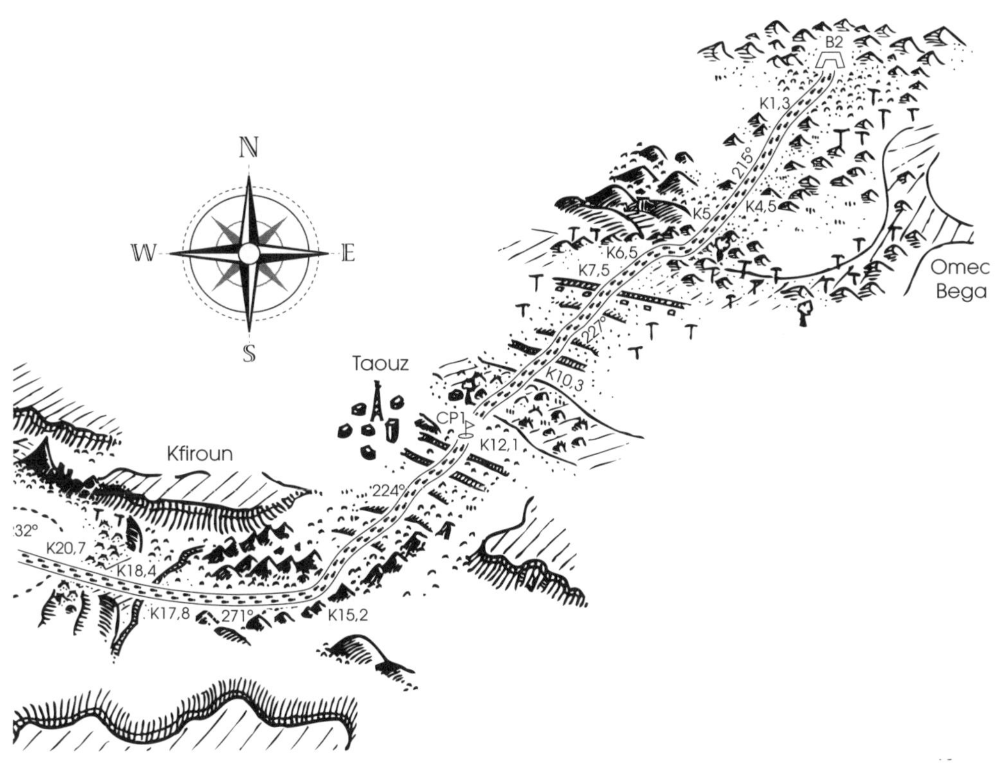

head to the side, as though that would help the answer come to her.

"I am trying to find…" she was thinking intently. "I am trying to find my knife, which I need to cut the tape, which I need for the blisters on my feet." It had all come together again for her, and we lost our opportunity for further humor as she discovered her knife and went back to work.

Trying to feed the mood, I stopped in the center of the tent and addressed everyone: "Hey, guys, I know that we're in the middle of the desert and that this is sort of hard for everyone, but I haven't even been gone for ten minutes." I paused just long enough for perplexed looks to appear. "I'm willing to look the other way this time, but whoever it is who keeps throwing sand on all my stuff when I'm away, just please stop."

I got a few sympathy chuckles and a few more groans. The joke was more painful than it was funny. Sand was everywhere, all of the time.

"Oh my gosh, right?" Karen chimed in immediately. "It's everywhere. I tried for a while to keep myself clean, but now it's just disgusting. My hair is so gross."

As though a symphony conductor had instructed all of the women to speak, Michelle, Andrea, and Georgia echoed Karen's hair comment.

"I'm so sick of sand," Jeff offered. His tone seemed to sarcastically acknowledge the fact that we had five more nights and an equal number of marathons to go.

I prepared my freeze-dried granola with blueberries and milk; it was just as good as it had been the first morning. Others rifled through their packs, searching for Band-Aids, tape, or other items to fix their feet. I seemed to have less to do than my tent mates, so I ate, lay down, and waited.

After a while, I wondered aloud if Andrew would be starting the stage. Karen suggested that I check in with him again, so I walked over and found him fully dressed, standing over his pack, and actively discarding items. He looked like a runner, and I smiled.

"I have so much stuff I don't need," he said. "I've already gotten rid of a dozen or so Powerbars."

"You ready to do this?" I asked.

"I'm gonna try." He had a little bit of confidence in his voice. Mentally, at least, he seemed interested in finding out what he could do. He attacked his bag like a TSA agent. "Oh, I totally don't need this. In the trash it goes."

As it neared 8:30 a.m.—time to assemble at the starting line—everyone was a bit slower than they had been on the first day. The dunes had injured us. They had humbled us. Shoulders were a bit slouched and feet a bit heavy. The second stage was being billed as the "easy stage," but few people felt as though twenty-four miles through rock flats and 120 degrees made for an easy day.

Mick Jagger started singing. It is fascinating the way that certain songs seem to transcend cultural boundaries. "I can't get no!" a Frenchman to my left yelled. "Sat-is-fac-tion!" rang the chorus around him. I still felt sluggish, but the music helped to improve my mood. Furthermore, I looked around and took stock of the situation. With the exception of the eight hundred people in my immediate area, there was no sign of life for miles. *Who would ever think to come up with such a ridiculous event?*

During the countdown to race start that morning, I was optimistic. I felt bad, but I took comfort in something that I overheard Jay tell another runner: "Everyone feels bad; don't worry about it."

The stage began with my least favorite terrain: wadi. It seemed never-ending with its sandy-then-crusty unpredictability. I slugged through it, losing myself in thought about nothing.

I was jolted alert by a Toyota Land Cruiser driving ten yards to my right. A cameraman sat in the back seat. The window was down, and he was taping as they drove by. A few hundred yards later, they came to a stop, and the cameraman jumped from the Toyota and set up directly in my running path. I could see his tan press jacket that the race organization had issued. I assumed that he was French—most of the media seemed to be. One of them said "merci" to the other, confirming my suspicion.

As I ran by, I offered a slight wave. I had seen previous years' videos on the race organization's Website, and it was obvious that they often taped random people. I chuckled at the thought of my girlfriend, friends, and family visiting the Website and actually getting to see me run. I wondered how bad I looked on my fourth day without a shower.

Not more than a minute later, the Land Cruiser passed me again. And, like before, it stopped a few hundred yards in front of me to allow the cameraman to position himself in my path. This time, I offered a wave and a weak "bonjour," thinking that perhaps I would get chosen for the Website because I spoke a word in the dominant language. It was not that I wanted media attention, but I knew that certain people back home would enjoy seeing me. It gave me an opportunity to reflect on what my friends and family would have been doing as I struggled through wadi.

Of course, since it was not yet 10 a.m. in Morocco, it was approaching 1 a.m. in California. Everyone I knew would have been sleeping. I realized that I would have to return to the thought later in the day if I hoped to actually piece together what they were doing.

The Land Cruiser passed again; I assumed that it was headed to the first checkpoint. But it stopped again! I was shocked that I, an American, was getting so much attention. It was a bit flattering. They repeated the process a fourth time. At that point, I was perplexed. ABC, the media outlet from my own country, had not followed me for a single step, but I was being treated like a superstar by a foreign land's crew.

I scolded myself for my pride, reasoning that I came to Morocco to run and learn something about myself, not to communicate with the media. But a small piece of me felt wounded. If I was going to receive attention, I had hoped that it would be from the American group.

Immediately following the first checkpoint, I began to feel fatigued—not a good sign with nearly eighteen miles remaining. A man a few years my senior but with my same build ran up alongside me.

"English?" I asked.

"Why, yes, actually. Just outside of London." He was somewhat surprised.

"I've sort of figured out the bib numbers and have an idea who speaks what languages," I explained. It was nice to have someone to talk to. At this point during the previous day, I had been lost in the sand dune version of Babel.

"How did you fare yesterday?" he asked. It was a logical question since we had not seen one another during the first stage.

"Twenty-ninth overall. You?"

"Forty-second," he answered. "You had a good run yesterday, huh?"

"Yeah, I felt good. But today I'm struggling. My plan right now is to hang out with you for as long as I can keep up." I laughed, despite being entirely serious. He understood.

We spoke a while about our respective journeys to Morocco. I had received an instant message from a coworker, and he had decided that his life had settled into a routine. As much as he liked his job and loved his family, he commented that something was missing. Really, his goal was simply to break the monotony. He expected the adventure in and of itself to be just what he needed.

"As-Salamu 'Alaykum," he yelled as we came around a small hill. There was a group of four children in their early teens.

"Salaam," they responded in unison, wishing their visitor peace. They took special interest in my running companion because he spoke Arabic. They yelled a few phrases back and forth.

"You speak Arabic?" I asked after we had passed beyond them. It was a stupid question, but I wanted to keep talking with someone.

"No, not at all," he chuckled. "I just learned a few phrases before coming over here. I figured that the locals would appreciate it if a Westerner took interest in their language."

"So, I guess that the next question is," I paused, "do you understand what you're saying?"

He laughed aloud. "Not at all! I knew what they meant at some point, but now I just know that they're greetings!" We both laughed some more.

He then told me about London's transformation during his lifetime, noting that the Muslim religion and culture were playing increasingly more powerful roles in society and government. He took care to offer all of the politically correct disclaimers, noting that all cultures are valuable and have a place in a free society. He even went so far as to suggest that the dominant English culture should change to welcome its newest residents.

"Londonistan," I commented. His was an argument I had read in a book by Melanie Phillips. The English were losing their culture, she argued, because they were unwilling to assert the value of Western culture. They were unwilling to admit the serious problems that had brewed for years as radical anti-Westernism had flourished in London. London had, the author argued, become the Western world's center for anti-Western terrorist activity.

He was surprised at my comment—not offended, but surprised.

"Yeah, you could say that," he offered, slowly. "But, nobody does. You're not supposed to say that. Nobody does. It's the dirty little secret, the elephant in the room." His tone had changed from reverence to longing. He obviously believed in the popular precepts of multiculturalism, but he was struggling to give up the England of his childhood.

"I see kids today, and they're so different from when I was growing up," he said. I knew that I was in for a retrospective. I could almost hear my father getting ready to talk about going to McDonald's for the first time or stomping around the Iowa cornfields.

"So many of the kids who've come from other countries don't embrace the culture or language at all. And then they struggle when they try to get jobs. It's sad, really." Something else was on his mind. We ran in silence for a few minutes.

"I think of my kids—one's starting college, and one just finished—and I'm so lucky. They're smart, hard-working, great kids. Struggling a little bit, sure, but they're trying to make the most of themselves. I sort of wonder if so much of the rest of the country has the same approach."

We passed another group of children, and he greeted them in Arabic as well.

The conversation then fizzled out; perhaps we had expended too much emotional energy. We spoke about trivialities—trips we had taken, running objectives, and more. The serious political and philosophical discussion had been put on hold as we refocused our energy on running. The temperature was approaching 100 degrees already. He wiped his brow, wished me luck, and stopped to walk.

As I ran ahead, I thought about his daughter—a recent college graduate who was a "good kid" but struggling somewhat. It made me think about my sister, Amy. Ten days earlier she had flown to the Utah desert to participate in a nature treatment program through the backcountry. No doubt she was going through an experience similar to mine—struggling through varied terrain, contending with heat, and questioning why she had come.

I wondered if the painful road to alcoholism was the same as the lost path of youth in multicultural Britain. Was it a decadent, easier lifestyle that caused people to lose focus? Did hatred drive someone to the bottle the way that some found themselves called to jihad? I thought about the religiously symbolic aspects of Amy's substance abuse program. Could wandering through the desert cause would-be terrorists to find their way as well?

I stepped on a large rock, stumbled, and nearly fell. My vision was blurry from the sweat pouring off my forehead. I used my shoulder to wipe my face, and I shook my head to try to restore some clarity to my thinking. I was obviously not thinking clearly—as evidenced by the stream of consciousness that attempted to connect my sister to England, Muslims, Jesus, Utah, and terrorism.

I heard footprints and heavy breathing behind me and assumed that the Englishman had returned. Instead, it was Didi Touda, a Moroccan and the woman who was favored to win. She plodded along at a consistent pace, her pack swishing from side to side with every step.

I looked over and smiled at her. She nodded—slightly. It was not rude, but short. She was acknowledging me while expending the least amount of energy possible. Though I was hurting, I found it invigorating to run alongside a famous athlete.

I wondered how long she had been running behind me.

It was then that I came to a startling realization. No doubt, she had been behind me for quite some time. And no doubt, she had been the reason that the French camera crew had been stopping every few hundred yards to film. It had not been me at all; I had just happened to have been running in front of her. They had been following Didi—all four of the times that they drove by and stopped—and I kept getting in their way.

I realized that I would not be appearing on the Website after all. In fact, they were quite possibly not even filming each time I had run by and waved hello. Even more depressing, if they had been filming, they would likely edit the tape to cut me out of the picture so as to get an Unobstructed Didi Experience. All of my mental machinations were for naught; the French media did not care for this American.

Chuckling, I wished that I could share the joke with her. The humor really was thick. I wanted to know how to speak French—or to have her speak English—so that I could admit my crime. Someone needed to know how embarrassed I was; someone needed to know how my self-absorption had come back to bite me. Someone needed to get a well-deserved laugh. But, when I turned and asked her a question, she just uttered something in French and shook her head. But at least this time she gave me a tiny smile.

I decided that, as I had done with the Englishman an hour before, I would use Didi as my pacer. I settled into a rhythm, allowing her to set the pace. I watched her body move, and it was almost mechanical. Each step, each pump of the arm, each breath seemed calculated. We ran together through the second checkpoint and found even more wadi to struggle through. I ran with her for well over an hour—at her side nearly the entire time—but I wondered if she even noticed. Do machines actually take in their surroundings?

We were approaching the third and final checkpoint of the day, and I was in a great deal of pain. My calves burned, my torso felt as though it was on fire, and my feet were starting to blister. She reached over and waved to get my attention. Surprised, I looked at her and wondered how we would manage to communicate.

She looked intently at me and thought. Finally, she pointed toward the checkpoint, half a mile away and just beyond the few mud huts that comprised the small town of Jdaid, and spoke: "Zeece…uh…zeece sree?"

She must have felt as though my eyes were burrowing into her face as I tried to decipher the question. She had offered enough inflection for me to gather that she was asking for something.

"Zeece sree?" She held up three fingers.

I realized that she was asking about the checkpoint: "This three?" In other words, "Is this checkpoint number three?"

I nodded yes.

"Zen…" she stopped and made a criss-cross X-motion with her hands. She was asking if that was the final checkpoint. Would we be done afterward?

I again nodded yes, and she responded, "Goot," letting out a gasp of air and wagging her tongue to show her exhaustion. She had confirmed my suspicions: She was in fact a machine. She had no idea where we were in the stage but had just started running that morning when told to do so. She no doubt would continue until someone told her to stop.

Upon learning that we were only a few miles from the finish, she picked up her pace. We turned onto a small dirt road in Jdaid and ran the hundred yards or so up to the mud buildings. As we turned the corner, I was unprepared for the cheering that ensued. Several dozen girls sat on a small wall; when we turned the corner, they began shrieking and clapping.

I turned to Didi, raised my eyebrows, and pointed at myself. She looked confused, so I motioned again, suggesting that the girls were cheering for me. My father had taught me that breed of humor.

She laughed aloud, a wide smile covering her face as she shook her head and wagged her finger back and forth. When she stopped wagging, she pointed at herself. She wanted there to be no doubt that they had come to see her. Hamming it up, I pretended to not be sure and again suggested that I had rallied the locals. In the end we agreed that she had been the main attraction.

The cheers gave her a boost of energy coming out of Jdaid. I waved goodbye as she sprinted up the rocky hill to the third checkpoint.

The final five miles of the stage were the most painful of the entire week. It began with an intense, rocky climb up a mountain and ended with a prolonged run through a valley of black rocks. I tried to swallow a salt pill, but my gag reflex shot it back out, and I watched it fall to the rocks. I would later hear varying figures regarding the day's high temperature. Someone's watch had registered fifty-five degrees Celsius—131 degrees Fahrenheit. The race's official number was a much cooler 120.

I walked off and on, trying to muster the strength to proceed. Yet, each time I ran a few steps, I felt a new type of pain and resumed walking. I was twenty miles into the stage and forty miles into the overall event, and I became demoralized as one runner after another passed me. It was not so much that I resented others beating me. No, it pained me as others ran by because it suggested that I was the only one struggling. Everyone else seemed strong as I simply prayed for the finish line. When it finally came, I had been further humbled. If there is a way to run two marathons without showering for days—and then exude pride in the process—I certainly had not learned how.

As I collected my afternoon's water rationing and walked back to the tent, I was grateful that the day's running was over but terrified of what was to come. Moments after arriving at the tent, I heard a friendly voice.

"Ted, how'd it go today," Jeff asked. I was surprised to see him because the previous day I had been able to return to the finish line and watch him arrive.

"Oh, man," I trailed off.

He looked outstanding. Sweaty, yes, but more importantly, he wore a confident smile.

"Not good, huh?" he asked. He was genuinely concerned. He felt great, but he wanted to talk about my day. That attitude seemed to be such a powerful theme. Caring for others paid considerable dividends for everyone. I shook my head, partially in pain and partially in disbelief that I had found such great people in the middle of nowhere.

"Oh, whatever, it's done," I responded, not wanting to fixate on my whine. "You sure look good. Heck of a day, huh?"

"Yeah, man, I felt good today. I can't believe it: I was sixty-second." I remembered our discussions before the race. Our coach had told him to shoot for the top fifty, but Jeff was convinced that it would be nearly impossible for him to break into the top 100. On the second day, he was not only there, but also looking good.

"That's awesome, man." I was feeling better already. It was invigorating to be around energy, pride, and strength. I could have been lying alone on the ground, thinking about my own discomfort. Instead, I was recharging by tapping another's success.

We talked about the heat, the fact that the terrain was more runnable than the previous day's dunes, and the points at which we had begun to question our reason for coming. I then recounted my experience with Didi in Jdaid.

"Hahaha! That's hilarious! I wonder what she thought of you, trying to take credit for all of the girls who look up to her. That's funny."

We sat and mixed our powdered recovery drinks in our water bottles and removed our shoes.

After half an hour passed, I was feeling somewhat better—and motivated to see others. I invited Jeff to accompany me to the finish line, but he declined.

As I left the tent, I saw Brendan lumbering in. His grey shirt had solid white, vertical, crusty streaks from dried sweat. He, too, had finished quicker than the previous day, and we talked about the stage. "It is *really* hot out there," he stated, looking to me for confirmation. I agreed. It was the type of heat that could not possibly be real. We had to look to one another for proof that it actually existed.

As I returned to the finish line and searched for shade, I thought about the kids I had seen during the stage. *They live in these conditions every single day of their lives*, I realized. Sure, few of them were foolish enough to run marathon distances during the day's worst heat, but nonetheless, my experience—my visit, my vacation, my journey, my snapshot in time—was simply called life for them.

The finish line was a mix of bodies. Half of the people felt like I had while the other half mirrored Jeff. The sheer difficulty of the event had begun to settle in. Even those who were not limping, those whose feet were not blistered, and those whose backs had not blistered from their backpacks—even they showed signs of wear. The strongest of the runners conveyed through their body language that they had already sweat out more life in two days than many people experience in a lifetime.

During the Marathon Des Sables, I lost entire chunks of time—not deep in thought, contemplation, or conversation, but in an odd trance. Halfway between heat and death, positioned between self-preservation and elation, hours passed by. Those were moments that I could have been savoring. They were moments that should have been committed to memory. They were opportunities to taste life, and yet I had less sensation than during an average night's sleep back in San Jose. I gave two hours to the finish line that day—and though friends later thanked me for cheering them in, I have no recollection of sitting on that wooden box and leaning against the sponsorship signs.

Fear began to set in when I walked by the registration tent and saw my day's ranking. Though I had slipped to fortieth for the stage, I had only fallen to thirty-second place overall. I had hoped to be closer to number fifty so that I could run slower during the third stage and ensure an overall ranking outside of the top fifty at the start of the fourth stage.

Being fifty-first had a special meaning at the Marathon Des Sables. For as long as the race has been run, the Marathon Des Sables organizers have thrown a twist into the fourth stage. It affects only the top fifty male and five female runners. At the beginning of the fourth stage, all but those runners begin at the normal time of 9 a.m.

The top fifty runners, however, would have to wait. As punishment for having done well, the elite runners are not permitted to begin until noon. We were only a stage away from finalizing who those top fifty runners would be, and my thirty-second place ranking placed me in the middle of that danger.

My fear coming into the event was that I would end up running at night; of course, most runners do, because they are unable to finish the forty-five-to-fifty-mile stage during daylight. While mentally preparing for the event, I had concluded that I could finish in less than ten hours, which meant that a 9 a.m. start would guarantee that I would finish a few minutes ahead of the Saharan sunset. If my starting time were to be noon instead of 9 a.m., I would have to finish the forty-seven-mile run in seven hours—an impossibly fast time for the terrain and conditions.

The prospect of running at night terrified me—not because of ghosts, the boogeyman, or mysterious sand goblins, but because of ankles. Following a quarter century of soccer and a few misplaced years of basketball injuries, I struggled to run on flat surfaces. In the desert, I had to watch each step, and on more than one occasion I had thought that perhaps my ankle would give out. At night, with limited depth perception, I had no idea how I would hold up. *Does God answer ankle prayers?*

"Hey Ted!" I could hear Rahwa yelling to me. My mind had taken me back to my freshman year in college, and Rahwa was a gal who lived a few doors down in Granada, my dorm. Puzzled, I walked down the hallway and looked in her room.

"Hey."

"Hey."

"How did you know that I was down the hall?" I asked. No one else had been in the hallway, and I had not said a word.

"Oh, I heard your ankles clicking."

It was then—twelve years before the MDS—that I had decided it was time to stop playing soccer. A day would come when I would have children of my own, and we would want to run around in the grass.

I looked at my thirty-second place ranking, thought of the night, and worried about my ankles.

"Where are you at?" Mike, who had been the third coach in Death Valley and was sharing a tent with Jay during this year's race, had walked up and jolted me out of my college retrospection.

"I'm in thirty-second."

He smiled, cocked his head to the side, and pursed his lips. He exhaled—his way of saying that I was running well.

"I'm not happy about it," I responded.

"What did you run today?" he asked. He assumed that I had wanted to be ranked better.

"Fortieth. Twenty-ninth yesterday."

"Yeah, but that's nothin'. It all comes down to the long stage. Don't worry about it. You're gonna do awesome."

"Oh, I'm not upset about my ranking," I corrected him. "I'm worried about starting later during the long stage. I *really* don't want to run at night."

He smiled even wider. "You're not going to have much of a choice."

"Well, I'm thinking of taking it *really* slow tomorrow so that I fall out of the top fifty. That way I'd start at nine with everyone else and get to finish the entire stage in the daytime."

"How far would you have to fall?" It was a practical question. I looked back at the rankings.

"About thirty minutes."

Mike cringed. "That's tough. Lots of people in that forty-to-fifty range might be thinking the same thing, and you don't want to slow down and then learn that you're in the top fifty after all."

Jay walked up. He was limping somewhat, and his face told me not to ask. I did anyway.

"You okay?"

"Yeah, it's just my knee, and the heat is getting to me," he replied.

"Ted's in thirty-second," Mike announced. He had another grin. He took pride in my accomplishment thus far, but he was enjoying watching me be uncomfortable.

"Good work, man. Looks like a late start on the long day," Jay added. It was an obsession that everyone had.

"I think that I'm going to take it slow tomorrow to get out of the top fifty. I don't want to run at night." I was repeating myself now, trying to talk myself into it. *What a strange twist to a race,* I thought. I just wanted to run, but this late start threw so many other factors into consideration.

We walked back to our tents, discussing the merits of holding back.

Back at Tent 77, Michelle was sick. Her face was sunburned, and she had white goggle eyes. She and Jeff were talking about their days; listening to her made me grateful for how I had held up.

"It's just my stomach," she said. "Sometimes I get really bad stomach problems when I run, and I can't keep anything down."

Just two days earlier, a race official had stopped by the tent and ordered Michelle to doping control. Having won a few fifty- and 100-mile races in the United States, Michelle was on their watch list of contenders who might be able to win the event. They were just taking precautions, but we in her tent had taken the opportunity to poke fun at her.

"Hey, Andrea," I had yelled. "Did you hear that we've got a druggy in our group?"

"Michelle Jen-son!" Jeff had interjected, trying his best French accent. "Doping control!"

Now two days into the event, Michelle looked broken. She was nowhere near contention; in fact, she was struggling to eat. But she never complained. I realized just how strong she was. Nothing had gone wrong for me, but I had nonetheless struggled all day. She, on the other hand, was contending with serious health problems—and she was still persevering. Impressive.

The late afternoon and early evening went just as they had the day before. The sky gave way to the yellows and pinks; the stringy cotton clouds began to glow. We relaxed, talked of sore feet, and finally got relief from the miserable heat. Andrea and Karen came in, and Georgia arrived shortly thereafter. It was good to be reunited, but the mood was somewhat more somber than the previous day.

"The heat was ridiculous today, eh?" Karen asked.

"I was dying out there. I had to ask for more water. I told them that I didn't care about the time penalty—just give me the time penalty—'cause I needed the water," Georgia said. She was flustered.

We talked about the rock flats, the temperature, and the lack of wind. I had finished first in our tent with some members taking more than twice as long to complete the stage, and yet I understood each of their comments. As on the first day, I could have been walking alongside them.

"Ted," someone said from outside the tent. It was Terry and Jay. "Have you seen Andrew?"

I shook my head and looked at my watch. It had been nearly ten hours, the maximum allowable time for the stage. I had not seen him, and given his condition that morning, we all suspected the worst.

"We're going to walk to the finish line to see if he comes in," Terry said. "Want to come?"

Five of us walked to the finish line and then a few hundred yards beyond to the top of a small mound that gave us a view of the last half mile of the course. The allotted time for the stage had elapsed. Even if Andrew were to finish it, he would be eligible for disqualification. We waited an extra fifteen minutes until it was completely dark. We saw no headlamps in the distance.

"Nobody's out there," Mike said. We had all been hoping to see someone emerge from the darkness, but he was right.

"I'll bet he dropped."

"I'm sure he dropped."

We walked back to our tents, lamenting the fact that Andrew would have to return another year if he wanted to finish the Marathon Des Sables.

"Tough kid," Terry said. "I can't believe that he got up and went this morning."

"Yeah, he is, but it's tough when you haven't done many races," Jay added. "He trained hard, but it's one thing to train and another thing to run races. At his age, it's tough to know how much your body can do, how much pain you can endure."

I wished Terry, Jay, Laurie, and Mike goodnight and walked back to my tent. It was glowing. It looked almost like a disco. Lights swirled underneath the black fabric. I poked my head in, and everyone was tucked into their sleeping bags with their headlamps turned on.

"E-mail delivery!" Andrea yelled, extending her arm in my direction and waving a piece of paper. "These are for you," she said. I looked around, and everyone was staring at a piece of paper. She explained that a race official had stopped by moments before with a stack of printed pages for our tent. I looked at mine and was pleased that a handful of my friends had evidently figured out how to use the race Website's "E-mail a Competitor" feature.

"I got an e-mail from my son. He says that I'm crazy. Teenagers," Georgia scoffed.

"Okay, so listen to this," Jeff said. "'Hi, Jeff, I'm a friend of your mother's, and we've never met. But I heard about the race, and I wanted to let you know how great it is that you're doing it.'" He paused, looked up so that his headlamp blinded us all, and continued. "So, I got a random e-mail from this woman I've never met who knows my mother—but nothing from my mother!"

We all laughed. I thought about the TV show, "The Biggest Loser," in which weight-loss contestants are given an option of different prizes. Receiving letters from family members was a popular gift because they needed the support of loved ones to continue on. I, too, was eager to get to reading.

"Ha!" was all that Andrea offered of her mail. When asked for more details, she just snickered. When a few of us protested that it was not fair for her to tease us, she simply snickered again.

I quickly unpacked my sleeping bag and climbed inside. I read quietly. Half a world away, it was moving to read the words "I love you," "I'm proud of you," and even "I still think that you're absolutely crazy for doing this…break a leg…uh, never mind. That's a bad wish given the circumstances." There was an obvious time delay; they wrote of just having seen the first day's results. But their love could not have been more current.

Everyone else had finished reading and put their lights away.

"Okay," I said. "I've got a friend who's given a riddle, and I'm the worst at these things. Can you guys help me so that I don't stay up all night trying to figure it out?" Everyone agreed. "Okay, this is the entirety of the riddle: How is an island like the letter 'T'?"

"That's it?"

"That's it."

We sat in darkness for a little while, talking of iced tea, T-shirts, and other types of 'T.' We reasoned, like doctoral candidates in a seminar, that 'T' must be a play on words.

While we were thinking, Jay stopped by our tent. "Andrew came in," he said. "He's okay and feels great. He's going to give it another go tomorrow. That's great, huh? Anyway, good night."

Great indeed, I thought. What a perfect end to a difficult day! We had seen so little of Andrew because he had been out on the course for so long. But he had become an inspiration to me—a symbol of what was possible through determination. I smiled.

"They're both in the middle of water," someone said.

"Huh?" I responded, lost in awe of Andrew's accomplishment.

"The answer to the riddle. An island and the letter 'T.' They're both in the middle of *water*."

9
Letters Home

A few years ago, I read somewhere that the French government had banned the word "e-mail." Instead of the American abomination, all government agencies would be required to use the more linguistically sophisticated "courriel." The decision was considerably more significant than the anti-Americanism on its face: this one word was a symbol for the preservation of French culture. The French way of life had been threatened by this encroachment, and government had swooped in to save the day.

Imagine my surprise, then, when I learned that, during every day of the Marathon Des Sables, the race organization would set up "e-mail" stations on a daily basis. I felt guilty as I stood in line to send messages to my friends and family, but as the service was free to all (i.e. subsidized), I quickly convinced myself that they had maintained the true spirit of French culture despite their use of such a dirty word.

I had heard about the e-mail tent, but I had wondered how long the lines would be. But, as I was one of the faster runners, I was lucky. E-mail was available starting around 2 p.m. daily. By three o'clock, it was common for there to be a long line—in direct sunlight and during blistering temperatures. But, since I had finished earlier than most competitors during each stage, I was able to send a few messages without suffering through the lines. Of course, the French keyboards and ten-minute time limit made things difficult. The messages that made their way to my friends and family were full of errors, contradictions, and confusion.

***

March 30

After two horrible nights sleep because of sandstorms at the first Bivouac, we began, exhausted already, in the largest sand dunes in North Africa. Oh, and as if 8 miles in the dunes to start was not enough, we ended in them as well. I finished the 19.75 mile stage in about 3:32. This was a much tougher beginning than I had expected: Race veterans have universally agreed that this was the toughest first stage ever. I do not yet know my ranking for the day but it was pretty good . . . I did force myself to slow down considerably after the dunes because I had gone out too fast: It is important to remember that this is a week long event. That is all: My inability to find the proper punctuation marks on this French keyboard is driving me nuts (once an English teacher, always neurotic about grammar).

***

March 31

Whew, what a difference a day makes. Yesterday I finished in 29th place, and today I was considerably slower, probably around #50, but I will not know for a little while. I am a little worried about the prospect of being in the top 50 after tomorrows stage, since that would mean starting three hours later during the long stage on day 4. I would rather be the 51st man than the 50th. So, I think that it is a good idea to take it ultra easy tomorrow, which will be a tough stage with more sand dunes.

Todays stage was billed as the easy stage, but it hurt. Aside from a 9.5km stretch in the middle, which I completed in 50 minutes, I felt horrible much of the day. It was considerably hotter (110 is the rumor), and though we did not have many dunes, there was a 6 mile section of junky, crusty shale of some sort that broke through to reveal sand beneath. This section also had rapid cycling mini hills, which was tough.

LOTS of kids appeared out of NOWHERE today to cheer.

***

April 3

Well, peeps, the past two days have been good ones. After getting lost in another set of dunes on stage 3, I finished the stage 21st. The long day (47 miles) I completed in 8:21, which was good enough for 14th on the day. I am not sure where that puts me overall, but it is better than I had expected.

The long stage was brutal. Not only were there the requisite dunes, salt flats, and rock plains, but we also got three extremely large mountains to climb; and I mean CLIMB: Several times the grade was more than 25%, and we were forced to go hand over hand in mixed sand and loose rocks. One thing that has become obvious is that this event is not just a run: The terrain has been such that running is impossible in many places.

My pack is down to 14 pounds or so, which feels much better than the original 22.

One crazy note: As I type this it is 9:15 a.m. Thursday, and I finished the long stage around 8:35 p.m. last night. I have several friends who are STILL going, for 24 hours now . . .

***

April 4

I am in awe of the grit and determination that so many have shown. We ran a marathon today, through sand and shale, after having run 115 miles over the previous three days. Some friends' feet are little more than mush, and yet they persevered, never thinking of quitting.

It's a short 11 mile finish tomorrow, and then we'll get to shower. Racing is over: Reflection can begin.

This is the most grueling event I can imagine. Temperatures topped 100 every day, we had no showers, we got no beds, and we carried our weeks' worth of food on our backs. And we will have run 152+ miles through the most scorched, God-forsaken terrain on the planet. How the children I've seen throughout the event can live in these conditions is beyond me.

Thank you all for the emails: They have been a great source of inspiration. One thing that I haven't mentioned is that ABC has been following we Americans all week, so you will get to live this event on national news and Good Morning America. Fun.

***

The race organization's e-mail system was a funny thing. In addition to not being able to find punctuation marks, I worried that my messages might not be delivered at all. Each day, after clicking "Envoyer" (which I assumed meant "Send"), I received a notification that my e-mail had been sent. But there had been no screen refresh and no typical signs of an e-mail having been sent. The reason, I was told, was that all e-mails were stored on a central server and then sent later once they could establish a satellite link. Sometimes the e-mails would be sent within minutes, and sometimes it took nearly a day. I was told not to worry, and I didn't. I was so impressed that the race had set up computers in a tent in the middle of the Sahara Desert that I decided that actual delivery of the e-mails would be the proverbial icing on the cake.

Even if the e-mails were not delivered, I told myself, the act of writing had always been cathartic for me. Those moments each day served as a valuable reminder of where I was and what I was doing. The contrast between the ten minutes I spent in front of a keyboard and screen, and the other twenty-three hours and fifty minutes of my day was staggering. I was living out of a twenty-two-liter backpack, wearing the same clothing for a week, not showering, sleeping on rocks, and running over God's scorched earth. The unimportance of typing on a keyboard for a few minutes each day put everything into perspective.

Meanwhile, back in the Land of the Free and Home of the Paranoid, a chain of e-mails and phone calls had been stirred to a flurry.

"Oh my God—they haven't posted the race results! What do you think that means?"

"We got Ted's e-mail mid-morning yesterday, but nothing came in today. Is he okay?"

"Do you think that he missed the e-mail hours today because he couldn't finish the stage?"

"Where are the results?"

"Have you gotten an e-mail from him?"

"Why am I obsessing about this so much? What is wrong with me?"

10
The Third Stage

"You've got to be kidding me, Matt," I said. It was 6:30 a.m., and I was returning to the tent after having gone to the bathroom. The ABC crew was filming my long, slow return, complete with a shot of the roll of toilet paper in my left hand.

"How's it going this morning?" Matt asked as I neared the tent.

I shook my head and rolled my eyes. "Okay, let's make this the last time that we film my trip to the loo," I joked, using the British word for the benefit of the British crew. "I hardly think that America is interested in what's going on in my intestines."

"What is going on? Anything we should know about?" I was uncertain if he was serious or not.

"Oh, come on, Ted," Andrea interjected. "That's what American reality TV is all about, right?" She did have a point, I thought. Worries about ABC's presence humorously crept back into my mind. *What if they do an entire segment on national TV, and all they show of me is a trip to the bathroom?* Frankly, I would not have been able to blame them. It would probably sell.

Karen laughed at Andrea's observation. It was a moment of Canadian bonding.

"Sure, eh, it'll be called 'Survivor in the Sahara,' and it'll be all about how nasty people smell, how horrible our feet look, and how often we go to the bathroom."

"Now you're giving them the color commentary they need, Karen," I laughed.

Andrea added, "Hey, guys, if you really want to know what's going on in everyone's intestines at this race, you really should go see for yourselves. I mean, just walk over to the holes in the ground. I *promise you* that you'll get some footage that'll shock the folks back home."

Bruno, the producer, laughed and said, "No thank you. We'll stick to footage of you guys."

Having ABC around had become a pleasure. We had moved beyond our initial excitement, and we had stopped playing to the cameras. They had let their guards down as well. We were no longer subjects to be filmed, but instead friends. When the camera was off, they would ask how we were doing and lament that they could not give us extra food or water. We enjoyed their company and checked in to ask if they were getting what they needed. Just as they wanted us to succeed in our running, we wanted to help them succeed in justifying the budget they had requested to take a crew and expensive equipment to the middle of nowhere for an obscure event that most Americans had never heard of.

And yet, despite our mutual respect, I doubted the need for footage of my return from the toilet.

"Do you guys need anything?" I asked in the spirit of helping them out. "Or are you just grabbing footage? 'Cause I was going to go see how Andrew's doing."

"Just getting general footage. We'll catch up with you later."

"Come back and let us know how he's doing," Karen added. Others echoed her request.

As I walked to Andrew's tent, I expected a repeat of the previous morning: him, huddled, still in his sleeping bag, and miserable. In fact, he was just the opposite: standing, active, and wearing an enormous smile.

"Feeling a bit better today, huh?" I asked.

"Oh, I feel great!" he responded. "I mean, my feet are torn to shreds, but other than that, I'm feeling great. Yesterday went really well. I just took my time, went slow, and finished feeling great. Man, I am so happy that I didn't quit yesterday morning."

I congratulated him on the finish, and I took care not to show my surprise. The truth was that I was amazed that he had recovered

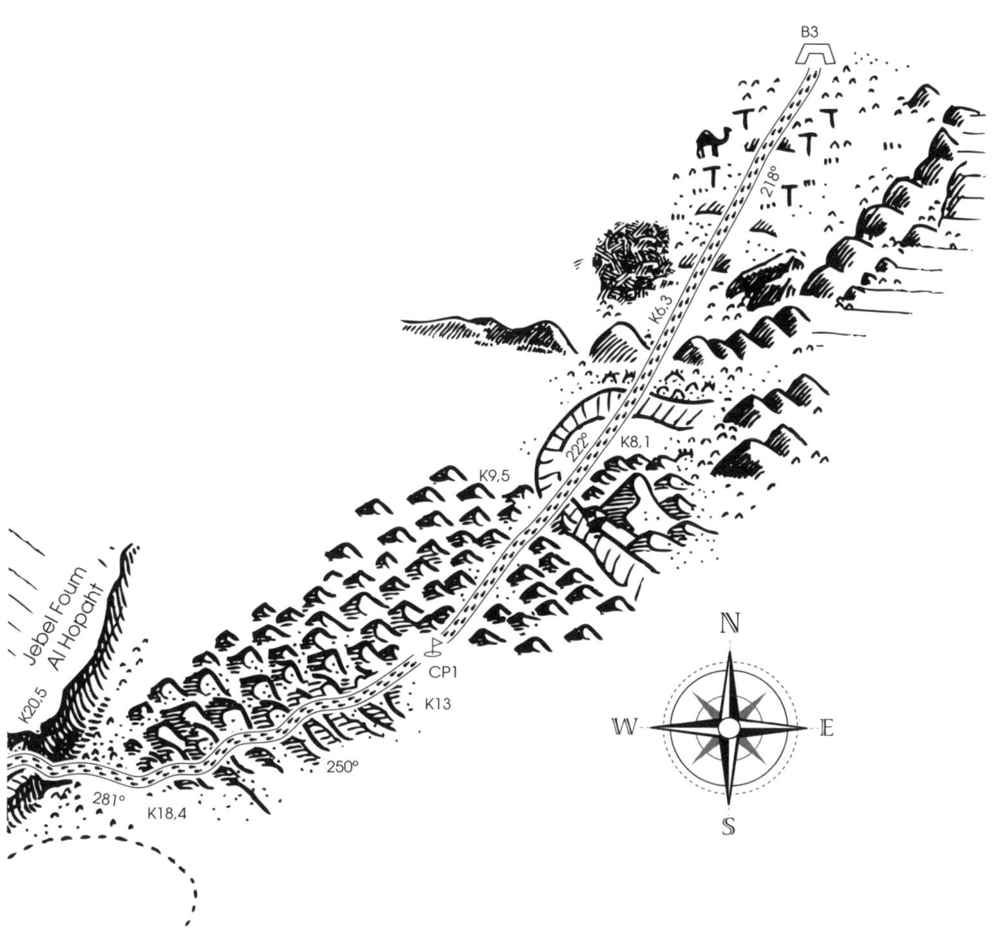

so well after having spent twenty-two of the previous forty-two hours walking in the open Sahara. I did my best to show nothing but happiness for him, for he seemed to have persevered in a way that we had all hoped for but had believed unlikely.

"And, what's better, they're gonna let me continue today even though I missed the cutoff."

"That's great to hear," I responded. I was glad that he brought it up. Knowing that he had visited medical following the first stage and missed the second day's cutoff by half an hour, I was nervous that he might have been disqualified. I watched him as he searched his bag for something to eat.

"Removing nearly ten pounds of food yesterday morning was key," he added.

"It ended up being that much?!" I asked. His pack had been heavy, but I had no idea that he had been carrying double the food of the average competitor.

"Just about. I tossed out so many Clif bars. It was ridiculous. I don't know what I was thinking. Nobody could possibly eat so many of those things." He laughed. In every way he was a different person. His color had returned, his voice was upbeat, and his attitude was uplifting.

I wished him luck and returned to my tent to report the good news. We sat, watching what was left of the sunrise and eating what breakfasts we had.

We talked awhile about our thoughts and fears for the day. From the looks of the hand-drawn picture in our race book, half of the day's twenty-five miles were in sand dunes. Memories from the first day surfaced. I began to recall the importance of balancing quick steps (to avoid sliding back down the dune) with the need to walk slowly in order to conserve energy.

We tended to our feet, double-checked the seals on our gaiters to prevent sand from getting in, and resigned ourselves to another grueling day. My mind had already gone to the fourth stage, and I talked openly about my fear of running at night. Mostly people just listened.

As we walked to the starting line that morning, the pace was the slowest it had been. Some people dragged one leg behind them; others clenched their guts or leaned on a walking stick.

"Hey, Ted," Clarissa of ABC said as she appeared from the side. "We're going to sort of follow you today if that's okay. Matt will run with you a little at the start, and then we'll see you throughout the course."

I looked at Matt, or rather, I looked at the enormous camera he was carrying. "Sure," I said. "But, it's probably a bad day to follow me. I'm going to take it extremely easy today." I recounted the plight of the top fifty, my fear of running at night, and to top it off, my incredible discomfort.

"That's all right," she said, disappointing me. I had thought that a promise of a slow day would have discouraged them from picking on me. "We're just following someone different each day, so you just do what you need to do."

By 8:50 a.m., half of the runners had not yet arrived at the starting line. Patrick Bauer and his translator, perched atop a Land Cruiser off to the left side, kept yelling into the microphone that everyone needed to hurry. Announcements had taken nearly half an hour the previous day, so it was a certainty that we would be starting late this morning.

The thought of further delay upset me as I lumbered toward the starting line. My body had been in a spiral of pain all morning, and despite painkillers, I was feeling increasingly worse. I just wanted the race to start so that it would finish. There was no doubt in my mind that I would walk much of the way. I knew that, in my current condition, I would be poorly prepared to tackle the following day's stage.

Then a funny thing happened. AC/DC began playing, and the speakers did in fact shake me all night long. My adrenaline started pumping; my competitive spirit got the better of me. "You're here to race," a voice inside me said. "Who cares how you feel? Who cares if you're in pain?" I began hopping up and down, alternating feet. I threw my arms back and forth across my chest. "You're here to race. Start racing! Forget about holding back. You'll only regret it." I rolled my neck from side to side.

"One minute to go!" the translator thundered overhead. Inches from the speakers, I was shaking from the vibrations. A man to my left was wearing earplugs.

Maybe it was the music, maybe it was the voice inside me, and maybe it was just my foolish pride. Or perhaps it was simply as shallow as having caught the ABC camera out of the corner of my eye. Whatever it was, one thing was clear: I had decided that I would be racing. After two days of feeling out the Marathon Des Sables—attempting to make friends, or at least peace, with the desert—I chose instead to conquer it or die trying.

I ran briskly and headed toward the front of the pack. Only a handful of runners were ahead of me. The sand was packed tightly, and though there were reasonably large rocks, my feet seemed to naturally avoid them. Matt, the ABC cameraman, ran alongside me. He shuffled sideways, and then ran backwards at what seemed like a full-out sprint—all the while with his eyes in the camera's viewer. Beads of sweat coated his forehead, and he panted. The ground was as rocky as images from the moon landing, but somehow Matt managed to avoid tripping.

The course rapidly turned junky: miles of mushy wadi followed by rolling sand dunes. But today was different. I ran smarter. On the steepest dune sections, I walked in others' footprints. Otherwise, I ran side to side—avoiding others' paths altogether and instead skirting the edges. I felt stronger, and I gained slowly on a few runners who had passed me during the initial wadi.

I approached one runner, Ian—the extremely affable Englishman I had spoken with the day before. He was slightly faster than I, but we had joked during prior days about how much he struggled in the sand. He was angrily stomping at the ground, seemingly hoping to beat it into submission. He was moving extremely slowly as I confidently approached.

"How's it going, Ian?" He turned his head and nodded. "Run with me," I continued, hoping to provide him with a reason to get through the dunes more quickly.

"It's just this sand. It's bloody awful," he said. We crested a dune and enjoyed the downhill.

"Plant your feet flat," I offered. "Don't let your heal dig in, and don't try to push off with your toes." It was valuable advice that my coach had given me in Death Valley, and with a day's practice under my belt in Morocco, I was becoming much more efficient. I wanted to help.

"Ugh, yeah, maybe. I'm gonna need to get you to show me how to do this sometime. I think that if it weren't for this sand, I'd be up in the top ten."

I had no doubt about it.

"Are you going to keep up with me?" I asked, wanting to move faster but also hoping that he would pace off of me. Didi and the other Englishman had helped me so much the day before, so I was encouraging Ian the only way I knew how.

"Naw, go ahead. I'm just going to suffer through this stuff," he responded.

Disappointed, I joked, "All right, well, I'll see you soon: I'm sure you'll catch me on one of the flat sections." He had often done so during the first day.

"I sure hope so," he chuckled, half out of hope and half with a competitive twinge. He had mentioned that morning that he had received e-mails from back home. Friends who had seen the first days' results instructed him not to let the American beat him. We had had a good laugh about it.

Coming through the first checkpoint, I realized that I was somewhere near fifteenth position. The Spaniard from the first day's dunes was just in front of me; one of the Frenchmen was just behind.

"Quatre-cent-quatre-vignt-douze," I heard one of the race officials yell. I had learned enough about French numbers to know that they were yelling the number 492. The pronunciation caught my attention: "Catre-son-catre-van-dooze." *Dooze!* I liked the sound of the number. It had a lyrical quality, and I repeated it over and over again in my head.

"Hey, what happened to running slow?" I heard to my right as I got my water ration card punched and picked up my water. It was Clarissa and Matt of ABC. They were waiting for me.

"Yeah, about that," I said, chuckling. It had not been a lie when I told them my plan, but I was feeling guilty. "I decided just before the race started that I needed to start racing. I'm not sure what's going on, but I feel really good."

"Is the heat affecting you much?" Clarissa asked.

"No. I feel good," I responded as I refilled the water bottles strapped to the front of my pack.

"We're probably going to follow you here during the flat section for a while," she said.

I waved and nodded as I poured the leftover water on my head. I departed the aid station within a minute and quickly resumed running. Matt had decided to run with me.

After a few hundred yards, I could not help but marvel at his running. I estimated that I was running at about eight mph; he was keeping pace with me—holding a camera and running backwards.

"How do you do that?" I asked. It would ruin their ability to use the shot, but I had to know.

"I...trained...in...Afghanistan...to...run...over...rocks.... You...always...need...to...get...the...shot." Streams of sweat poured down his brow. I admired his commitment.

"You should tell the folks at ABC that you deserve a raise," I responded. He laughed and asked me to repeat that on camera later. I said that I would, and he let me continue on.

"I don't know how you run so fast," he said as I continued on. The feeling was mutual.

We ran on flat ground for a short while, but I did not notice if ABC's Land Cruiser had been following me as Clarissa had suggested.

"Catre-son-catre-van-dooze," I repeated several times, deriving strength from the repetition.

Within minutes, we were thrown back into sand dunes. I caught up to the Spaniard and paced off of him. There were two other runners in front of him a ways off, and a pack behind us. He had a camera in his left hand, and he was snapping photos as he went. Sand was in every direction, but there were a few points where we could see mountains in the distance or a small shrub off to the side.

At the top of a major dune, we came across a woman and her three children. The woman was in a full black burka. Her eyes were visible in the small slit of open fabric, but other than that, not even her feet were visible between the edge of her gown and the sand. The three children—two girls and one boy—were around ten years old. Their clothing was Western. One of the girls had a Jordache logo on her jeans; the boy had a small crocodile on his breast.

The Spaniard marched up to each and contorted his body in order to take a photo with each.

I half expected a protest of some sort, but each of them, in turn, looked at the camera and put their arms around the man. Even the woman—dressed to remove her body from the eyes of men—rested one hand on his shoulder and waved with the other, revealing a little of her arm. The Spaniard waved and ran along. I waved as I walked by, but the children seemed disinterested by the absence of a camera.

"Catre-son-catre-van-dooze," I muttered as we approached and then summited a rocky hill.

"Catre-son-catre-van-dooze," I repeated as I fought my way downhill, trying to avoid the scree that scattered beneath my feet. Ian the Englishman scampered past me like a mountain goat, undeterred.

"Catre-son-catre-van-dooze," I repeated as we reentered the dunes and I again flew by Ian and caught up with the Spaniard.

Our seesaw action was fun. We were like NASCAR drivers losing and then retaking the lead. I wondered to myself if our race would be decided by an extra pit stop.

A mile later, the dunes opened up into somewhat of a bowl—the largest dunes on the outskirts, with smaller hills in the middle. A few of us plodded along; we were following the tracks from the other runners—or were we? I looked down and noticed that we were following camel prints.

In the process of repeating my new favorite French word, I had stopped paying attention to where we were running. I looked in front and then behind. I was running with the same group that had lost its way during the first day. But this day's dunes were not quite as large, and the map promised a valley in a short while, so I was not particularly worried.

As we climbed out of the sand bowl, we could see the promised valley not far in the distance. The problem, however, was that our race book showed the second checkpoint positioned immediately outside the dunes. None of us could see a checkpoint, and a number of my companions stopped and looked at one another.

Preferring to remain in my French-numbered daze, I marshaled on. *Catre-son-catre-van-dooze*. Part of me was unconcerned because an open valley was within sight; part of me was incredulous. Continuing was one way to prevent myself from focusing on our collective idiocy. Evidently none of us had learned anything from the first day's scare.

"Catre-son-catre-van-dooze," I said aloud, this time giving the "dooze" extra verve. I ran beyond the final line of sand dunes and continued running into the open valley. To my right, around the curved edge of a dune, I could see the blade of a helicopter in the distance. A few steps later, I could see the checkpoint. We had missed it by a mile or more. Our inability to navigate had certainly cost us time today. I stopped briefly and waved the other runners onward.

"Catre-son-catre-van-dooze," I thought. It had become my soothing mantra, a baby's lullaby.

Nine of us passed through the checkpoint; I took a few additional moments emptying my powdered energy drink into my water bottle. Immediately following the second checkpoint, we were thrown back into yet another set of dunes. I looked at the other runners as we approached and then passed a posted sign with the words, "Cap 313," meaning, "Head at a compass bearing of 313 degrees."

Not a single runner brought out his compass. Twice in the first three days, we had gotten lost; today the error had cost us nearly eight minutes. Flustered, I removed my compass from my bag and decided that it was time to start paying attention to the signs that the race organizers had put up for our benefit. I recalled Terry's comment before the start of the race—"You'll never need a compass, just follow the footsteps"—and I shook my head. That only works when there are footsteps to follow, I thought.

"Catre-son-catre-van-dooze," I said, calming myself down.

"Do you know how to use that thing?" the Spaniard asked, in Spanish.

Perplexed, I held up my compass. "This?"

"Yes. Do you know how to use it?" Had he cracked a smile, I would have assumed that he was kidding. But he looked earnest.

"Yes, I think so," I responded, wondering if my attempt at a Castilian accent was improving or hindering our conversation. "Yes," I said more confidently. "I know how to use it."

"Good," he said, stretching out the word. "I'll follow you, then." He was happy that he would no longer be getting lost, and he was content to go slower, if necessary, to avoid it.

He had never learned how to use a compass, I realized. I thought back to my first experience in Death Valley. It had not been too complicated, but I had required a refresher course when I arrived in Morocco. I had never considered starting the Marathon of the Sands without being sure that I knew how to use a compass. Evidently that sentiment was not a universal one.

The Spaniard and I pressed forward, he telling stories about running, and I rechecking our heading every minute or two.

"What is your fastest marathon time?" he asked.

"Two hours and fifty-six minutes," I responded.

"Really?" He was shocked. "That's it? I run two hours and twenty-eight minutes." A minute per mile faster. My marathon times were in fact slow compared to the times of the other runners around me.

"Yes, that's it. It's a lot slower than many people here," I responded.

"But you run well in these conditions," he said. "And I predict that you do not slow down much on longer distances. Tomorrow, you will do very well—the first twenty for sure." I thought his pronouncement a bit odd, but I liked the thought of it.

We eventually exited the dunes and rounded the corner of

an enormous mountain on our right. The ABC Land Cruiser was positioned at the base of the mountain and began filming as we passed.

"Go England!" the Spaniard yelled at the camera after grabbing my hand and lifting it into the air.

"American," I laughed. "I am from the United States."

The Spaniard's eyes grew wide, and he repeated my nationality. He was surprised to be running with an American. There was no hostility, though. Was the surprise a result of his own misconception, the fact that fewer Americans run the event, or the fact that we tend to be slower? I never did find out.

"Go America, then!" he yelled, again in English, even though we were several steps beyond the camera.

We ran out into a vast expanse of sand and stunted trees. For some time we ran, the ABC truck nearly half a mile in the distance. The hills in the background, I tried to imagine what the African landscape looked like from their perspective. What did I look like from half a mile away, running through shrubs, and with never-ending desert valley in the background?

I thought of myself as part of a Discovery Channel special, and I pictured myself as a cheetah. It was an image that my cheetah-obsessed mother had long ago planted in my mind.

My legs extended out in front of me, my arms swayed back. I could almost see my spots, complete with a tail flopping behind me. No doubt a middle-aged, deep-voiced British man in the Land Cruiser was providing the requisite voiceover: "The cheetah can reach speeds faster than 100 kilometers per hour, but it only runs when chasing prey. This young cheetah seems to have spotted a Spaniard just a short ways off and is going in for the kill."

Proud of my wit, I smiled before falling back into my trance: "Catre-son-catre-van-dooze."

By the time I reached the final checkpoint, I felt nervous. The stage had gone so incredibly well considering its tenuous start. I began to again think of the following day's forty-seven-mile stage.

Above: A pit stop on our drive out to the Saharan starting line.

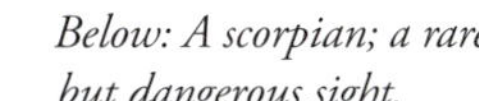

Below: A scorpian; a rare, but dangerous sight.

Above: The dusty ring of tents at a typical bivouac.

Below: A Saharan sunset's beauty can mask the desert's pain.

Above: Tent 77 (from left) Jeff Grant, Michele, Andrea, Karen, Ted, and Brendan. Georgia was missing.

Below: Georgia, the final member of Tent 77. She's definitely "glowing."

Above: A pre-race water distribution checkpoint.

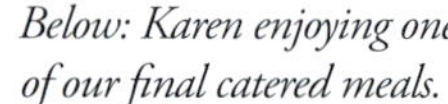

Below: Karen enjoying one of our final catered meals.

Above: Clarissa Ward of ABC conducting a pre-race interview.

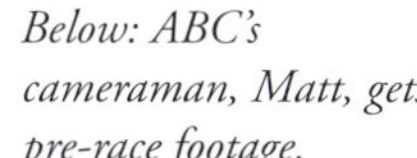

Below: ABC's cameraman, Matt, gets pre-race footage.

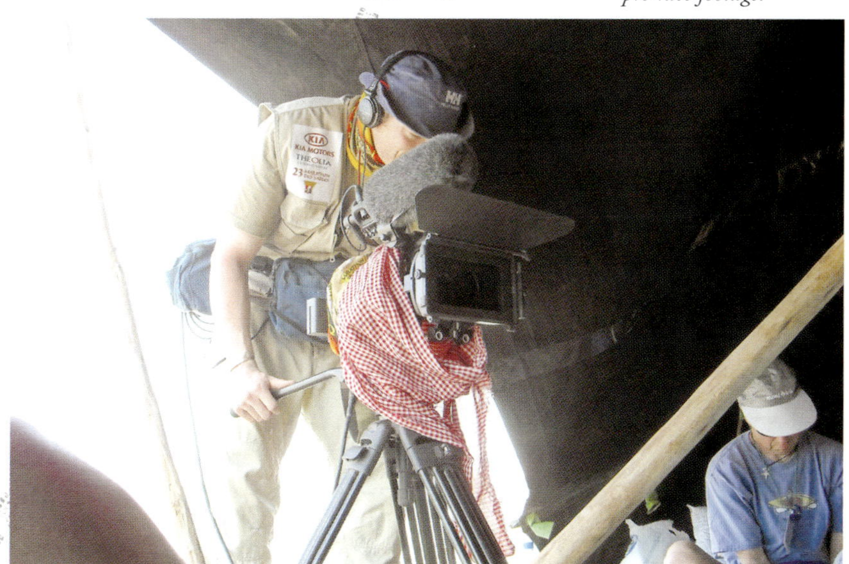

Above: Pre-race, the waiting is the hardest part.

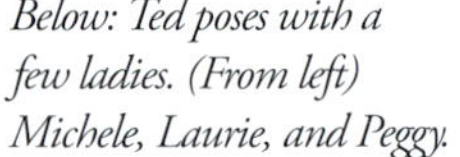

Below: Ted poses with a few ladies. (From left) Michele, Laurie, and Peggy.

Above: Mike and Leigh, smiling...obviously before the race has begun.

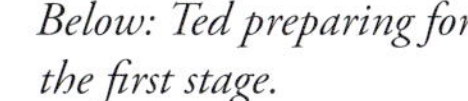

Below: Ted preparing for the first stage.

Above: The starting line on day one.

Below: Jay Batchen, sporting his exceptional hairdo, at the starting line.

Above: The Erg Chebbi dunes confronted us on the first day.

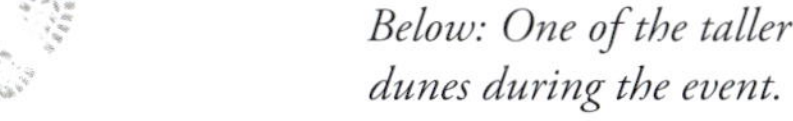

Below: One of the taller dunes during the event.

Above: A typical, never-ending, expansive flat.

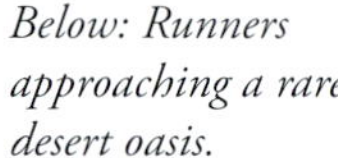

Below: Runners approaching a rare desert oasis.

Above: The long stage's daunting climb that led to the naming of this book.

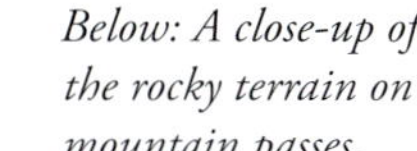

Below: A close-up of the rocky terrain on mountain passes.

Above: A view of Ted running by during the long stage.

Below: A rare hut, this qualified as a "town" in the race book.

Above: After nearly thirty hours, Steve Wolk finishes the 47-mile long stage.

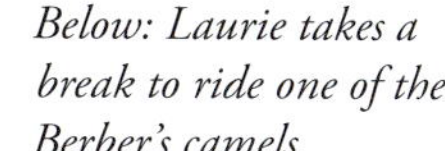

Below: Laurie takes a break to ride one of the Berber's camels.

Above: Bunny, proving that a week in the desert leads to hygienic inconveniences.

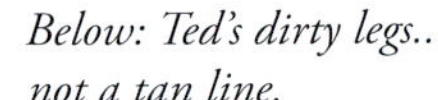

Below: Ted's dirty legs... not a tan line.

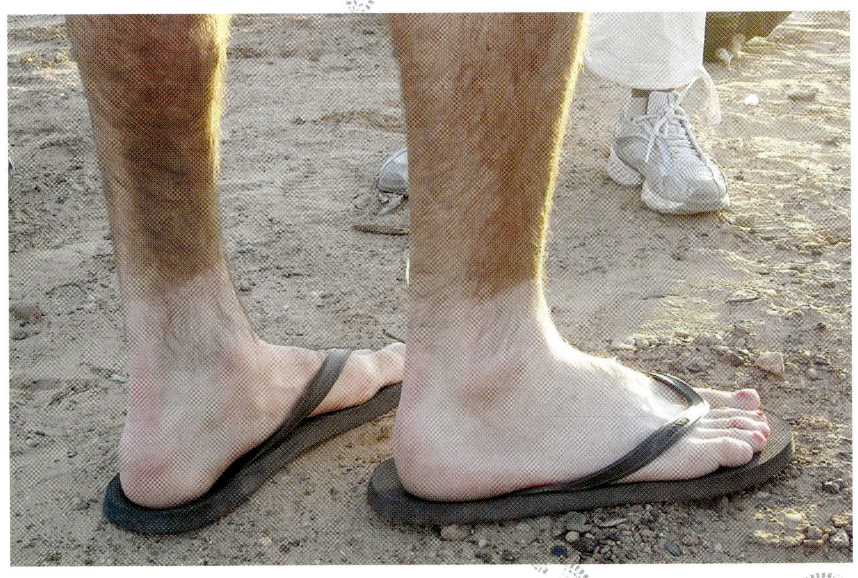

Above: A surprise Pepsi on Day Five. (From left) Aaron, Ted, Jeff Arricale, and Andrea.

Below: Following a stage, Ted being interviewed by ABC at the finish line.

Above: A not-so-rare site in the Sahara.

Below: Confident, happy, and excited American and Canadian runners.

No doubt I would be starting at noon, but I wanted to make sure that I would be as fresh as possible for the long day. In fourteenth place for the day and staring at a long stretch of wadi, I decided that I should put on the breaks for the day. Certainly I could expend my energy in the wadi and save a few minutes—but at what price? I knew that I could suffer an injury or just be fatigued. Slowing down, though it would cost me a few minutes, was the prudent decision for a week-long event.

The final run into the bivouac seemed to drag on indefinitely. The terrain sloped slowly downward, and the tents were visible for miles just above the tops of the shrubs. Seven runners passed me in the final miles, but I could hear their heavy breathing as they passed. I moved easily. I could not believe how good I felt just three and a half hours after intending to walk most of the day.

"Catre-son-catre-van-dooze," I again repeated, enjoying the way that the words rolled off the tongue. "Catre-son-catre-van-dooze," I said to myself as the wadi opened up to compact, rocky sand, and I sprinted toward the finish.

I crossed the finish and looked at my watch. The day's stage, despite being a mile longer and consisting of much more difficult terrain, only took an additional fifteen minutes over the previous day's run. More importantly, I felt good, not as though I wanted to die.

I let out a scream at the top of my lungs. Everything had gone ideally: I had run comfortably, but well; painlessly, but fast; intelligently, but hard. To date, the only positive part of the experience had been the friendships made in the tent and beyond. That moment—from the perspective of running—had been what I had come for. It was the perfect moment, where I had run within myself but triumphed over the conditions. I had no words to describe the satisfaction at having reached that point, but a scream certainly sufficed.

"You feel good, then?" It was Bruno of ABC, with Matt and Clarissa by his side. Evidently, they had been entirely serious about their intention to follow me the entire day. I thought about the previous day's experience with Didi's French camera crew and felt even sillier. Now I was getting attention but mostly unaware of ABC's presence.

"Oh, yeah," I responded. "Today was a very good day. A *very good* day."

"What made it so good? Why was it better than other days?" Bruno asked.

"Who in the heck knows," I said, careful to use PG-rated language. "In all honesty, I have no explanation. This morning I had planned on running slow. I felt horrible. I was miserable. Then I started moving, and everything just clicked."

"Why do you think that happened?"

I paused and looked into the camera. "There's no explanation for it. Seriously. I know that's not what you want to hear, but it's the truth. None of it makes any sense. I felt incredible today, but all initial signs pointed to a struggle."

"You don't have any ear buds," Matt commented from behind the camera. "Everyone else seems to be running with music, but you don't. You must think about a lot out there with all that time."

I looked at Matt and said, "Honestly, I think of nothing." He pressed me, insisting that something had to be going through my mind. I proceeded to discuss *catre-son-catre-van-dooze* and explained that I had repeated the number either aloud or in my head for two hours. "So, Matt, that's what I did with my brain for two whole hours today." I saw them laughing, trying not to snort and mess up the interview.

Back at the tent, I repeated my ritual. I removed my shoes and socks, mixed a recovery drink, and snacked on some beef jerky. Lying down with my feet elevated, I could not wait to begin the following day's stage. Not thirty minutes prior I had finished a twenty-five-mile run through heat and dunes, and yet, I was already looking forward to more running. What a difference a day made.

My tent mates trickled in, though more slowly than in the first few days. First Jeff, then Brendan, and then a struggling Michelle arrived. She continued to walk awkwardly. Her stomach was still a concern, and she was suffering from other signs of weakness. She threw her bag to the ground and said a weak hello. Her water bottles dropped, and she sat down. Her goggle-shaped sunburn had worsened, and she was shaking.

Over the course of the following hour, she worsened. With temperatures above 110 degrees, she climbed into her sleeping bag and began to shiver.

"Michelle, what do you say we get you to medical?" I asked. "Maybe they'll have something to help your stomach and your chills."

"No, I just need to lie here and hope that it goes away," she responded. I looked at Jeff, and his face reflected my worry.

"Michelle, maybe Ted is right. You don't have to get any treatment that would get you a penalty, but just let them look at you," Jeff pleaded. Michelle again declined, even rejecting a suggestion that we get someone from medical to come to see her in the tent so that she would not be forced to move.

For Jeff and me it was a dilemma. We knew about pride, competitive spirit, and stubbornness. And we knew that Michelle was considerably more experienced than we were. Part of us wanted to concede that she deserved the right to be stubborn, but as we looked at her shivering, worry took over.

"I'm going to go get Jay," I whispered to Jeff. "Michelle won't feel that she can say no to him."

Jeff liked the idea and stayed with Michelle as I walked off to find Jay.

It was a well-engineered ruse, really. I returned to the tent and had a normal conversation with Jeff. Jay followed a few minutes later, pretending as though he was visiting all of our group's tents to check in. When he noticed Michelle in her sleeping bag, he suggested to her that she needed to go to medical, and she begrudgingly agreed. As they walked off together, Jeff and I felt a bit proud of ourselves for so deviously arranging for good.

The result was a good one. The doctors indicated that she was significantly dehydrated and gave her some sort of rehydration salts with fifty ounces of water. When she returned to the tent an hour later, Michelle was still not healed, but she appeared to be improving.

The afternoon was hot, but my spirits were high enough. It was a struggle, though. Suffering was everywhere. We had run seventy miles over three days; we had spent nearly five days cleaning sand from our teeth and shifting around at night to prevent rocks from digging into our skin. Most feet had developed blisters on top of blisters, which would pop open to reveal a mess of dying flesh. Every part of our bodies was coated in a thin film of greasy sand. Muscles burned. Sunburns were common. I was noticeably thinner but had begun to look with revulsion upon the food that I had left in my pack. I scanned what I could see of the camp from my prostrate position—from Michelle's motionless slumber, to a man on all fours, to a woman barely able to walk—and was amazed that this event had taken place for twenty-three straight years.

In spite of all of the misery, we continued and felt all the more alive for doing so. We had found a place between suffering and death that reminded us how fulfilling life could be.

Georgia arrived back at the tent. We were surprised; she had come in much faster than on previous days.

"Holy cow, Georgia," Jeff said. "Strong day, huh." He was congratulating her, but Georgia's face was not filled with pride. She informed us that she had withdrawn from the race. Shaking her face, she was noticeably angry.

"Geez, sorry to hear that," I said. Brendan and Michelle, who had appeared to have been sleeping, both turned over and looked up.

"Are you okay?" Michelle asked.

"Yeah, I'm fine now. Now I'm sort of pissed for pulling out given how I feel now." She tossed her things somewhat erratically into the tent. More than anything else, her spirits were wounded.

"At the time, in those dunes, I just struggled so much," she sighed. "I had run out of water with more than a mile to go to a checkpoint, and when I got there I just broke down."

There was no way for us to respond. We were grateful that she was okay—defiant, in fact. We had seen the helicopter airlift out a few competitors who had needed serious medical attention, and we had all heard the story about the man who had died the year before. Georgia moved quite well now, but we all felt sorry that her journey was over. She talked about the desert and her pain; we imagined how difficult it must have been to endure the suffering—and how much more difficult it would have been to tell the race organization that the end had arrived.

"What happens now?" someone asked her.

"Well, I wish I could continue; I wish I hadn't withdrawn. But, since I did, they took all of the food out of my backpack so that I couldn't give it to you guys, and they're going to feed me with the race officials now. They gave me the option to leave or spend the rest of the week in the tent with you guys. I decided to stick around to remember how this feels." She paused.

"Sorry, Georgia," a few of us echoed. Those closest asked if there was anything they could do.

"You know," she said, "it's a good thing that I'm already registered for next year. I'll be better trained and know how to manage my water better. And, I'll get to do it with Monte." She was referring to her husband, who had later regretted missing the registration deadline because of his indecision.

We sat awhile in silence.

It was a moment that all of us had feared—and yet, as I reflected, I realized that it could have been worse. As sad as it was to watch Georgia throw her shoes to the ground in disgust, I was grateful that she was with us, and not seriously injured.

After a while, I walked over to a neighboring tent to see how others were doing. Not having traveled to the finish line following the day's stage, I wanted to get my dose of other competitors. "Toby," I called out to the crass Englishman, hoping he could lighten the mood. He had just finished for the day and was tossing his gear into the tent.

"There he is. How are you doing today, sir?" He had a near beard and sunburn, but a wide grin.

"Doing pretty well, actually. Feeling pretty darn good." I paused. "Georgia had to drop today, though, which sucks."

Toby winced and shook his head. "It's really brutal out there. Some people are really struggling. That's too bad." It was a genuine, softer side of a man who had become known for fart jokes and ridiculous proclamations. One of our group's two adopted Englishmen, he was beloved for his humor. But beneath the jokes was a deep sense of caring and compassion.

"I struggled a lot today, too," he said, confidently. "Nothing major, but it's tough."

I listened to him talk about the day and offered consolation where I could.

"I hear that you sort of screwed up on your goal of taking it slow today," he needled, a bit of spark returning to his voice. I had gotten a number of playful insults from people for my quick finish after having declared that I would be taking the stage slowly.

"Heh, yeah, that sort of didn't happen, did it?" I chuckled. "I don't know what happened, Toby. Yesterday I felt horrible, and for no apparent reason, today I felt great."

"Sometimes it's like that," he said. It was matter-of-fact and somehow wise. "Hey, how's that Andrew kid doing today? Has anyone seen him yet?"

I responded that he had not yet arrived, but noted that there was still an hour before the day's cutoff time. Toby shook his head as I spoke.

"He's a tough little twit, huh?" he asked, affectionately calling attention to Andrew's perseverance. "I thought he looked really bad after the first day. I'll be honest, I didn't think that he was going to make it yesterday, but good for him."

Having run the race five years in a row, Toby had a perspective that none of us had. He was hardened, wise, knowledgeable. Things that bothered all of us tremendously, Toby did not even notice. He knew exactly what to pack with him, exactly when to eat, and exactly how he would feel at various points. He had also developed a perspective on the environment around him. He had seen countless runners struggle through the Marathon Des Sables, and he was good at identifying the warning signs in another's walk, the weather, or a myriad of other factors. From his gait to the look in his eyes, Andrew had many of those signs.

Night fell, and the deadline passed. All but one runner in the American/Canadian/Australian contingent had arrived. Sadly, Andrew was nowhere to be seen. As we had the previous night, a few of us searched for him at the finish line, asked for clues at the registration desk, and checked in with medical personnel. The truth of the matter was that we could do nothing. Sure, we felt better walking from structure to structure to ask questions, but the reality was that we were homeless souls in the middle of nowhere. The race officials had their comforts, and though we could see them and ask questions, there was nothing we could do to alleviate our or another's suffering.

We were informed at the registration tent that the day's deadline had in fact been extended an additional hour, which meant that Andrew actually had another twenty minutes to arrive. Yet, as we stared off into the darkness, it seemed unlikely that he would arrive anytime soon. It was pitch black, but we could not see a single headlamp in the distance. I remembered the wadi in which we finished that day, with the scraggly trees that shot up six to eight feet into the air. I suggested to others that he was perhaps obscured by the vegetation and thus a lot closer than we knew. I was grasping, I knew, but it made me feel better.

The revised deadline passed. A few Land Cruisers trickled in from various directions, and we peered in the windows looking for him. Most of us figured that if Georgia had been unable to make it, Andrew's blistered feet would prevent him from finishing as well. Still nothing. The officials at the finish line had no record of him crossing, and the rest of the personnel were holding the night's final meeting in the registration tent. The little college student who could was nowhere to be found.

After 9 p.m., as we were all settling in for bed and awaiting the night's e-mail delivery, we heard a few cheers with his name.

"Andrew!"

"Hey, Andrew, all right! Welcome!"

"You're actually looking good!"

As he got closer, he announced to one of the tents, "Oh, yeah. I finished. I took a little while, didn't I? But I finished. I actually feel great—absolutely great. It's just that I got lost with this other guy. As soon as the sun went down, we wandered off course a few miles until we figured things out and ended up finding the camp. I would have been here an hour or two ago if we hadn't gotten lost."

None of us in Tent 77 could see him, but we listened to him recount the day and talk about how good he felt. He had been out in the desert for more than twelve hours, most of that time alone, in temperatures that had started around eighty degrees, climbed to 120, and dropped fast to the present fifty-five. Somehow, despite all of the misery, he was in good spirits.

"All right, I've got to get something to eat," he announced. "'Cause I think that I'm going to need the energy and sleep tomorrow." It was as though someone had replaced the kid from Tennessee with a grizzled mountain man—and then found a way to make him giggle.

Our nightly e-mails arrived as Jeff and I were talking about how incredible Andrew's resolve was. We had been back at camp for seven or eight hours; Andrew was removing his pack for the first time all day.

Georgia was in better spirits. She talked awhile about her lingering disappointment, but she had begun to place things in perspective. She was proud of what she had accomplished—and motivated to conquer the event the following year. "Now I just want to see all of you kick butt," she said.

It was then that I realized something that made this journey different from any other athletic event: mutual admiration. Jeff, Brendan, and I were racing, and our times thus far had ranged from three and a half to five hours. Andrea, Karen, and Georgia had been mostly walking and had taken at least twice as long to finish each stage. Michelle, being sick, was stranded in between. But one thing was evident: each of us was in awe of the other. The girls could not comprehend how we were able to run so fast; we were impressed at the resolve and hard work necessary to keep moving for such a long day. There was no room for arrogance. Each of us marveled at the other's effort.

"Listen to this," Georgia yelled out. "It's from Coach Lisa. She says, 'Georgia, you're glowing!' What in the heck does that mean? I haven't had a shower in five days—that's called gross, shiny skin!"

It felt good to laugh and be together, but we were all preoccupied. No one discussed the following day's menacing long stage, a forty-seven-mile trek that would force many of us to run all day and then through the next night.

11
Packing

My foot tapped nervously as my eyes scanned the TSA security line. My bag disappeared into the X-ray machine. Just after it passed beyond the rubber separation strips, I shot a look at the woman who was responsible for examining the contents of the carry-on luggage.

I was hoping that she would not notice that I had twenty-three Ziploc baggies full of white powder. I had separated them as best as I could, trying to mask them with other food items and clothes.

The woman looked disinterested as my bag passed through, and I breathed a sigh of relief as it emerged undisturbed on the other side. Not wanting to chance a more thorough examination, I rapidly slipped into my shoes and scuttled along.

A few days earlier, I had sat in my living room with two canisters of Heed energy drink, packages of beef jerky, jars of macadamia nuts, more than a dozen freeze-dried meals, and assorted clothing. I spread them out across the floor and looked at the pathetic packages that would have to sustain me for a week.

I had spoken and e-mailed with a number of the Americans who were preparing for the Marathon Des Sables, and those conversations had led me to believe that my plans were more efficient than theirs. Others planned on bringing thirty-liter packs; mine had only a twenty-two-liter capacity. Others talked about bringing additional changes of clothes; I had only a few extra pair of socks.

I looked out over the various items and felt confident that everything would fit without complications. I was so certain of this that I began packing without any modifications, stuffing entire jars of nuts, along with entire canisters of Pringles potato chips. Sure, I reasoned, there was a bit of extra weight and air, but I reasoned that I could deal with that because I was surely bringing fewer items than anyone else.

Boy, was I wrong. After having stuffed only four days' worth of food into my pack, along with my flip-flops and extra socks, it was full. I could barely close the zipper, and three days worth of food remained on the floor. It was time to reexamine my methodology.

I started by rationing out individual servings of Heed energy drink into snack-sized Ziploc baggies. After pouring two scoops of powder into each bag, I was careful to seal it completely and remove the excess air. When all was over, I had twelve pouches of orange- and eleven pouches of lemon-flavored drink mix. Without their original bags, they took up slightly less space, but it would obviously still be a daunting task to further reduce the mass of my belongings.

I removed the nuts from their jars and portioned them into individual baggies, estimating how many cashews or sunflower seeds I would want on a particular day. I did the same with Pringles potato chips and was careful to take the time to smash them into crumbs so that I could reduce them to the smallest possible amount of space.

Dried cranberries are a good choice when sucking the air out of the bag is one's objective. A little jiggling of the bag causes the various pieces of fruit to press against one another in just the right way, almost concealing every other berry. However, despite their efficient spacing abilities, cranberries offer a poor calories-per-ounce ratio, which is a dangerous trait when the overall packing objective is to be as light as possible.

Macadamia nuts, by contrast, offer an incredible 190 calories per ounce—more than double that of cranberries. Getting them to compact into a smaller amount of space, however, is a bit trickier.

Thus was the exercise—with freeze-dried lasagna, blueberry granola, and pastas; chips; nuts; drink powders; and other assorted snacks. I weighed, measured, and compacted foods in hopes of maximizing the number of calories that I could fit into a given space and weight.

The night before my flight to New York City (which is where I would catch my flight to Morocco), I sat on the floor of my living room with plastic baggies strewn throughout the room. I stared at my chosen backpack, which had a capacity about that of an oversized women's handbag.

Somehow, I would have to pack everything I would need for a week into something smaller than a gym bag.

I first took my sleeping bag, a $300, seventeen-ounce, tightly-packed bag I had ordered special online. It went to the very bottom because I had read somewhere that a sleeping bag belonged at the bottom of the pack. It took up about 90% of the width of the pack, making it convenient to shove a few pair of socks down the sides.

My flip-flops were next. They were cardboard thin and weighed little more, and they easily slid upright behind the sleeping bag and up along the rigid portion of the pack. My girlfriend had found them in an Old Navy closeout bin for $2.50. It had been the best dollar-for-dollar purchase of anything in my list of gear. At size thirteen, they nearly touched the top zipper.

I then began stuffing gallon-sized Ziploc bags, each filled with smaller baggies that totaled a day's food ration. One lay horizontally atop the sleeping bag, three stood vertically across the width, and a fifth barely made it under the top of the pack. I zipped up my pack, straining to get the final inches to close.

I looked across the floor and saw two days worth of food, an inflatable sleeping mat, a long-sleeved shirt I had planned on changing into as the nights closed in, two water bottles, and an assortment of compulsory items mandated by the race organization.

The only spaces remaining in the pack were three neoprene pouches—one on each side and a larger one in the back. I started indiscriminately shoving items into the various pouches.

My compulsory medical items—salt pills, antiseptics, a snake venom pump, and an aluminum blanket—went into one of the side pouches, along with a Ziploc bag full of Advil, Tylenol, and electrolyte tablets. Into the other pouch went my final pair of socks, a spoon, some Band-Aids and athletic tape, safety pins, spare flashlight batteries, a butane lighter, and the required steel-blade knife. I tucked my compass and headlamp (both required items) into the zipper pouches that wrapped around the waste belt.

With only the back pouch remaining, I shoved the food into the bottom, tucked the spare shirt around the food, and then extended the strap that connected the neoprene to the top of the pack by way of a small plastic clasp. I wrapped the strap around my sleeping pad, adhering it only via compression, and successfully locked the clasp.

My girlfriend returned to the room and laughed when she saw the pack. It bulged in areas that definitely should not have been bulging. The back of the bag alone looked like a hunchback riding a camel. I looked at her, then at the bag. Shrugging my shoulders, I picked it up and threw it across my shoulders. Like a wicked step-sister hoping to get her prince, I squirmed and twisted to try to make it appear a comfortable fit.

"Looks comfortable, babe." She had a wide grin on her face and was shaking her head in disbelief. I knew that this would be another story she could tell others when she announced that her boyfriend had signed up to run "The Marathon du Crazy People."

Weighing closer to thirty pounds than the twenty-two I had hoped for, it was nowhere near comfortable. But, with only twelve hours until my flight, it would have to do. I would repack it once I got to Morocco—and repack it, and repack it, and repack it.

12
The Long Day

When the Berbers arrived to tear down our tent on the morning of the fourth day, we were already awake. The night had been calm, but we struggled nonetheless. We had trained for half a year or more for this experience, and we had built our expectations around the fourth day. This year's monster would start on flat ground but included three major climbs, the first of which had been incorporated into the previous year's event as well.

I thought about what Toby had said about this particular climb: "My brother got to the base of the mountain, threw his bag down, and quit. He just said that there was no way he could do it, and he stopped."

Before we could get on with the event, we awaited the decision from the race officials as to whether or not Andrew would be allowed to continue. After the first stage, he had gone to medical. After the second, he was half an hour beyond the allotted time. And he had missed the stage three cutoff by more than an hour.

Andrew walked around the camp and was nervous. He looked stronger than he had the entire event—his cold gone, his face a normal color, and an air of confidence—but he still walked with a pronounced limp. He wanted so badly to be allowed to continue, but all he could do was wait.

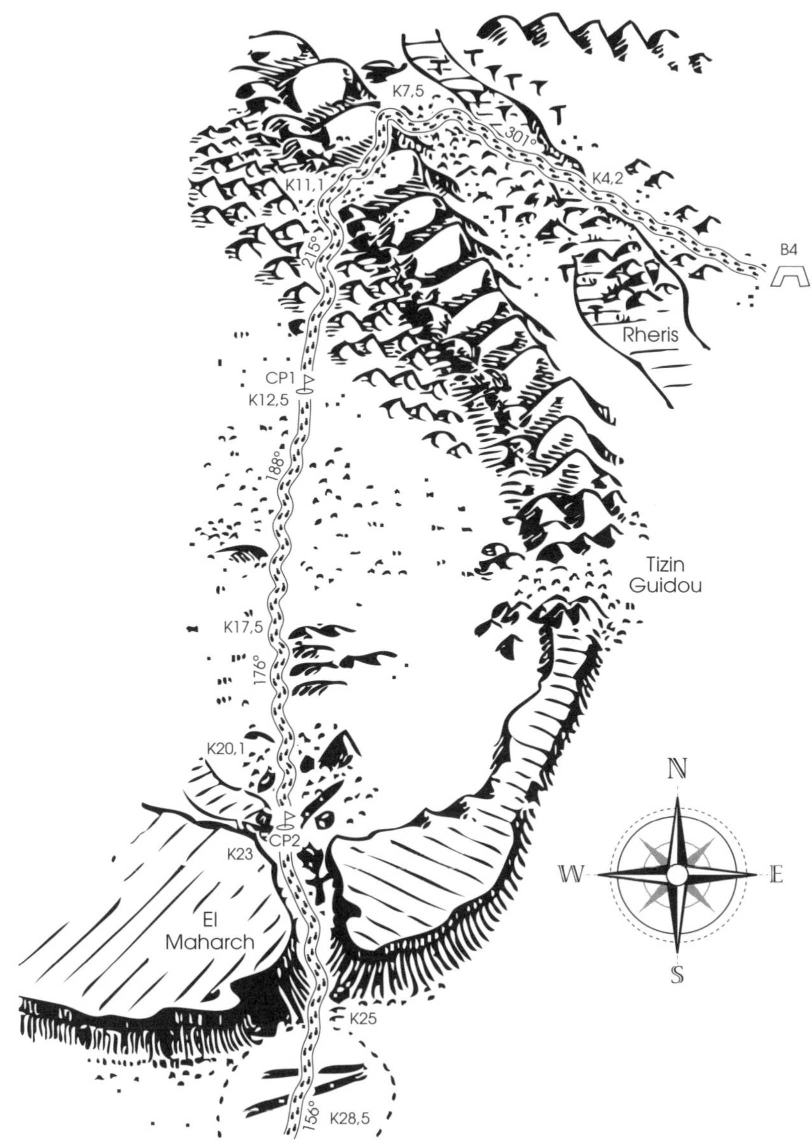
K7,5
301°
K4,2
K11,1
215°
B4
Rheris
CP1
K12,5
188°
Tizin
Guidou
K17,5
176°
K20,1
CP2
K23
El
Maharch
N
W
E
S
K25
156°
K28,5

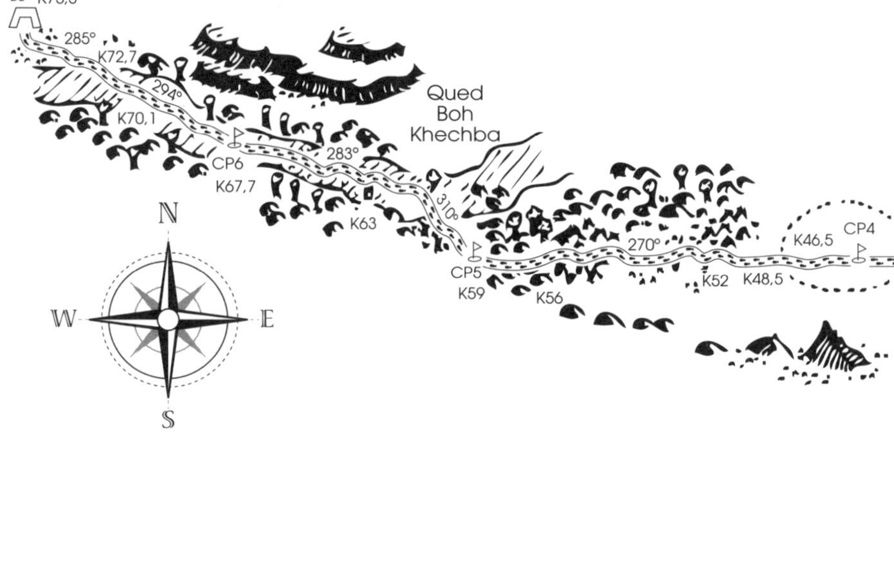

***

There is a balance in extreme athletics. The bar should be set high, and no exceptions should be made for the elite athletes. But what is the right course of action for the non-elite? The vast majority of the field had no aspirations of competing to win. Their competition was internal. They had set an objective of conquering the world's toughest footrace, and for them, finishing time did

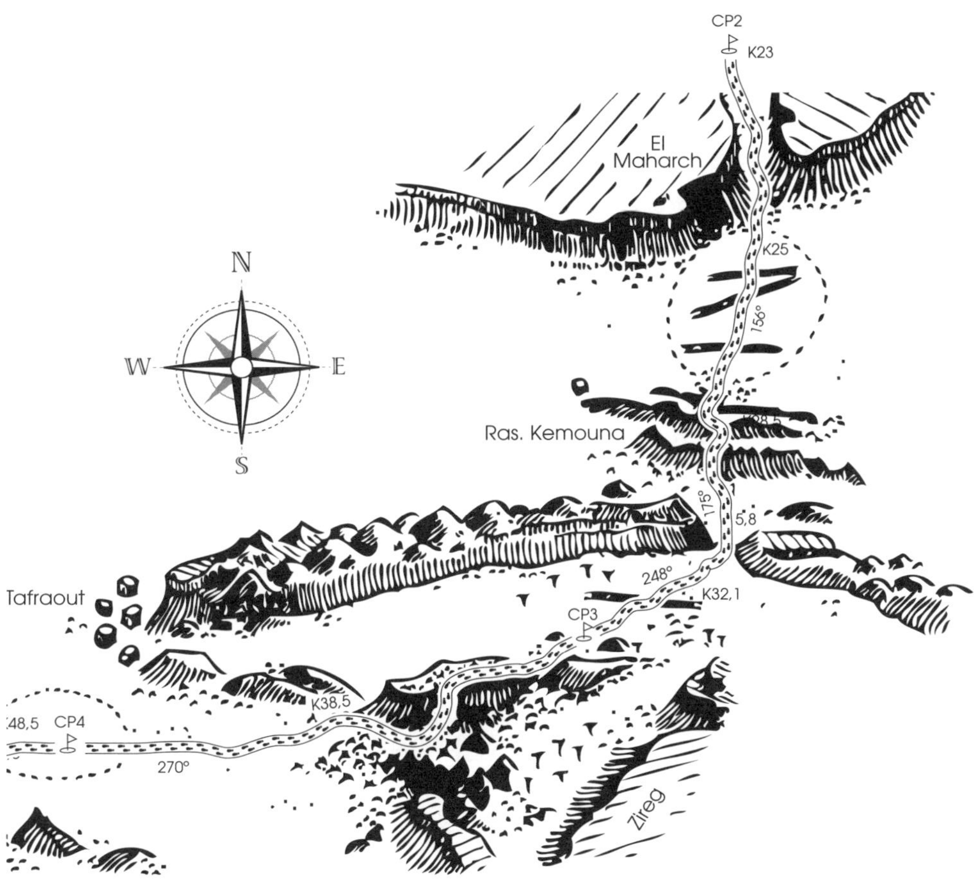

not matter. Coming in, most of us had no idea how long it would take us to complete a twenty-mile run in those conditions. What we wanted, however, was to feel satisfied—complete—when we finished each day. We wanted the knowledge that we had prepared, persevered, and did what our bodies would allow us to do. Races should allow for these aspirations. They should permit the hard-working athlete the option to reach for greatness—even if their definition of greatness is vastly different from that which is glorified on ESPN.

And yet, there is a flip side: A race is an event with standards. Rules exist to preserve order and maintain the sanctity of the experience. For more than two decades, runners from all around the world had been traveling to Morocco to participate in an experience that promised to be difficult but possible. They expected a chance, but not to be coddled. Bending rules, then, necessarily becomes a delicate art. Looking the other way to help someone succeed is admirable, but one must be careful not to damage the reputation of the event by allowing certain athletes too much leeway.

These were the issues that the officials no doubt debated. These, and safety. We were entering the most daunting phase of the event, and it would be imprudent to put someone in undue danger. Everyone waited for a decision to be handed down. Andrew, of course, was most nervous of all. He packed his bag, ate breakfast, and waited.

I meandered around the camp, doing none of my normal preparations. The previous day's run had ranked me in the mid-twenties overall, which meant that I would be starting at noon instead of the normal 9 a.m. It was lonely to watch the other Americans prepare. I felt as though I had been reprimanded for my performance. Everyone else was being allowed to go do something together, but I had a three-hour "time-out" to contend with. I imagined myself in a corner, wearing a cone-shaped hat, and sobbing.

Everyone walked toward the starting line. Wanting something to do, I followed. Besides, I needed to know where I would be put for the three hours in between starts.

As our group lumbered toward the starting line, Jay walked up to Andrew and whispered something in his ear. Andrew immediately shook his head and removed his glasses. He was crying.

"Did you tell them that I'm okay?" he whispered. "Did you tell them that I really want to continue?" He choked out the words in between sobs. Moments before he had been no different than any of us—his bag on his back, his water bottles filled, and his outfit ready for action. Now, he was dejected.

"Sorry, Andrew," Jay responded. "I really am. I told them all of that, but they just said 'no way.' They're really concerned about safety heading into the long stage, and they're not willing to take any chances."

He offered a few weak protests, and a few of us asked if perhaps they would reconsider. But the decision was final, and Jay had the ugly responsibility of taking Andrew's race bib from him. No doubt someone from the race would be by shortly to confiscate his food so that he could not help any of his countrymen.

"Sorry, Andrew," I offered. There was nothing constructive to say. He had been one of the slowest competitors throughout the event, and it might very well have been dangerous for him to continue. And yet, he so desperately wanted to go. I muttered a few words about how he should be proud. I reminded him that he had gathered strength for two more stages after wanting to quit the first day. He nodded but continued crying. No words could mean anything at this point. He handed his race bib to Jay, and they walked off together to check in with the race officials.

After watching Andrew's hopes get crushed, the mood darkened briefly, but people refocused quickly. Under other conditions, distractions might be permissible, but it would be irresponsible to do anything but focus on the day's task.

In the middle of a vast valley, with hundreds of miles of death in every direction and mountains visible for 360 degrees, there were three lone black tents standing to the side of the finish line. Long ago our tents had been thrown into trucks and driven off. Hours earlier the registration tents, Land Cruisers, and all other signs of human life had been removed. All that remained was a starting line and three black tents. Those, I presumed, would serve as my home for the following three hours.

My friends disappeared, listened to AC/DC, and sang a few rounds of "Happy Birthday." The wind was picking up, and the sand began shooting across the barren plane, so I dropped myself into one of the tents. Inside were men I had seen but did not know. Like the London subway, no one talked. Part of it was the language barrier, but part of it seemed to be that same sense that traveling Brits emit during their commutes: life was tough, and establishing a connection with another human being would only serve to make it tougher.

Shortly after nine o'clock, the race began. Lying down, I waited for them to pass, and within moments energy swept by. Jeff was near the front, Brendan just behind him. As the trail of runners grew longer, the scene shifted: some carried flags, some screamed, and some made airplane or monkey gestures. It looked more like San Francisco's Bay-to-Breakers run than the Marathon Des Sables. I kept looking, half expecting to see naked people, a family dressed as fish, a fraternity doing keg-stands, and a traveling Hawaiian-themed Tiki hut.

The crowd thinned, and the walkers passed by. They talked, laughed, and gestured as though they were in a neighborhood park. I thought of my brief human contact during the first few stages, and part of me wished that I could have shared each day's experience more fully with someone I knew.

Then, the camel walked by. His job was to follow the last competitor, and his joints ached along as the older couple slowly plodded forward.

Moments later there was nothing but the sound of the wind against the black canvas of our tent. Fifty of us remained, but we sat, motionless and conserving energy. There was no conversation. I found myself listening for the rustle of a backpack so that I would know that life existed.

It helped to sleep. I had set the alarm on my watch to wake me, and I drifted in and out of consciousness. Each time I heard the wind, I quickly rolled over, praying that I could get back to the friendly thoughts in my head.

With more than an hour before we were to begin, I stepped outside the tent and looked around. It was complete desolation. Complete isolation. As I stood to the side of the tent, I could not see a single person in any direction. If I had blocked out the tents, I would have been entirely alone—with a 2,000-foot-high mountain ridge to my left and endless valley stretched out before me. Only hours before, this had been a small city, but there were no longer any signs of that.

When it was finally time to begin, a Land Cruiser emerged from behind a hill and drove to where the starting line had once been. A race volunteer pulled two metal stakes from the back of the vehicle and pounded them into the cracked earth, about twenty feet apart. He then tied a yellow plastic rope between them, forming a three-foot-high starting line. A companion distributed a bottle of water to each competitor, and fifteen minutes before we were to begin, I could feel a bit of adrenaline course through my veins.

Race Director Patrick Bauer made fun of Mohamad Ahansal, who was currently in first place. Other Frenchmen joined in. People stretched, made last-minute adjustments to their packs, and nibbled on a few final morsels of food.

Just past noon, Patrick whistled and motioned for everyone to assemble. I expected the day's announcements, a few birthdays, and a few jokes. Instead, he plainly informed us that we would start in a minute, and two of his volunteers stood ready to drop the rope. He counted down in a calm voice—no microphone and no music—and we began. The long stage of the Marathon Des Sables, what should have been a momentous occasion, for us began with a whimper.

The course was flat—compact sand with only an occasional rock, which made the pace quick. Fear drove me to run faster than I would have otherwise. I had no desire to be anywhere near the back of the group. Unlike the 9 a.m. contingent, we had no Berber atop a camel to follow the final competitor. If the final runner in our group lost sight of the others, he would have been completely alone, with no one for hundreds of miles behind.

As usual, Mohamad led a pack of five runners. Clustered in a tight group, they slowly pulled away. A few more of us ran in a loose grouping as we entered an area of small, rolling dunes with small green shrubs. To the left, a few hundred yards away, was a mountain range. Flat on top, it reminded me of the tepuis scattered across the Venezuelan countryside: exceptionally steep mountains that rose rapidly from the valley floor and stood independently. But, unlike in Venezuela, there was no rich, green vegetation atop these Moroccan monsters.

I knew that we would at some point be headed through the mountain. It was only a matter of time until we turned left. I looked ahead, searching for a spot in the mountain that had an easier slope. It was at that moment—just as I thought to myself that it would be impossible to climb the sheer faces of sand and rock to my immediate left—that a little yellow plastic sign directed me to do so. I stared upward and felt what Toby's brother had felt: *There is no way that anyone can make it up that hill.*

The slope was at least 25%, and the first several hundred yards were nothing but sand. I looked up and saw Mohamad & Friends struggling—walking—just above. The world's best could barely walk it; how could any of the rest of us be expected to climb? With each step, my legs burned. The sand was even softer than it had been in the dunes. I lost half of each step and had to balance my hands along the side of the mountain to avoid sliding all the way down. It helped to follow in the footsteps of the runner ahead of me, but not even that prevented me from slipping.

After several minutes of excruciating difficulty, the slope worsened, but it was easier going. There was still sand, but there were also some rocks, ranging in size from tennis balls to goldfish bowls. With each step, I tried to jump to a new rock. They still slid, but not nearly as quickly as the sand alone. I became Frogger: The Sahara Version.

Slowly, the sand dissipated, and the terrain was increasingly rocky. Still uphill, I found myself using all four limbs in order to make progress. Hand over hand, I held onto rocks and lifted my feet to a higher ledge. *Please, oh Lord, please let this rock hold.* As I knocked my knees and paused to catch my breath, I could not believe that the other 750 runners had already passed this way. A few small rocks fell past me; it was a miracle that boulders did not dislodge. I wondered if anyone had been hurt going up. I wondered how many had withdrawn.

It was inappropriate. This was no longer a race, but a dangerous climb. We had trained to run, trained for heat, and trained to carry a week's worth of supplies on our backs. But none of us had carried climbing equipment or clamps for our shoes. None of us felt comfortable with the prospect of rocks raining down upon us.

Mohamad was no longer visible, which made me happy. *The top must be near.*

The entire climb took more than twenty minutes of intense, non-stop upward movement. There were no switchbacks, no trails, and no steps. It had been carved by God and cursed by the devil.

My anger and frustration at the race officials for their dangerous selection disappeared when I reached the summit. It was one of the most beautiful panoramic views imaginable. The two-tone tan-brown, hazy mountains in the distance were obscured by heat waves across the vast oceans of never-ending wavy sand. Black rocks, as leopards' spots, tickled the countryside. Never before had death felt so alive.

With more than forty miles remaining, I did not want to pause for long, and so headed out across the rocky ridge in search of a path that would take me down the other side of the mountain. My gratitude at having reached the summit did not last long. Going downhill was just as difficult as walking up. Nature had not been particularly considerate. The steps were of varied distance, loose terrain, and steep. I found myself traveling even slower on the way down, afraid that one wrong step would cause me to pop an ankle or lose a knee. I had reached the top of the mountain in ninth place, but I watched another nine runners scamper by me, including Ian the Mountain Goat.

Within minutes of summiting, I passed the last runner from the first group. Moments later, I came upon a familiar frame in a long-sleeved green shirt. Steve Wolk was slowly plodding along. I had been running just over an hour; he had been traveling for more than four. I yelled as I approached, and we said our hellos. But our goals for the day were different, and as much as I wanted to stop and talk, I knew that I would be tempted many times as the day went on.

So I continued running. At a 6% average grade, I would ordinarily be able to sustain a reasonable pace. But I felt as though I was running in a dried-out coy pond, with loose rocks, varying levels, and uneven surfaces. I stepped carefully, continually worried that I would lose my footing and sustain an injury. My knees ached as the downhill continued, but I was grateful with each step that I was still vertical.

But, alas, even miserable experiences can get worse.

Through a steep and narrow ravine—with a twenty foot wall of boulders to my left and uneven terrain to my right—a short, stocky runner came barreling through and slammed into my shoulder as he passed. My footing already shaky, I fell forward—quickly. My knee scraped along a jagged rock, but I broke my fall with my left hand. I lay on the ground, stunned. Looking left and right, it took me a few moments to realize that I was conscious. Once lucid, I proceeded to wipe bits of sand from my mouth and check myself for obvious injuries.

The palm of my left hand was mangled. A half-dollar-sized chunk of flesh had been flayed, sand had embedded itself, and it stung tremendously. My knee throbbed, and an already-dry trickle of blood had soaked its way into my sock.

My attacker simply ran onward, undeterred. Evidently I had been in his way.

I lifted myself up and rubbed my knee; I looked forward at the man and thought about sprinting until I caught him, pushing him to the ground, and watching him suffer. But then I realized a powerful fact: it was the first time during the entire event that I had experienced such a lack of caring. Up until that point, my every experience had been that my fellow runners—from the best Moroccan to the slowest American—were kind, caring, and supportive. Everyone had universally seemed more interested in collaborating than conquering. Getting forced to the ground by the exception to the rule helped me appreciate just what an incredible group of people I had been running alongside.

I wiped my left hand as best as I could and licked my right fingers to try to clean my left knee. Then, with a determination that was half rebellion and half resignation to the fact that there was no one around to help me, I pressed forward.

I could see the first checkpoint in the distance, just beyond a set of small dunes at the base of the rocky mountain. In time, the terrain became more navigable, and I finally began to develop a rhythm. Yet, in my excitement at finally being back on flatter ground, I grew reckless. I turned the corner out of the final rocky section and came across a cactus. Trying to jump out of the way at the last moment, I nearly dodged it. But my left shoulder collided directly with one of the barbs, and I could feel the spike burrow deep into my muscle. Almost as quickly as it happened, the spike withdrew, and I continued forward. My shoulder throbbed, my knee had gone numb, and my hand was bloodied. The left side of my body was in need of repair.

As I crossed the final sand dunes and unscrewed the caps to my water bottles, I worried about my shoulder. I remembered a story that Jay had told us about a woman in a previous year's event who had made the mistake of running through a field of shrubs. The following day, he said, her legs "were black and blue, filled with puss, as though someone had beaten them with a baseball bat." Evidently, the plants in the Sahara could be poisonous. I imagined my arm swelling, circulation getting cutoff, and passing out from the pain. But, given my determination to plod along and see how well I could compete, I dismissed my paranoia and decided that I would continue without checking in with the medical staff.

"How's it going out there?" a woman yelled from the checkpoint.

Surprised to be addressed in English, I looked up and surveyed the volunteers. It was Clarissa and cameraman Matt of ABC. They explained that the entire crew had actually climbed the horrendous mountain that day to get an idea of what we were going through.

As I ran up, I held out the palm of my hand, putting it directly into the camera's lens.

"I fell," I said. "My knee and shoulder hurt. My hand's bloody and stinging. And I've got one and a half marathons ahead of me." I had hoped that my tone conveyed enough humor. I really had started to feel better as I got out of the mountains, but I could not tell if my attempt at charm had gotten through. Undeterred, I said goodbye and ran off.

"Ted!" It was a man's voice, and I looked over my shoulder to see Bruno, ABC's producer, running after me. "I have a message from Coach Lisa!" I stopped and turned, looking inquisitively at him. "She said to leave nothing out here—to save absolutely nothing for tomorrow."

"Thanks," I said. It was the right advice—even if it had come via satellite phone from a woman back in Tucson, Arizona, who had chosen to sleep in her own bed instead of competing this year. I amused myself by imagining this world-class athlete lying on the sofa, eating bonbons, and watching daytime soaps. I enjoyed the exercise and spent a little time resenting her for not being with all of us in Morocco. Then, I remembered her two young girls, both under five years of age, and realized that my day might be easier than hers after all.

Once through the checkpoint, the race took on a different feel. Unlike the start of the run, in which the uninhabited wasteland stretched out in front of me for miles, I now had a human map. Speckled throughout the landscape were little human forms, stretched out into the distance and becoming ants near the horizon. It provided a different take on running through the desert. Navigation would be absolutely unnecessary today.

As the valley became flat and fast, it was energizing to pass other competitors. They limped, carefully placed their walking sticks, and talked to one another. But they provided companionship and encouragement. As I ran by, everyone offered a "well done," "good work," or "keep it up." I had heard from competitors in previous years that it energized the slower runners to see the faster group charge through. It certainly seemed to, and it definitely gave me the incentive necessary to continue running at a brisk pace.

A short while after passing through the first checkpoint, I saw Karen and Andrea ahead. Side by side, they walked steadily along. Karen's gesticulations suggested that they were deep in conversation.

Andrea turned to the side and slapped her thigh; the sun glistened off her face and revealed a sparkle in her eye.

"Looking good, ladies," I yelled as I approached. They continued along with their conversation. Either they had not heard me, or they had chosen to ignore the presumably chauvinistic male approaching. "I mean, looking *really* good," I said as I was steps from their heels. They stopped talking and turned.

"Holy cow, Ted!" Andrea yelled. "You rock!" Karen offered a few friendly Canadian "ehs."

"Aaaoooooowwwww!" one of them yelled after I had run by. It meant that they definitely had not been offended by my initial comments.

Just ahead were George and Leigh—George steadily chugging along, and Leigh out for a daytime stroll with a glass of lemonade. George just so happened to turn as I approached, and he waved hello. Tapping Leigh on the shoulder, he pointed in my direction. But Leigh seemed disinterested. I felt a little neglected that she hadn't given me an enthusiastic greeting.

"My goodness, that's an attractive top," I commented—a reference to Leigh's pre-race fashion fixation. Leigh looked at me, perplexed as I passed, and then realized who I was.

"Oh my gosh…Ted!?" she screamed. Her tone was half shock, half encouragement. "When George pointed, I didn't know it was you!" I looked back and trotted sideways for a few moments, flashing a wide smile and waving at her. I then turned back around—not to be rude, but because I was concerned about stumbling on the floor of the Sahara. "Ted, Ted, go, go! Oh my gosh, you're flying! Keep it up!" The excitement in her voice gave me the energy I wanted.

Every thirty to sixty seconds I passed another runner—occasionally someone I knew, but mostly strangers fighting for a common cause. Everyone was different, but everyone was the same: an oddly dressed form fighting nature for no reason other than to look inside oneself and take pleasure at knowing that, if only for a moment in time, self-actualization was real.

After the first checkpoint I was able to average seven-and-a-half-minute miles despite the terrain, temperature, and backpack. It seemed that mere moments had passed when I reached the second checkpoint, which was positioned in the middle of a small oasis. Ten or so palm trees offered a bit of shade to the weary.

It looked like a refugee camp. Dozens of people were strewn across the ground; other emaciated bodies limped in search of food. Around the perimeter lurked officials with official-looking clothing, but they could offer nothing to the masses, who sat blocking the rays and swatting at insects. As my water ration card was punched and I was handed a bottle of water, I felt as though I had crossed enemy lines. A member of the Red Cross, I would be allowed to observe only, but in no way to assist the occupants in their quest to make it to the other side.

I poured water over my head and quickly scanned the landscape for a family member I might know, someone for whom I could carry a message to the other side. But no one looked in my direction.

"Holy crap!" someone to my left screamed. "Ted! Holy crap!" It was Bunny. Her pack was elsewhere, and she was walking around the makeshift camp in search of a trashcan. "You're already here!" she screamed in disbelief. It was good to see her, and I wanted to stay and chat, but I felt as though I needed to leave as quickly as possible to avoid being sucked into the lethargy. The second checkpoint was flypaper: few seemed to be passing through without staying awhile.

"Hey, what's up?" I asked. "How are you doing?"

"This sucks," she responded. "I mean, it's so damn hot, and…" she paused, and then, as though startled again by the sight of me, blurted, "I can't believe you caught me already! Holy crap!"

I chuckled and muttered something about how good I was feeling.

"Get out of here! Go!" she exclaimed, shooing me along in such a way as to encourage me to succeed. I replaced my cap and waved to her as I continued on.

It felt good to leave the dozens of stranded warriors; I imagined myself leading a charge and encouraging them to follow me. No one budged.

During my brief pause at the checkpoint, Ian the Mountain Goat had passed me. As he had always done when we crossed paths, he offered me words of encouragement, displaying the true mark of a good competitor and all-around decent person. I looked at the upcoming sand (his nemesis) and knew that I would pass him shortly. The stage was progressing well. I was about fifteen minutes ahead of when I thought I would hit the second checkpoint, and by my count I was in fourteenth place. I had little doubt that my body would break down at some point, but I enjoyed the period of strength as I surged to catch Ian.

Just beyond a mile of sand was an expansive valley of softball-sized rocks. I could see for miles, and the runners in the distance seemed to have lost their way. They were spread out over a plain several miles wide, and as I looked into the distance at the next mountain we were to climb, I was surprised at how far out of the way many runners seemed to be traveling. The majority seemed to be following a loose trail, one that had been carved by a flash flood and reinforced by the day's footsteps. Plenty of other runners were taking even more circuitous routes, but no one seemed to be traveling in a straight line toward the next mountain.

Navigation in the desert is tricky. It is often more efficient to travel a longer distance because of the terrain and hills. But, as I scanned the entire valley I could not understand the reason for the wide deviation. I assumed that the rest of the runners had noticed something, but *efficiency be damned*, I thought, *I am taking the most direct route toward the hill.*

It proved to be the right decision. I passed runners at an even faster rate, and those who had been close on my heels had disappeared by the time that I crossed the rock flat. Perhaps it was superior navigation on my part, but perhaps it was merely that others were suffering more during the hottest part of the day. Whatever it was, Ian and I headed into the first of two 500-foot hills separated by a short valley. We traded places on the first hill, with my passing him on the way up and he passing me on the way down. Following a brief valley, I again caught him and expected him to pass by me as I descended the second hill. But I looked back and saw no one. Somewhat disappointed, for it had been more rewarding to run with another competitor, I pressed forward. I figured that I should take advantage of the times when I felt strong, for I assumed that a time would come when I would need to slow down.

The third checkpoint suddenly appeared. Four hours into the longest stage of the event, I could not believe how quickly it was going. I tried to relive the details of the day, flashing back to the giant mountain, Andrea and Karen, Bunny, and playing leap-frog with the Englishman. But little came to mind. Everything seemed to condense into a few brief moments. I looked at my watch to confirm how long I had been running and shrugged my shoulders.

The checkpoint had fewer refugees than the previous one, and all of them were huddled in a few black tents that the race organization had erected for shade. I was surprised to see the tents: It was an unexpected luxury from a group that prided itself on providing no assistance or comfort to the competitors. I saw no one I recognized. I popped a few salt pills, poured my excess water out over my head, and ran toward the rocky hill that meandered up toward a pass that we would have to climb.

Looking ahead, I noticed a familiar form. After spending nearly a week in Tent 77, I knew my tent mates' outfits well.

"Michelle!" I yelled.

She turned around, saw me, and looked at her watch. "Good going," she said softly. Something was wrong.

"Are you okay?" I asked. She was cradling two large water bottles in her arms.

"No, not really," she said. She looked as though she was out of energy, walking on sinew alone.

"Do you want me to get help?" I asked. I was surprised by her comment, given that she had just chosen to leave a checkpoint full of medical personnel.

"No, no. I feel terrible, but I'm going to make it. I haven't eaten anything all day because I can't keep it down. But I've come this far, so I'm gonna make it. Good luck."

She was tougher than I. I may have been running faster, but only because my body had not shut down as hers had. I could not fathom her predicament: She had been traveling for more than seven hours, and more than twenty miles, without eating anything. Her insides must have started consuming themselves.

"Stay tough," I said. A silly response, really, as though someone who had pressed through a three-day sickness needed my two words of encouragement, but I could think of nothing more.

"Thanks. Go get 'em. You're going great."

She felt horrible and was struggling to continue—and yet she cared about my progress.

After a manageable but difficult climb up a rounded, rocky mountainside, I reached the top of a ridge and got another view of the splendor in the distance. To my left, I could see a valley that had cut through the mountain and emerged on the other side. How much easier it would have been, I realized, for all of us to have avoided the mountain altogether. But the road book had directed us to summit the ridge, so I ran for several minutes in exceptionally rocky terrain. A small trail had been rubbed along the top of the ridge from the hundreds of runners who had passed by. Each time I passed a fellow competitor, I did so cautiously, out of fear that deviating from the "trail" might cause me to sprain an ankle.

The ridge narrowed as it continued gently uphill and met with a second mountain. Soon there were rock walls twenty feet in both directions, and I fought to keep my balance over body-sized boulders. The top was only a short ways off, and I could see that the rocks would soon give way to soft, golden sand. As I reached the top and looked down, it was strange: the other side was not a mountain, but also not a dune. I had my choice of a sandy chute in one direction and more rocks in another. Tightening my pack, I opted for the sand and began gliding downward.

Oh the joy! The wind rushed through my hair, and the sun disappeared behind a mountaintop. With each step, I slid ten feet or more, gently placing my heels into the sand and allowing it to take me away. My arms swung back and forth, and I felt weightless. The glide was smooth, like sliding on fresh ice; it was downhill, but there was just enough friction to prevent me from feeling out of control.

Alas, the downhill fun came to an end, and the sand was not nearly as fun along the side of a ridge leading out to the valley. But I could see the fourth checkpoint in the distance—how soon! Though it was many miles away, out in the center of an expansive salt flat, my route appeared to be downhill the entire way. Less than a quarter mile away, the rock/sand combination on the side of the mountain stopped, and the path opened up to a wide-open area with occasional three-foot-high shrubs. It seemed like only minutes had passed since I had left the third checkpoint; this segment was destined to be the fastest of the day.

I hit the wide open area and lunged forward, planning to surge the entire distance to the next checkpoint. However, my foot sank to mid-calf, and I nearly fell. I stopped momentarily to get my bearings, and I walked off to the side, hoping to find more solid ground. I began jogging again, but within a few steps, I again melted into the surface. It was sand, but unlike any other terrain in the race. I again sprung to the side in search of solid ground, but I met the same fate.

Over the next forty-five minutes, I suffered through the unrunnable terrain. Every few minutes, I would try to jog, but the exercise always ended the same way: with a leg sinking to the calf and my blood pressure boiling. I had been making such good time, but the desert was preventing me from continuing. My body felt good, my legs were capable of running. I felt like Ian, cursing the impossible sand and angrily pounding each step into the ground.

By the time I reached the end of the sand and entered a hard, compact salt flat, I realized that my view from the top of the mountain had been a mirage: The path to the checkpoint would not be downhill the entire way. As I resumed my running, I knew that I was headed at a slight upward incline. My legs hurt as I increased my pace, but I felt as though I needed to run harder to justify my lethargic pace over the past hour. After so many frustrating steps, the pain felt good. I ran briskly, munching on a bag of beef jerky along the way.

I realized that it had been well over an hour since I had last seen one of the elite runners. Though I continued to pass runners from the 9 a.m. group, most were weary by this point. No one's pace in my vicinity approached mine, which was simultaneously invigorating and disappointing.

I looked at my watch as I entered the chute at the fourth checkpoint: 5 p.m. Assuming that there had been an error, I toggled to the stopwatch function, but it confirmed that I had only been running for five hours.

Before the race began, a few of us discussed our respective strategies for the long day. Someone had asked me what my plan would be if I had to start the stage at noon; I hoped aloud that I could reach the fourth checkpoint within six hours and the fifth checkpoint by dark. "Then," I remembered saying, "it appears to be relatively straight and flat for the remainder of the stage—and my chances of getting lost or injured would go down." I was an hour ahead of that schedule.

That realization caused me to power through the checkpoint with only a pause.

The sun was a well-defined yellow ball, and I ran directly toward it. It was that late afternoon, blinding haze, the moment just before the pinks and oranges begin settling on the horizon. The mountains to the sides looked black, and only a few stringy clouds dotted the skyline. Heat still bounced off the ground, but the Sahara had begun to cool. With only twenty-nine kilometers to go (just over eighteen miles) and the heat fading, the worst of the day was over. *I can finish. I can do this.*

I could only see a few runners now in the distance. With the sun ahead, they were difficult to see—just black splotches with shadows as I neared.

Despite my progress and upbeat outlook, the day began to

take its toll. I was hungry and reached into my pockets for some macadamia nuts. My back ached, but shifting my pack no longer seemed to help. Worst of all, my mind started to drift. Until that point, I had been so focused on the day and determined to proceed that I had forgotten to think about discomfort. But it settled in now. I wondered how much longer my body would hold out. I wondered if my bloodied hand and pierced shoulder were infected. I worried that my numb knee might be seriously injured.

"Catre-son-catre-van-dooze," I said aloud, returning to the mantra that had been so helpful during the previous stage. I enjoyed listening to the French say the number twelve—"douze"—because it offered such playful energy.

I began bargaining with myself. "All right, Ted," I promised. "All you need to do is make it to 5:30 p.m., and then you can walk."

When the time came, I renegotiated the terms: "Another fifteen minutes will probably get you to the halfway point between the two checkpoints. What do you say?"

Then, when the new time arrived, I again constructed a reason to keep running: "You might be able to make it to the next stage entirely, which would enable you to walk the entire distance to the following checkpoint."

I imagined two figures on my shoulder—one counseling rest and the other insisting that I continue. However, I did not have enough energy to continue thinking about the little men; no, it was much sadder than that: I just mumbled to myself and then complained when I broke my own promises. I repeatedly became angry with myself for failing to keep my word. It never occurred to me that I was free to reject the idea to keep running. It never occurred to me that I could once again be in control if I wanted to be.

Just as I had reached my worst—at the moment when I could argue no more with myself and wanted to buckle—was when I saw two familiar forms ahead. Terry and Ed plodded along. Ed looked somewhat hurt, but they were talking, which was a good sign.

"Hi guys, keep it up," I muttered. I felt horrible but wanted to do my part not to sour the mood.

"Hey, Ted," Terry said. It was direct but respectful. "You're doing well, very well. Not too long: you might even be in the top ten." He was extremely matter-of-fact, as though he were explaining the importance of a museum exhibit to a young child.

I muttered something else, another attempt to pick up the mood. But it was obvious that, as happy as we were to see one another, neither of us had enough energy to give a proper greeting. I continued without much fanfare.

The wadi continued on, and the sun was low enough to begin sending other colors into the sky.

I continued to bargain with myself, picking points in the distance and promising—"this time for real"—that I would walk once I reached that point. Upon arrival, I would see another object in the distance and suggest that it was a more legitimate marker for a period of walking. Then, once again I would disappoint myself, continuing with my slow run to yet another imaginary checkpoint.

Finally, after more than an hour and a half, I arrived at the fifth checkpoint. It was still far from dark, which meant that I was still ahead of my schedule. I decided to remove my headlamp from my pack in anticipation of darkness falling.

As I passed through the checkpoint this time, one of the race volunteers snapped a glow stick and used a string to tie it to my backpack. She informed me, in broken English, that it was for the benefit of the other runners. She instructed me to follow the little green dots. Ingenious.

"Just more than sixteen kilometers to go!" one of the volunteers yelled. I did the math: about ten miles. As I exited the checkpoint, I informed myself that the next segment was the one that really mattered. "You can walk the final section if you want," I offered, "but from here to the next checkpoint is the turning point." I whined at myself but conceded that I was right: with only ten miles to go and some daylight remaining, it would be foolish to walk now.

I have no memory of the following five-and-a-half miles, which was the distance between the fifth and sixth checkpoints. At some point, it became dark, and at another I finished the remainder of the food in my pockets. Upon arrival at the sixth checkpoint, I was confused. I asked the race officials which checkpoint it was, and I checked my watch. Realizing that night had in fact fallen, it made enough sense that I was where I was. But what had I done? How had I felt?

I look back now at the race book and get few clues—some wadi, some "well shafts," and some trees. I could remember none of it. I was suspended somewhat between worry and wonder. *I must be sick or in some way out of it,* I thought. *How cool it is that I just traveled an entire segment without having to think about the pain,* I continued. I oscillated between the two sentiments and decided to check my body for injuries. I banged on my left shoulder, the site of the cactus prick, but felt nothing. My left hand was bloodied and crusted over; sand had embedded itself in the wound, but the stinging had stopped. My knee was tender to the touch, but no worse than I was accustomed to during training runs back home.

The sixth checkpoint was structured as though the race organizers were trying to send the message that the stage was nearly done. There was no traditional chute to run through, and just a single Jeep with water in the back. Only a few race personnel were on hand (not the dozen or more who had been at previous checkpoints), and the mood was subdued. I grabbed my water bottle and realized that I had been running for longer than I had ever run before—even after having traveled nearly seventy miles on the first three days. I could not believe that I was fewer than five miles from the finish.

The temperature had dropped precipitously. An hour earlier I had been sweating; I was now beginning to shiver. I looked to the heavens in search of the giant green laser beam that race veterans had told me to expect. I had even seen pictures of the powerful beam shooting across the sky, clearly pointing the runners in the direction of the finish. But this year there was no guiding green light; I looked into the distance and wondered how I would find my way. I searched for the bobbing glow sticks on my fellows' backpacks but saw nothing.

I thought back to the morning's loneliness. The only difference now was that I could try and run away from it. I pushed onward, deciding that eventually I would see some sort of guiding light.

It came in the form of a Land Cruiser summiting a small dune and stopping. I ran toward the headlights, and as it drove into the distance, I could see that the driver had left a dangling glow stick on a small wooden sign. It was no night-sky laser, but I was nonetheless grateful for the direction.

Another twenty minutes passed, and I could hear a distinctive voice ahead. It was Laurie, loud and chipper (as usual).

"That is so funny!" she said. I was dying to know the joke, dying to share in the conversation. But she did not continue.

"Hey, guys," I said as I approached. "Not long now, huh?"

Laurie cheered; it was Mike and Jay who accompanied her.

"You're doing awesome," Jay said. "You might be top ten, Ted. Keep it up, man, keep it up. Don't stop."

I wanted so badly to stop. I knew that the finish was only a mile or two away, but everything hurt so much that I questioned how it would be possible to get there. I had no food handy, my hips and knees ached, and the entire world seemed to be traveling at a different pace.

"Teddy!" Mike yelled, a throaty version of my name that seemed to convey praise. "Teddy, Teddy, Teddy!" I laughed to myself. Since the talking Teddy Ruxpin doll emerged in the 1980s, I had done my best to go by Ted. I sort of liked Mike's version, though. It made me feel like a kid, immature. I laughed some more when I realized the appropriateness of the thought: I wanted to throw a tantrum.

"Thanks, guys, I'll see you at the finish. Keep it up."

"Woo-hoo! Go Ted!" Laurie yelled. I wanted to know where she got her energy.

No more than five minutes later, I could see the lights of Reno, Nevada. During college, there was that moment coming over

Interstate 80 when, driving through complete darkness, we crested a hill. Out of darkness was an excessive amount of light—casinos in the distance offering me refuge from the cold if only I was willing to part with my cash. It was a time before Reno lost its charm, before all the people moved in. It was a time when Reno was nothing more than a downtown of burning lights. It was a time before the suburbs extended the infrastructure into a stringy system of dotted lights up the highway.

Yet no suburbs had moved into this part of the Sahara, so I saw vintage Reno: a highly concentrated island of lights with complete blackness surrounding it. I could feel the cold, and I knew that I was in that ring of blackness. I offered all of my money to be instantly transported there. I could taste that ninety-nine-cent ham 'n eggs breakfast, complete with hash browns and a murky cup of warm, dishwater coffee. I smiled as the fifty-eight-year-old waitress with the raspy voice walked by, an inch of ash dangling off her cigarette. I inhaled my breakfast at two in the morning and cursed the dealer who had hit twenty-one four times in a row.

And then I was done. I crossed the finish line to the sound of a generator and a French woman announcing, "quatre-cent-soixante-six, See-o-door Archer." I paused and took a 360-degree look at my surroundings to confirm that it was in fact the finish line. It was 8:20 at night, and I had run forty-seven miles since noon.

I tried to scream. I wanted to express happiness at having completed the most difficult physical experience of my life, but nothing came out. It was as though my scream were a party and nobody showed.

"Dooze," a woman said as she pointed at me. It was my favorite French number: How did she know? Was she mocking me? Had she heard me repeating it over and over throughout the desert?

"You are twelve this night, See-o-door," another volunteer offered.

It was fate. Of all the strange coincidences, how fitting that I would finish the stage in twelfth place! I enjoyed the moment not because the number had any significance, but because I would now have an official reason to speak the word aloud.

"No, sorry," she said. "Sir-teen, you are sir-teen this night." I thanked her and walked away graciously. Still proud of my performance, I wondered if the woman knew how much she had taken away from me. Never before in my life had I so badly wanted to be number twelve.

A man walked next to me, with his arm around my shoulder. He somehow managed to carry three water bottles with his other arm; there was enough light for me to read my number on the caps. *This man has his arm around me*, I thought. I felt awkward and wanted to know what he was doing. I had no idea who he was, but he was steering me toward a set of white tents.

The white tents are for the race volunteers—and for medical! I looked at the man and realized that he was the reason that I was able to keep my balance. Stopping, I looked back at the finish line and was surprised to learn that I had traveled so far.

I then remembered that, only moments before, I had asked to go to the medical tent. I remember having showed my bloodied hand to a nice woman and having her point me in the right direction.

Perhaps I am in worse shape than I thought.

The man helped to wash my hand just outside the tent. They had water bottles with soapy yellow liquid, and he sprayed it at me. It stung a bit, but I let him continue.

Once inside, a pleasant-looking woman of forty walked up and asked if I spoke French or English. She continued on in English, asking me to have a seat on the floor, just in front of a wooden stool. I looked throughout the tent, with bright bulbs dangling from the ceilings, and could see other doctors tending to other athletes. They were in similar positions—the athletes on the floor, and the medical personnel hunched over on stools.

"I need to eat something out of my bag," I said. I was definitely disoriented, and I convinced myself that perhaps eating something would help me return to feeling normal.

"Okay, take your time," she responded. Her tone was kind, but I was for some reason skeptical.

"No, you don't understand," I shot back. Her eyes grew wide, and she looked a little from side to side. "I need to take something out of my bag," I paused, searching for the next words. "And then I'm going to eat it!"

The poor woman nodded and sat on her stool. I removed my backpack and started rifling through in search of drink mix and a bag of nuts. Out of the corner of my eye, I noticed a Brooks Cascadia sneaker—the brand I wore—across the room. I looked down; I was barefoot. Focusing closer, I could see the other sneaker on the floor as well, along with both of my socks, which had been tossed in different directions. My shirt was at my feet. At that point, I was grateful to see that I had not removed my shorts.

I sat down and starting mixing my drink. As I nibbled on my cashews, I looked at the other runners in the tent, all of whom were having their feet tended to. *Do something original,* I thought. I looked around. *Did I say that out loud?* I looked at my doctor and was grateful that she was patiently waiting for me. I knew that something was wrong, but I was hoping that it was nothing serious. I drank my Recoverite and ate my nuts.

"I'm sorry," I said to the doctor, who was surprised to have me address her. It must have been a while.

She laughed aloud. "That is okay. You are fine. Just take your time." I smiled at her, and she back at me. I sort of liked the state of delirium. I felt safe with her around.

In time, I allowed her to clean my hand and examine my shoulder. She marveled at the depth of the scrape but said that it would likely be fine. She continually asked me if she was hurting me, but I felt nothing. I looked over and noticed that she was scrubbing vigorously with a cloth. *That should hurt,* I thought. But I felt fine. Though somewhat numb to the pain, I was starting to regain some sensibility.

"Everyone else is getting their feet looked at," I commented.

"Yes, that is because they have bad blisters," she responded. I realized that she had responded to my statement instead of my implied meaning.

"Maybe I should have you look at my blisters," I said. She smiled.

"Yes, that is next. You asked me to do that when you came in." She was so patient and so careful. I felt lucky to have such a nice woman tending to me; I looked down the way and felt sorry for the other runners because they did not have my doctor.

I have no idea how much time elapsed in the medical tent, but I felt good enough after a while to make my way back to the tent. She had bandaged my hand and placed gauze between my toes. I pulled my flip-flops out of my backpack—one luxury item that I had decided to bring with me—and put them on.

"You have a good night, and a good sleep," she said.

"Thank you, and again, I'm sorry for being mean."

"You were not mean," she said. I thought that it might have been a lie, but I was grateful for it.

I collected my belongings and adhered them to my pack. "Did I forget anything?" I asked as I picked up my scattered possessions. I wondered what else I had thrown—and where.

"No, that is all," she replied with a gentle smile.

I walked back out into the cold night, colder still since I had removed my shirt. There were clouds in the sky, so I did not get to enjoy the stars. The camp was mostly quiet, but there were occasional headlamps and a few lights dangling from officials' tents. I then remembered: from a distance, this had been Reno.

"Ted!" Jeff greeted me as I approached our tent. He looked good. "Damn, man, congratulations! I heard from Jay, Mike, and Laurie how well you did. That's incredible."

"Thanks," I said. I looked at our tent and felt comfortable. Though I knew that the ground would be rocky, it felt like home.

"Are you okay? They guessed that you must have come in about an hour ago."

"That long, huh?" I looked at my watch and realized that it had been at least that long. "Yeah, I guess. I've been at medical just having them look at me, but I'm okay. Hey, how'd you do today?"

Jeff's eyes lit up, and he had a grin from ear-to-ear. "I crossed the finish line second today. It took me just over nine hours." He waited.

"Damn, Jeff," I responded. It was by far his strongest showing of the week. He had taken full advantage of being able to run the entire stage during the day. I wondered what that time would do to his overall ranking.

"And I feel really good," he offered.

We sat and talked for a while, and he informed me that Brendan had finished strongly as well—in just under ten-and-a-half hours. We lamented that most of the runners would be out in the cold for much, if not all, of the night. Our reward for finishing quickly was a complete day's rest. Both of us looked forward to not being awakened by Berbers the following morning.

I mixed and ate my freeze-dried meal. The packaging said lasagna, but with cold water and no sun to warm it, it was just a crunchy red stew. It was wonderful. Following an entire day of running on sugar and sugar derivatives, I welcomed the texture of something other than a gel packet.

The day had been long, and the night had come quickly. I lay atop my sleeping bag and thought about the stage, which already seemed a distant memory. I was proud, but part of me doubted that I had actually run the event.

And then I slept.

13
Wanting to Die

"That's some get-up you've got there," said a man along the trail.

He was in his mid-forties and wearing a complete cyclist uniform—one of those tight, multicolored fashion mishaps that for some reason is accepted when someone is atop a bike. Granted, we both looked ridiculous, but I was a bit surprised at the authority with which he spoke.

"Pot calling the kettle black," I responded. I wore a large smile, and he nodded to acknowledge the hypocrisy.

"What're you training for?" he asked.

"What do you mean?" I joked. "A guy can't just head out for fun for a thirty-mile run with a backpack, straw-capped water bottles, and a flapped-hat?" The sarcasm felt good. I had been running for twenty-five miles, all the while carrying a phone book, thirteen bottles of Crystal Geyser spring water, and a sleeping bag. I had just emptied another pouch of drink powder into one of my water bottles and dumped an ounce of crushed potato chips down my gullet.

"Happens all the time. Sometimes I do it just to remember what it's like to chafe," he said. He was exactly what I needed at that point. It had been three hours, but for whatever reason I was in considerably more pain that I would normally be at this point in a run. I had 8.8 miles to go before reaching Beals Point, a boating area and campsite on Folsom Lake in Sacramento, California. That would complete my day's run—the entire length of Sacramento's American River Bike Trail.

"Exactly," I said. "I just saw the backpack and realized that it was being neglected." I wondered how long we could keep up the false premise before it became annoying. I decided not to find out.

"I'm training for a 150-mile race through the Sahara Desert. It's called the Marathon Des Sables."

"Oh, yeah, I've heard of it," he said. "I saw a documentary about it somewhere. It's a week long, right?"

He was the first American I had ever met who was familiar with the event.

"Yeah," I said. I was standing near a water fountain, a few hundred feet from the river. Just up the way was a bridge that would take me to the other side, where the trail would continue. I knew from past experience that from the bridge I would be able to see fishermen wading below the Nimbus Dam and casting their lines.

As a young boy, I often came down to the river. In the late fall, between Thanksgiving and Christmas, I would stand on the riverbank and watch the salmon fight their way upstream. There were thousands of them, and with the low water, I could see them at the surface. I could have walked out and picked one up had my father not been there to prevent me from doing so.

"Kinda tough to simulate that kind of weather over there, huh?" the man asked. "How hot will it be?" We both had experience with Sacramento summers, so we expected a certain level of heat.

"They say 120," I responded. "But, I sort of doubt that. Besides, with how bad I'm feeling right now, I can't imagine being able to make it if it's that hot."

"Where did you start this morning?"

"Discovery Park," I said. It was the beginning of the trail just outside of downtown.

"What time did you leave?"

"Eight o'clock." I looked at my watch. It was just after eleven.

"That's pretty good time. How far are you going today?"

"The whole way—Beals Point—but I'm not happy about it." I hunched over and balanced my hands on my knees. My breathing was heavy, I was tired, and I was out of food.

"It's been a while since I've run an ultra, but I used to run the entire trail every now and then. It took me a bit longer than it's taking you, though."

"Did you want to die twenty-five miles in while talking to a stranger next to the Nimbus Hatchery?" I responded. It was only partially a joke. He was complimenting my speed, but I wanted him to know the price I was paying.

He laughed and nodded his entire torso in agreement. "Oh, there were definitely times I didn't think I'd make it. The worst times were when I was running in the middle of nowhere and realized that I had no choice but to continue because no one could come get me. At least here you could get a ride home if you needed it."

"Speaking of which," I said, "my girlfriend is supposed to pick me up in a little more than an hour—and I can't imagine I'll make it by the time I said I'd be there. I should get going so that I don't worry her too much."

He laughed again and wagged his finger. "No, no. Look at this as a test. If she doesn't get too mad and is supportive of your running, she's a keeper. Heck, I can't tell you how many times I've left my wife waiting for hours when a run took me longer than I thought it would."

"Yeah? How'd that couch work out for you?" I shot back.

He bared his teeth and cringed. "You've got a point. You should probably get going!" We laughed a bit, and I shook his hand goodbye. He was headed in the other direction, planning to finish where I had started that morning. I cinched my backpack a little more and readjusted my cap as I trotted up the trail.

I crossed the river and began jogging alongside Lake Nimbus. Not a single part of my body felt normal. My calves had sharp pains, my toes were blistered, my feet felt cramped, my ankles were swollen, my knees clicked with each step, my hamstrings were tight, my quadriceps ached, my hips pulsed, my abdomen was sick on the inside and being rubbed to open sores on the outside, my neck hurt from the weight of the pack and the straps, my arms felt somewhat dislodged from my shoulders, my fingers stiffened, and I had a headache. I had also forgotten to wear sunscreen on what had turned out to be a particularly sunny day. The backs of my legs, triceps area, and face were already red.

I struggled to maintain an eleven-minute-per-mile pace. Normally, even with a twenty-pound pack, I could run several minutes faster without much effort. I knew that I needed to keep moving to prevent my body from thinking that it could shut down.

Nearly an hour after my encounter with the awkwardly dressed cyclist, I heard heavy breathing behind me. A young woman in her early twenties was slowly catching up to me. She was easily fifty pounds overweight—and hardly taller than five feet.

I smiled at her as she came alongside. She smiled back but said nothing. I could hear Jane's Addiction blaring from her headphones. I decided that she would have to become my pacer. Nearly thirty miles in, I was searching for every reason I could think of to stop, search for a cell phone to borrow, and figure out how to abandon the day's run. At that moment, she was my only hope. I ratcheted up my pace and struggled to keep up with her.

It worked reasonably well for about twenty minutes. I figured out how to temporarily block the pain; by focusing on taking one step for each of her steps, I became lost in a trance. Things seemed to be going well.

Then she removed her headphones and heard my footsteps. She turned her head and was clearly startled to see the man she had passed twenty minutes earlier.

It was a bit of an awkward moment. In all of my discomfort—in my need to grasp any conceivable amount of help or hope—it had not crossed my mind that a six-foot-three man wearing a funny hat and carrying a backpack full of heavy items could be threatening to a single woman. To make matters worse, I realized, we were the only two people visible on the trail in either direction. The lake was to our right, and a steep, rocky hill with oak trees was to our left.

"Oh, don't worry about it," I said, wanting to assuage her concerns. I felt a bit worried that I had perhaps caused the gal a certain amount of fear. "I just really wanted to follow you."

Her eyes grew even wider. She stared at me intently, as though she was afraid of what might happen if she averted her look. I repeated my comment in my head, but I struggled to make sense of much of anything.

"No, no, no, that's not what I meant. It's not so much that I wanted to follow you. I *needed* to follow you," I responded, pleased with myself for clarifying the situation. But I realized that because of the pain I was in, I was grunting and speaking in a much deeper voice. Moments before, I had not thought it possible for a person's expression to be any more agape than hers had been. I was wrong. As I said "needed," all of the skin on her face tightened and pulled backward to her hairline.

"No, no, no! Oh my gosh, I am so sorry!" I stopped jogging, and she did too. "Okay, I'm really sorry. I just realized that this is either awkward or frightening or both for you, but I promise I didn't intend for that to be the case!" She just stood, looking at me. "Listen, I started my run more than four hours and thirty miles ago. I'm carrying twenty pounds in this backpack to train for this crazy race. I'm really sore, I'm tired, and my mind is playing tricks on me."

She kept staring.

"So, seeing another person—anybody else—is nice at this point. I'm looking for any way to motivate my body to just keep moving. And then you came along," I paused, trying not to find the wrong words. "When you came running by, I wanted to stop, but I figured that if I could just keep up with you, I'd get done faster. That's it." I stopped talking and looked at her, hopeful that she would understand—or at least not pull out a can of mace and spray me down.

She started laughing and nodded yes. "Okay, I gotcha. That's funny. Well, sorry to break it to you, but you're going to lose your pacer just up the trail here 'cause that's where I get off. But you're free to follow me until then." She put her ear buds back in, cranked the music back up, and jogged along. With her blessing, I followed her for the few hundred yards until a defined trail underneath a footbridge. She waved as she went down the trail, and I continued along toward Beals Point.

The final mile or two were excruciating. By allowing me to remove my mind from the thought process involved in placing my own steps, the girl had been doing the mental work for me. My legs were Jell-O, and without her, I had reached the point where I was unable to override the pain. I knew from past experience exactly how far away my final destination was, and I just put my head down and moved my body as much as possible. I was no longer running as much as I was floundering under the assumption that enough movement of any sort would in some way propel me forward.

As I finished, I tossed my pack to the ground, looked down, and watched as my legs shook uncontrollably. My muscles convulsed. I braced myself against my girlfriend's car, and she offered all the consolation that she could. I knew that everything would be all right eventually—possibly even later that same day—but at that moment I needed something to take my mind off of the pain.

I looked at my watch and then thought of the awkwardly dressed cyclist. I was only two minutes later than I had predicted, which meant no woman's wrath for the day.

14
A Day of Rest

Even before the race began, I had been thin. In the weeks leading up to my departure for Morocco, friends and family had commented on how emaciated I looked. After four days—and 115 miles—I had become sickly. Each of my ribs was clearly defined, and the muscles in my arms were nondescript. There was no scale to step on, but I had lost enough weight to be able to feel my own bones against the desert floor.

The ground was no firmer or rockier than it had been on previous nights, but I could not find a remotely comfortable position. The thin layer of fat that had once insulated me from the elements was no more.

***

A series of dreams drifted in and out of my mind throughout the night. I could hear pounding feet accompanied by the rhythmic beatings of tribal drums. There was a steady cadence but also competing forces. At times the drums were subdued, mellowed, while at others they pounded heavily, almost angrily.

I saw faces of the children I had seen the previous day, as well as children I had never seen. They were laughing; they were crying; they were expressionless. I knew that they could not hear the drums, but I also knew that they were aware that my feet were producing them.

"Hi, Ted." It was my sister, Amy. The drums had faded into the distance, but I had continued to run. I wanted to stop and talk with her, but I was forced to continue running. She remained by my side, peaceful and calm. She was not running, but she somehow kept up with me.

"Hi, Amy. How did you get here?" I asked. I was not sure where I was, but I was surprised to see her.

"Oh, you know. I just got here." On its face, her response made no sense, but since it fit her pattern of evasive answers, it seemed like a perfectly logical response under the circumstances.

"How are things going in Utah?" I tried to do the math to figure out how long it had been since she had first traveled to the program. I looked at the children, as though to ask them, but they shrugged their shoulders. I contented myself with the conclusion that it had been longer than a day but shorter than a year.

"Utah? What are you talking about?" she responded. She looked at me, concerned. "Are you okay, Ted?" Her face conveyed worry, kindness. I felt a sense of panic that perhaps I had done something that I should not do.

"Uh, well, Utah. I thought that you were going to an addiction program in Utah, but I guess not?" I had decided at the last minute to turn my statement into a question.

"Oh, *that* Utah," she said, relieved. I felt better because she no longer seemed puzzled as to my state of mind. "That place, like, so wasn't for me."

My cheeks drooped and tears welled in my eyes. *It doesn't matter if it's "for you" or not. You've just got to do it!* I tried to scream, but nothing came out of my mouth.

I looked back at Amy; she was frighteningly skinny. I could see her femur and every other bone that was not covered by clothing.

"Oh, yeah, I've lost a lot of weight. It's all of this damn running through the desert. It's impossible to get enough calories." She spoke so calmly, so in control. I struggled to make sense of her comment. I was running, but she did not appear to be. I spent a few moments trying to remember if she were actually a runner. I decided that she must be. Why else would she be with me at the Marathon Des Sables?

The little children ran away without saying anything, and I knew that it was because I had not given them any candy. I was pleased to be left alone but felt slighted that my conversation or character had not been interesting enough for them. The drums returned, though, which provided me with a steady rhythm to continue running. Amy had disappeared, but I thought little of it.

"Welcome back, girls. How'd it go, Karen? Andrea?" I could not tell where the voices were coming from, but I tried to tune them out because it was getting more and more difficult to see the ground I was running on.

"Well, it feels good to finally be done. More than a day, but it's done. Time for sleep, eh?"

"I can't imagine what my feet look like. I'll drink my wine later. I don't even want it."

"It's good to have you back. Do you need anything before you conk out?"

I looked at the faces of the children. They were the same, except they now looked like Karen, Andrea, and Jeff—my tent mates in Tent 77. We were no longer in Morocco, but in Death Valley, somehow sitting at a table eating dinner at my favorite San Jose-based pasta restaurant. My tent mates were hungry but would not tell me if it was because they were starving children or because they had been running. Puzzled, I asked the waiter how he had managed to move his restaurant to Death Valley, but he just looked the other direction and walked away.

"I don't get it. I don't know you guys in Death Valley," I said, looking at Jeff and Karen. "I know you in Morocco."

They looked at one another and shrugged their shoulders. They went back to eating their meals; both seemed to be eating meatloaf—something that was not even on the menu.

***

It was then that I turned over, opened my eyes, and realized that I had been dreaming. In my haze, I thought about my sister, and then I struggled to make sense of the drums and children in my dream. But I decided that it had been a meaningless hodge-podge of visions, finally broken up by Karen and Andrea's return to our tent after twenty-five hours of struggling through the fourth stage.

"No, we just need to get some sleep. It's past ten on the rest day, and unlike you guys who got to sleep all night, we've been out and suffering through the Sahara." It was Andrea responding to Jeff's question about whether they needed anything.

I checked my watch. It was 10:30 a.m. I had tossed and turned most of the night, but I had been in my sleeping bag for nearly twelve hours. My head ached, and I was sweating. It was at least eighty degrees already. I unzipped my bag and grabbed a water bottle.

After taking some time to gather my senses, I sat up and looked around. Jeff nodded at me, and Michelle appeared to be sleeping. Neither Georgia nor Brendan was present.

"How're you doing?" Jeff whispered.

"You guys totally don't have to worry about whispering," Andrea said. "I'm going to be out so fast that it won't matter. Seriously, don't worry about it." She was lying on her side with her back to me.

"*How are you doing, then?!*" Jeff said loudly, exaggerated for humor's sake.

"I've got a headache and some sort of head-fog," I responded. I rubbed my face and eyes, trying to understand for myself how I felt. "I'm not sure what this fog thing is; I don't know how to explain it."

"How is the rest of your body?"

"I don't know yet," I chuckled. "I haven't tried to walk anywhere. But it seems to be surprisingly good, actually. I just hope that this head thing goes away quickly. How are you?"

"I feel pretty good." Jeff seemed to be getting stronger as the race progressed. "Sure, I'm sore, but that'll work itself out. All things considered, I feel good."

"Do you feel like you've run a hundred and fifteen miles over the past few days?"

We reminisced a bit about the stage, expanding on our brief conversation from the previous night. He reaffirmed his performance—the second person to cross the finish line—and recounted how strange it had felt to be running at the front of the pack instead of fifty or 100 runners behind.

"For the first few days, all of you guys were in front of me, and I could always see footprints. Yesterday, there was nobody. I basically ran alone," he explained. "It was sort of lonely, but also liberating. It was definitely a different and neat experience."

We discussed my thirteenth place finish and laughed at my disappointment for not having been *dooze*.

I mixed my freeze-dried granola with blueberries and milk, but the thought of eating it made me want to vomit. Something was clearly wrong with my body: Even when ill, I have never lost my appetite. Knowing that I needed the calories, I forced myself to eat despite the nausea and then followed it up with my morning's package of Pop-Tarts.

I got up to walk around. My headache persisted, and fog filled my brain. I figured that a stroll might help things. And, I wanted to check in with my friends to see how they were doing.

"Hey there, grumpy!" someone yelled. It was a woman's voice, and a happy one at that. It had to be Laurie.

"Hey, how're you doing?" I responded. It was a silly question; she had a giant smile on her face.

"You know, I'm feeling pretty good. You?"

"I'm feeling pretty crummy, to be honest. I'm not all that sore, but I'm sick in other ways."

"So you're still as grumpy as you were last night?" It was a question, but there was also a subtext. I looked at her and tried to figure out what she was referring to. She had a wide grin, and a thought entered my mind that we had talked about something the previous night.

"Uh, did I say or do something last night?" I knew that I had, but I could not place what it was. Laurie laughed.

"Yeah, you could say that. You scolded me for being happy all of the time."

The conversation came back to me. I suddenly remembered my drunkenly walk back to my tent after my visit to the medical team. I had walked by their tent, heard Laurie talking, and rudely asked if she always needed to be so happy. In the grand scheme of things, it was not that big of a deal—Laurie would forgive me—but I wondered what else I could not remember. What had I done to the doctor?

"Oh, geez. Now that you mention it, yeah, I remember that. Sorry. You know, at the time I think that I was trying to be funny, but looking back, it was just sort of pissy."

"Don't worry about it. It's totally fine. It was obvious that you were pretty out of it last night."

"Well, thanks. I definitely was out of it, but I still feel bad."

"You ran really well yesterday, huh?" she paused to wait for an answer but then blurted out with a follow-up thought: "What place were you in?"

"Thirteenth."

"No way! That is incredible! Well done! How does it feel?" I decided that I would try a little humor again—admittedly a risk, given the previous night's failed attempt.

"Well, to be honest, I'm somewhat disappointed. When I crossed, they told me that I was twelfth but then later modified it to thirteen." Laurie understandably looked at me as though I were crazy.

"Twelfth, thirteenth, what's the difference?!"

There is a fine line between humor, arrogance, and graciousness; it is probably not a line I navigate well. This was one of those moments where it was important not to come across as boastful. The problem in this situation was that I felt so bad, and I had convinced myself that generating a little humor was the most likely way to win my senses back.

"Oh, in English, they're basically identical. I couldn't care less. The problem is that in French, twelfth is *dooze*, which is a really cool word. I've been repeating it for days now."

Her expression changed to ridiculous disbelief.

"That's ridiculous. You are too funny." Without warning, she decided to change the subject. "Is everyone in your tent back?"

"Yeah, Karen and Andrea got back this morning, just a little while ago. They were the last ones. Everybody made it, but a few of us are paying for it."

"That's great. Yeah, everyone in our tent made it back, but Toby had a bit of a scare. I'm sure he'll give you more details, but I guess that he stopped to help some guy in the middle of the night and ended up getting hypothermia."

"Oh man," I said. I stared at her, my way of asking for the conclusion.

"He's fine, though. The doctors checked him out, but he's getting some sleep now."

The doctors. I remembered the poor woman who had put up with me the night before. Even if I had not remembered any details, I figured that she deserved an apology.

"Oh, geez, speaking of doctors, I was a little bit rude with the medical staff last night, too. I think that I'm going to go apologize."

Laurie gave me some final grief for causing trouble, playfully reprimanding me. I deserved it.

The medical tent was a zoo. Emaciated, sore-footed creatures traveled in twos. I walked around until I saw the woman who had helped me the night before. We made eye contact, but she did not seem to recognize me. As I apologized, she remembered our interaction and laughed. Her reaction reinforced how positive an experience the volunteers had made this event. It was a miserable, painful, and wholeheartedly stupid thing to attempt; without such a kind and supportive staff, it would have been unbearable. I walked away and for a moment felt better.

With no stage to run on the fifth day, people roamed aimlessly around the camp. The camp was home to the walking dead. People walked with heads down—ostensibly to shield their eyes from the sun, but equally likely was that they were suffering from a weakening of the neck muscles. The men mostly went bare-chested. Many had unnaturally thin frames with exposed ribs. Others had taped various parts of their abdomen and spine in hopes of preventing sores caused by the friction of one's backpack. I had done this, and it seemed to help; but after four days, much of the tape had dirtied, crusted, and bloodied at points. Feet looked universally tender. One in two runners wore little medical foot coverings that they had received during their visit to the medical tent. Even from afar, I could see the blood-red iodine stains.

"Anybody know when e-mail is open today?" Michelle asked. I had returned to our tent.

"Yeah, it starts at noon," I responded. I had seen a sign while returning from the day's second apology.

"I'd really like to send an e-mail today. The lines have been so long, though. Did you see how the lines looked?" she asked me.

"No lines at all. I was actually planning on grabbing my shirt and then going over. Wanna go?"

Given the day's circumstances, the e-mail tent should have been a different experience from previous days. But when we arrived I saw the same dozen people I had seen on other days. Ian the Mountain Goat was there, and we talked a bit about the stage. The Spaniard lamented that he had fallen apart during the previous day but congratulated me on my performance. Michelle was the outsider, but she did not seem to notice. Her reddened face looked painful, and she still had not eaten anything. It had been thirty hours. In between conversations with a few of the other runners, I watched her sitting on the ground. It was obvious that traveling to send an e-mail was a painful but important mission for her.

When we had walked in, the other runners had informed us that we were numbers seven and eight in line, which boded well since the tent had ten computers. Once the race officials opened things up, we would be quickly seated.

I baked on the floor. I tried to focus my mind on pleasant things—my girlfriend back home, a bath, a burrito—but I kept fixating on my discomfort. My head hurt more; I was impatient.

"Number seven," a volunteer announced as he stepped away from a computer. It was Michelle's turn, but a Frenchman jumped up, ran over, and sat down. It was the same man who had cut in line during two previous days, and I had said nothing. But with my headache and the heat, I had reached my breaking point.

"Hey!" The Frenchman turned around and looked at me. We both knew that he didn't speak any English. "You're nine—neuf," I said, making my best attempt at French. "—and you're after her," I said, pointing at Michelle. I had only remembered his place in line because he had walked to the center of the tent and asked aloud; I had heard "nine" in four languages.

Michelle very quickly realized that she had no interest in joining the fray. She whispered to me that it was all right and that she would just wait for the next computer to open up. We both knew that it was a matter of moments, but there is something about the way that discomfort can feed sanctimony. I convinced myself that I was on a noble mission. Confronting him helped me deflect my attention from my own discomfort.

"You're nine, and you've cut in line for days now. We're all tired, we're all sore, and we all want to get out of here. But you don't see us trying to cheat. Why? Because we all respect the fact that we aren't the only ones uncomfortable." I paused. I had no idea what my point or purpose had been. I could see the next PC coming online. "That's *her* computer," I emphasized.

"Oh, shut up," said a man from the other side of the tent. His tone was impatient, haggard like mine. "Just calm down and sit down. Who cares? What do you care? Just shut up and wait for the next computer. It'll only be a minute." It was a Canadian man, someone two tents down from me. I had tried several times to make conversation with him during previous days, but we had not gotten along. I had avoided a confrontation earlier in the race, but in that e-mail tent on the fifth day, I completely lost my composure.

"I'm not trying to be rude to you, but let me be very clear: I wasn't speaking to you, and if I do speak to you, you'll know it. My problem isn't so much waiting; it's that the same guy has been disrespectful for three straight days."

Two more computers freed up, and Michelle tugged my arm. It was providence. Things would have gotten worse if I had continued speaking.

I sat down and began typing. As I recounted the previous day's events, I realized just how bad I was feeling. My mood was so sour. I knew that I was right about the cutting Frenchman, but I also knew that the Canadian had a point. Under normal circumstances I would have deflected the situation and not thought anything of it. After six days in the desert, four of which I had spent running 115 miles, my fuse was short. I was disappointed in myself for the outburst but worried about the implications. *How would I be able to recover enough to run the following day?*

Following a walk around camp to calm myself down—probably not a good idea with the sun directly overhead and the temperature topping 100 degrees—I made my way back to the tent. Everyone was there, and Andrea and Karen were awake. There was a little bit of pride, a little bit of whining, and a whole bunch of laughter. It was the middle of the day in the Sahara, and for the first time in days, none of us had anything to do. We were together. As we sat and talked, I was somewhat sad that we had not spent more time as a group throughout the race. Given our respective paces over the first four days, we had only been together at night, and I missed the opportunity to hear their stories. I was like a father hoping to hold onto his teenage children's attention, demanding that they make it home in time for six o'clock dinner.

"I have got to stink so bad," Karen said. It was odd not to hear an "eh."

"*You* do?" Georgia blurted. "I am absolutely disgusting. Remember how Coach Lisa sent that e-mail saying that I was glowing? Well, I'm glowing now from a layer of oily junk!"

Others took turns trying to lay claim to the worst hygiene. Brendan lamented that every article of his clothing was crusty from salty sweat. I smelled myself but noticed very little. That morning I had remembered smelling a little funk in my sleeping bag, but I was a little surprised at how little I could smell. I tried to place the others' comments, but they too seemed to be overplaying their conditions. After six days without showers—and undergoing intense exercise—I had expected it to be much worse.

"You know what?" I interjected. Everyone stopped talking, not out of respect, but rather, out of surprise because it had been so long since I had said anything. "I've got to be honest. I really don't think that we smell that bad. Seriously," I paused and looked around for confirmation. Instead, I found surprised looks, so I continued in an attempt to explain my position. "This is sort of a gross thing to say, but I can't smell you people." I nervously continued, "Not that I had any reason to think that you would be particularly smelly people by nature, but after all this time I would have figured that everyone would have been much worse."

"And why do you think that is, Ted?" Andrea wryly asked.

Jeff jumped in: "Yeah, that's a strange thing, Ted. Here we are talking about how bad we smell, and you're the only one who thinks we smell good. What do you think that means?" He too had a sarcastic tone. Everyone was on the verge of laughter.

"Okay, okay, okay," I acknowledged. "I freely admit that perhaps I'm the worst of all—and that my scent is so bad that it causes me not to notice anyone else." Everyone laughed, and I nodded to acknowledge my faux pas.

"But, here's why I don't think that's the case," I countered. "This morning I couldn't smell you guys. Now I can't smell you guys. But, on my way back from the e-mail tent, I walked by the French tents..." I paused for effect. "And, I'll tell you what," I added in my best redneck accent, "I'll tell you what: I've smelled better things walkin' through a trailer park on garbage day."

As everyone laughed, I took another swig of my coffee-flavored water; Andrea had gifted me a teabag with coffee crystals, and the caffeine was helping me feel better.

"Really?!" Karen asked. Michelle echoed the question.

"Yeah, really," I said, my voice lower and serious. "Seriously, I feel horrible for saying this because the race officials have been so darn nice, but the French tents had a continuously horrid stench. I didn't get it walking by the Moroccans, the British, or the Italians. It was bad."

"So you're saying that our B.O. smells like roses?" Georgia laughed.

"Why yes, Georgia, I think I am."

She lifted her arm and motioned over, offering me the opportunity to take a deep whiff.

"No thank you," I responded. "You're too kind. But, I'm not sure that I could handle so much sensory input in my weak condition."

At that moment, Jay dropped by the tent. "Hey, guys," he said, ducking his head underneath one of the side flaps. "The race organizers want everyone to go to the middle of the bivouac to exchange one of their bib numbers. It's something that they do every day before the marathon stage to make sure that the sponsors' logos are nice and visible."

We looked into the middle of camp, and a few Jeeps had assembled. Runners had begun lining up.

"Oh, and you're going to want to go do it," he added, showing us an obviously cold can of Pepsi.

***

I had heard the rumors, and evidently they were true. Toby had told me about that magical moment in 2007 when race personnel had surprised him with a cold can of Coca-Cola. Back home, Coke was an integral part of my diet. Coach Lisa had tried to get me to stop, but I kept sneaking cans, bottles, and fountain drinks. Coworkers were wont to ask what was wrong if ever I walked around the office empty-handed in the afternoon. My girlfriend would order me a Coke—

complete with a lime wedge—if she arrived first at a restaurant.

But Pepsi was another story. I simply refused to drink the stuff. In fact, there were a few restaurants I frequented often enough to become friendly with the wait staff; they knew that I would scold them for offering me The Other Cola, but company policy still required them to ask. "Have you started serving Coke?" I would playfully ask before requesting a glass of tap water.

For some people, a cola choice is a preference; for others, it is a toss-up. For me, Coca-Cola had become a way of life. As a marketing executive, my job is to create a brand and awareness that would hopefully develop customers with a firm attachment to my company's product. I knew the power of good marketing; I knew the impact of a brand. For this reason, I should have been immune to Atlanta's sway, but I had long ago given in to my physical and emotional addiction to the tonic.

I looked at Jay's can, complete with condensation on the outside, and I was torn. On the one hand, it was The Other Cola. On the other hand, it was cold and full of caffeine. I felt a little ashamed as my mouth began to water, but I realized that I could not turn down such a gift from race officials whose job it had been to ensure that we were living self-sufficiently. This Pepsi was a deviation from the rule. It was freedom in a can—even if it was a smaller, eight-ounce version.

Ashamed at first, I quickly found myself generously offering to drink others' Pepsis if they did not feel like drinking the caffeine. But, alas, even sick Michelle, whose stomach had refused everything for more than a day, enjoyed every last drop of the sugary water.

Prior to the start of the race, I had noticed that Moroccan Coca-Cola tasted differently than it did back home. They followed the European recipe, which, I had learned while in London the previous year, called for sugar instead of high fructose corn syrup. It was a small difference to some, but to a true connoisseur like me, it was a flagrant violation of the product's purity standard.

That day's Pepsi no doubt had the same deficiency, but everything about it was wonderful. I found myself joking to God that perhaps—just perhaps—the can contained a small piece of Heaven.

***

"So, there I was, bloody nighttime, and it was starting to get cold." It was Toby, and it appeared to be story time. A crowd had gathered to watch him raise his arms and pound his legs. "I'm walking fru the bloody sand"—I smiled at his substitution of the "f" sound for "th," which seemed to be a common Britishism—"and I see this stupid guy staggering off to the side of the trail, walking from side to side. I decide to go see how he's doing, and when I get over to him, I realize that he's got his flare out, and he's waving it around wildly." He stopped talking and waved his hands in an animated way.

"So I grab the bloody flare, and he's trying to shoot the fing off into my chest. So I went from wanting to help this struggling guy to trying to protect myself from a bloody lunatic. I finally got the flare out of his hands, and he's talking about how he's gonna die." He offered an exaggerated roll of his eyes before continuing.

"I'm thinking to myself, 'Oh shit, what am I gonna do? I can't leave this guy.' So I grab him and put his arm around me, and we're walking—the whole time he's trying to wander off in different directions. By the time we got to the checkpoint, I had lost at least an hour, and I was a little pissed off. I walked this geezer up to the medical personnel and told them that the guy had started going into hyperfermia. I went to move on, to continue because I had lost enough time already, and a doctor grabbed me and shined a light in my eyes. Then he told me that I was going into hyperfermia also, and he ordered me into my sleeping bag and told me that I could continue when the sun came up."

We were all laughing—not that there is anything funny about hyperthermia and human suffering, but because Toby's storytelling was so animated that each detail became so involved.

"So, I ended up losing several hours, which sucked. But, what was I going to do—leave the guy to die?" It was one of those touching, genuine moments when the sarcastic and witty Brit showed his sentimental side.

"Thirty minutes until the last runner!" a woman yelled through a megaphone. She had a thick French accent. "Thirty minutes until the last runner! Please come to the finish line."

The newbies looked at the veterans in our group, who explained the tradition of having all competitors at the finish line when the final runner came in. It was then that someone noticed that one American was missing from our group: cardiologist Steve Wolk. I remembered that he had been the first runner I had passed on the previous day.

We talked amongst ourselves to see if anyone had heard anything. A few dozen runners had been forced to quit during the stage, and we hoped aloud that Steve was one of the final runners who would be coming in. We walked back to the finish line, some of us with a few last drops of Pepsi remaining, in hopes of seeing the last of our group.

Within minutes of the woman's megaphone announcement, hundreds of people had assembled at the finish, forming a hundred-yard long tunnel leading up to the white, inflatable sponsor structure. Women with shredded feet and men with cherry-red sunburns made their way. I saw Mohamad and Mustafa out near the front. They had finished the stage in fewer than seven hours—compared to these competitors, who were approaching thirty hours—and yet they felt it important to be there with everyone else to welcome home the last runners.

I wondered how many professionals back home would take the time and expend the energy to cheer for someone whose athletic prowess was not even in their same league. Looking at Mohamad and Mustafa, I found it difficult to believe that either of them would be arrested for waving a firearm at a police officer. I doubted that they would drive a Cadillac Escalade with twenty-four-inch rims. They might just be what has become so rare in America: the athlete role model.

A husband and wife crossed the finish line, and we the assembled cheered. They cried and kissed as they limped across. Following a night in the desert and more than twenty-nine hours of exertion, they were suspended between pride and delirium.

By the time we watched the third competitor cross the finish, the crowd had developed an organized cheer. With the runner a few hundred yards away, everyone began clapping in unison. The claps were about a second apart and grew steadily faster as the runner approached. By the time the athlete was within spitting distance of the finish line, the clapping had escalated to a frenzy; as he crossed the line, the audience gave a perfectly-timed scream. Then we would begin anew for the next competitor out in the distance.

After about fifteen minutes and half a dozen competitors, we looked out into the distance and saw no one. Restlessness rippled throughout the crowd as we began to ask one another if, perhaps, we had seen the final runner. If it had been, it would have meant that Steve had withdrawn from the race.

Then a slender green figure crested a small hill in the distance; we could even see the tuft of white hair atop Steve's head. The American and Canadian runners began screaming. Several minutes must have passed, but in the excitement it seemed like mere moments before he was just a hundred yards away. He lumbered patiently along—like he always did—placing each step deliberately.

He stopped and looked upward. With hundreds of us screaming, it seemed implausible that he had not heard us. With the rhythmic clapping in the background, it seemed unlikely that he was unaware of his proximity to the finish line. But he simply stood there and stared in our direction, as if he had lost his vision and was trying to make sense of a cloudy mess in front of him.

"Steve!" someone yelled. "All right Steve! Woo-hoo!"

Steve looked at us and seemed confused. Then, without warning, it was as though he had spotted his friend across a crowded restaurant. His forehead flicked upward, his eyes opened wide, and he raised his hand in acknowledgement. Without warning, he began to sprint. It could not be more different from his methodical walk. His seemingly dead frame took on superhuman powers, and despite thirty hours of trudging through the desert, he broke into a full-out sprint toward the finish.

ABC had brought its camera out for what was perhaps the most magical moment of the entire event. A sixty-year-old American man, scanning the crowd from side to side as he passed, exhibited complete confusion as he barreled toward the finish of a forty-seven-mile nightmare. The cheers were louder, the screams more pronounced, and all the while Steve's eyes were wide open as he shook his head from side to side. After an eternity of desert solitude, he was learning what it was like to interact with people again.

Matt, the ABC cameraman, ran backwards as Steve ran the final fifty feet. Clarissa and Bruno asked him questions, which he ignored in favor of looking out over the audience. I am not sure that he had any idea where he was.

As he crossed the finish line, many of us lost sight of him. It was no longer about Steve's finish, but rather, our collective triumph. Steve completed our contingent; he was the best we had; he had struggled longer, pressed further, and accomplished more than any of us would ever know.

"How do you feel, Steve?" Clarissa yelled, hoping to capture some good footage for "Nightline." Steve said nothing. He continued to look around, glassy-eyed, in hopes of making sense of everything.

Matt interjected, "Steve, what are you going to do now…now that you've finished the longest stage of the Marathon Des Sables?"

At that question, Steve stopped and looked into the camera. With a confused look, he matter-of-factly proclaimed, "Get water. That's what I always do." Without hesitation, he walked beyond the camera toward the water distribution checkpoint, pulled out his water ration card, and said hello to people as he walked.

"Get water" was the perfect response. American advertising culture had taught us to think of going to Disneyland after triumphing in an athletic event. But for Steve there was no pretense. He had traveled to Morocco to run, and his goal was to do only what was necessary to aid that goal. He could have used his opportunity for fame to speak to the country, but he had not even considered it.

My headache was gone. Part of the reason was likely the caffeine, but I would attribute most of my recovery to the incredible emotion generated as Steve crossed the finish line. It put everything into perspective.

As I walked back to Tent 77, there was no breeze in the 120-degree heat. My muscles were sore, but I looked around and knew that I was in considerably better straits than the majority of the runners. Some struggled to shuffle their legs one foot at a time, and most walked with a pronounced limp. There were bloodied feet, scraped sides, and blistered backs. I saw sunburns that had deteriorated into open facial sores. Many of the athletes walked stiff-legged, as though they had no knees.

At the tent, I watched and listened as Andrea and Karen worked to repair their blistered feet. As they passed gauze, bandages, tape, and scissors back and forth, they asked the rest of us what they should do to tend to their blisters. I was closest to Andrea, and I looked at her feet. Less than half of the skin on her feet was normal. The majority was covered in blisters, blisters that had developed inside of blisters, and skin that had rubbed raw to reveal bloody tissue.

Their only concern was how to properly tape their feet so that they could continue.

Dear Lord, I thought. *How are we all going to run a marathon tomorrow?*

15
A Marathon

Even though I had persevered through times when I thought that my body could not continue; even though I had survived excruciating levels of pain in my legs, torso, and back; even though I was able to move much more easily than my fellow competitors, many of whom limped or shuffled without bending their knees; even though I had seen friends continue after having shredded skin pulled away from their blisters; even though many of us had continued despite diarrhea or vomiting; and even though my headache was no longer blinding; I still could not believe that I had to run a marathon that morning.

As the Berbers came around and felled our tents, no one moved much. Andrea and Karen rolled around and complained about their feet. Michelle clutched her stomach. I whined about my foggy head. Brendan, quiet most of the time, admitted that he was suffering. Even Jeff, the previous day's hero, commented that the fifth stage hurt before it even started.

After five days and 115 miles in the desert, we were exhausted. None of us had showered in a week. I itched everywhere.

We were decaying but nonetheless required to perform.

Each of my ribs was visible whenever I lifted my shirt. My pack

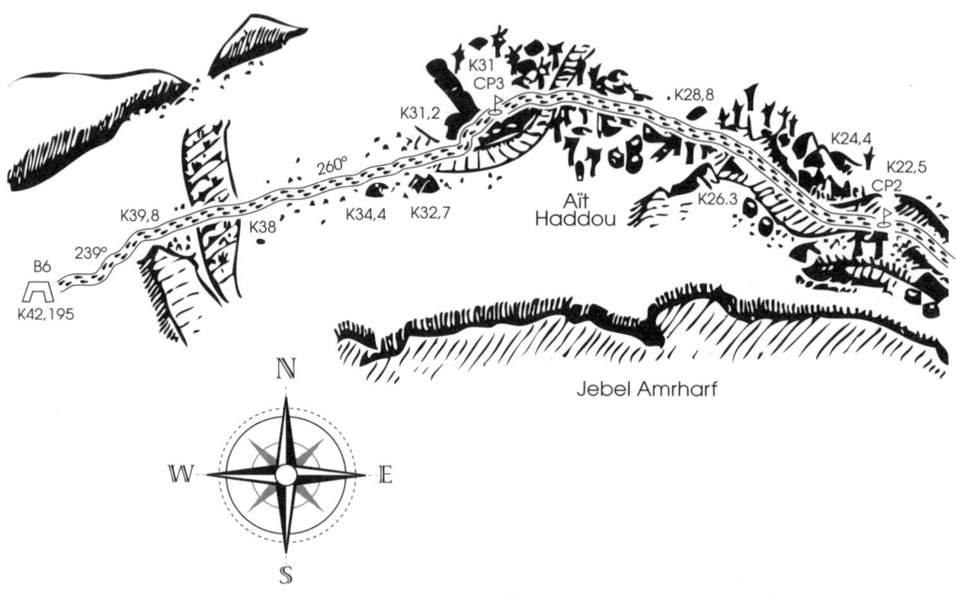

sores had multiplied, now coating my entire waistline and much of my spine. My muscles felt as though they had deteriorated, as though I was functioning with half of what I started with. The world looked foggy and slow. As necessary as food was, the mere thought of eating made me nauseous.

As I scanned the camp, I wondered if our bodies were beginning to experience a small part of what concentration camp victims suffered. I would certainly never equate the two, but I would have imagined that under such conditions, one would be driven to eat. Instead, we seemed to be shutting down. Though we needed food, most of us preferred to lie motionless and hope for some other cure.

I wanted to do things, but inertia was so much more comfortable.

"Hey, where's our wakeup song?" Andrea asked. The question was directed at me.

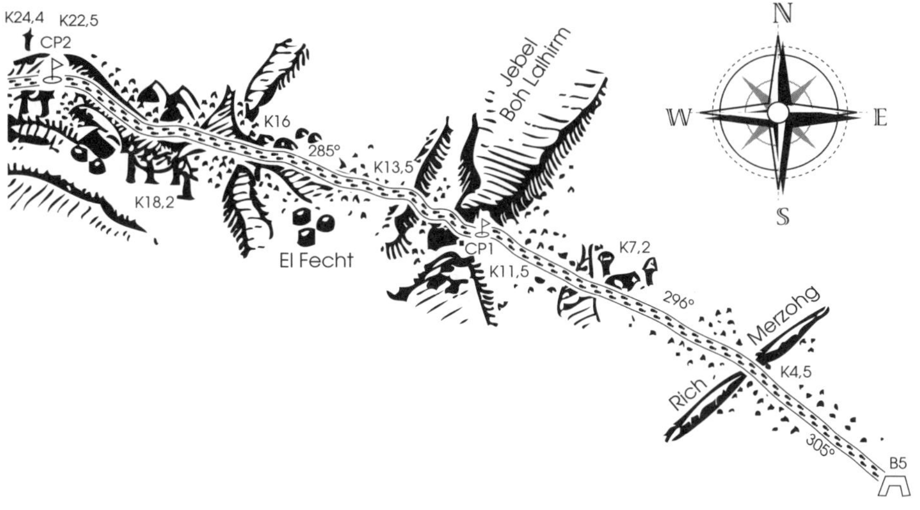

I wanted to chuckle, but I just lay there. It did surprise me, though. Everyone had groaned during my first few performances. I had not expected a call for an encore.

"Right, eh? We need some of that cowboy stuff," Karen added. "Just don't sing about bad feet."

I thought back through the week, recounting the Brad Paisley songs that I had sung. I realized that I had omitted one of his funniest. "Online" is about an overweight and ugly boy who uses the Internet to create a false identity, thus making himself more attractive to the outside world. I looked around the camp and thought that it actually had some relevance for us: lies would have been necessary for anyone to consider us sex symbols.

So I sang a little about afternoon snacks and basement bedrooms; six-pack abs and GQ magazine; playing the tuba; and having a three-way (chat) with two women at one time. "I'm so much cooler online…yeah, I'm cooler online," I sang. The lyrics were as absurd as previous morning's songs, but they had more of an impact this time. People liked the ridiculousness.

In due time, the dead began to stir their freeze-dried meals.

"Would you people please stop throwing sand on my stuff!" I said, with as much exasperation as I could muster. It was a recycled joke, but it was all that I had.

Georgia called me on it: "We told you earlier in the week that was the price you've got to pay for being allowed to stay in our tent."

I rolled around on the ground and then shook out my sleeping bag. I stuffed it into my backpack and smiled as I picked it up. After having eaten five days worth of food, my pack must have weighed less than twelve pounds. When I had started training, that would have seemed heavy, but that morning it felt good to have dropped ten pounds.

When it finally came time to start the stage, there was no doubt that our outlook was worse than on any other day.

We no longer rippled with nervous anticipation.

We had thrown out any hope that we could defeat the dunes.

The long stage no longer loomed in our minds as the imminent, powerful force to be conquered.

Simply put, the adventure had stopped being and the misery had set in. The emotion that we had invested into the first few days of the event—and the long stage especially—was drained. There was nothing new for us to gravitate toward. Each of us felt as though we had done what we had come to do—and yet, nearly forty miles remained before we could celebrate.

My blueberries with granola had been chalky; my Pop-Tarts were cardboard. Each time I walked ten feet in any direction, I waited for my brain to catch up.

The mood at the starting line was subdued. Patrick, however, seemed his normal self, which was unsurprising given that he had a helicopter, Hummer, and queen-sized bed to comfort him.

In a never-ending loop, a single song—"It's a Beautiful Day" went the chorus—played loudly overhead. It was by a French band living in Morocco, but the song was in English. The singer channeled Leonard Cohen, his deep voice eerily conveying pain and hope at the same time. The beats belonged in a nightclub, their trancelike, hypnotic repetition soothing the crowd and promising a better life. I wondered if I had been drugged. It would have been fitting.

The song continued indefinitely; I absorbed it and sought to channel its incessant rhythm for the day. Today, I informed myself, I would have to run on will alone, for strength had long ago left me.

I tried bargaining with myself: *Four hours of good running is all that I need, and then I can stop*. My other half fought back, rightfully claiming that it was unfair of me to inflict yet another day of punishment. I had succeeded in tricking myself for hours during the fourth stage, and I was trying to do it again before the fifth had even begun.

Unable to get an agreement for an entire day's effort, I knew that the entire marathon would need to be a point-to-point process. I knew that I could make it to the first checkpoint, and so this became my only focus. Once there, I reasoned, I could turn my attention toward the next checkpoint.

It reminded me of an old argument I had had for years with friends: "You can never be 100% full," I would joke. "You might *feel* full, but you can always manage to take just one more, teeny-weeny bite." I wondered if, perhaps, the same logic could be applied to running; could I indefinitely convince myself to run just one more step?

It was time to find out. The fifth stage began with considerably less fanfare than on previous days. Groans replaced cheers.

Despite my aches, the compact sand seemed more compact than it had been on previous days. The wadi seemed less wadi-esque. Where I would have ordinarily wanted to stop and walk, I was able to continue jogging. The first seven miles were at a slight incline with varying terrain. We ran toward the farthest point of a U-shaped ring of mountains, and as they closed in around us, it was obvious that we would soon be headed over the top. For miles, I could see the checkpoint in the distance, at the base of the mountains.

As the race began that morning, I had decided to follow the Spaniard. Though I had beaten him during the long stage, he had proven to be a stronger runner over shorter distances. I hoped that he would do the work for me. My goal was to not think about a thing, but rather to force him to navigate and set the pace.

His pack was also lighter, and he motored ahead at a swift pace. I checked my watch as we arrived at the first checkpoint. I had run my fastest leg of the race. It seemed inconceivable given how bad I felt, but my watch told a different story. I looked to the top of the mountain ahead and could still see Mohamad. He was only half a mile in front of me.

The climb to the top of the mountain was a relatively easy one. Only a few hundred yards high, it appeared to have a natural trail carved into the rocky façade. It reminded me of jogging up the Incan steps toward Machu Picchu, and I was surprised at the ease with which I scampered uphill. I hoped that it signaled my strong will, but I suspect that my lighter pack had more to do with it.

At the top of the mountain, I stopped. Though I had come to Morocco to race the Marathon Des Sables—and had planned on stopping to look at the scenery only before and after each stage—that moment was too incredible to forfeit.

The sandy valley stretched for what seemed like hundreds of miles. Mountains snaked around off in the distance, forming an endless trail of stitches on the belly of an obese man. But the valley very clearly was the dominant force. It was as though the mountains had been offered a lease. They were sharecropping—only for as long as the valley would allow them to remain.

The sun shone down on the valley and played tricks on my eyes. I saw little glints of light—small flickers, diamonds sparkling in the distance. There was nothing there but compact sand, I was sure, but as I stood atop a rocky mountain with patches of deep, soft sand, I looked out across the scaly landscape and tilted my head from one side to the next.

I enjoyed what looked like flash bulbs. I imagined that they were for me.

I was proud to be there, in Morocco, in the middle of nowhere, standing atop a mountain and imagining diamonds in the distance.

I stood and drank my Heed energy drink and felt the sun on my shoulders. For those twenty seconds I felt like a free man.

Yet none of it made any sense. Only an hour before, my head had been foggy, my hamstrings were cramped, and my stomach turned. There was no explanation, but I had somehow recovered. I had become a machine. As I began gliding down the sand on the opposite side of the mountain, I felt nothing but the wind in my hair.

As I slid down the soft sand, Ian the Brit flew by on my right. He scampered on fist-sized, loose, black rocks that dislodged and tumbled as he ran. As per his usual downhill form, he flailed out of control while traveling twice as fast as me. I watched him and marveled that he never fell. Just as I had learned how to be more efficient in sand dunes, he had obviously learned something about running downhill. He was gracefully chaotic.

After reaching the valley floor, I passed Ian again and began running alongside a Moroccan man. His legs were seventy percent of his height, and he had even less fat than I did. I could see the sinew stretching in his legs. It did not seem right for me to be running next to him, but I passed him anyway. It felt good to be running ahead of a man who had qualified to receive a single-digit bib number: three. Little did I know that he would overtake me in another half hour and continue on to beat me by a substantial margin. But I nonetheless enjoyed the moment.

I saw palm trees in the distance and wiped my eyes. Given my view of the valley from the mountaintop, it seemed implausible, but they grew as time went on.

The wadi thickened as we ran into a small town. There were no more than a few huts and a few meager areas for growing crops. The race organizers had marked the course with little strips of plastic—our warning to avoid stomping on the locals' food.

I looked at what they were growing—small green plants shooting up sporadically through the sand. Back home we would have traveled to Home Depot for some topsoil; here the farmers just prayed that enough of the crops would take to allow them to survive another season.

It was too difficult. It was unbelievable. I had seen the lush landscape as we had flown into Casablanca. It looked similar to the flight into London, with expansive patches of light and dark green as far as the eye could see. It had reminded me of the rows of corn and soybeans spread throughout Iowa, and I remembered running through my father's farmland as a boy. The Moroccan orange farms outside Casablanca were some of the world's richest. *Those were farmers*, I thought. As I looked at the troubled sprigs in this hidden hamlet, I wondered why people would subject themselves to such miserable conditions.

The Spaniard ran alongside me and commented on the farms. We both ran as close as we could to the palm trees to benefit from what shade they did offer. The heat had crept up on me that morning; in my wistful thoughts, I had avoided noticing the sweat.

Just beyond the town was a dried up riverbed. Likely millions of years old, I wondered how often it flooded. How much rain would it take? The oversized river rocks embedded in the crusty sand could have come from Sacramento's American River: smooth and polished.

On the other side of the river were a handful of children, all boys, ranging from five to fifteen years of age. They screamed as I approached, waving at the Spaniard and me and speaking in both French and Arabic. I held up my arms and shook my head, an attempt to tell them that I could not understand what they were saying.

They screamed louder, and the expressions on their faces ranged from pained to comical. I smiled at them, and they smiled and laughed back as they ran alongside me.

"Monsieur, monsieur!" they yelled before asking for something in an endless string of French. "Monsieur, monsieur!" they yelled while pointing at things that dangled from my pack. "Monsieur, monsieur!" they pleaded as they grabbed my hand and held it triumphantly in the air. I offered high-fives and shook hands. I was so tall, and they so short, that I imagine part of the surprise was my height. I wondered how often they saw a white person and wondered if that was part of the mystique.

"I'm so sorry," I yelled back. "I don't speak French. I don't understand what you're saying."

They kept yelling, only now they were more excited that I was responding, perhaps thinking that I understood something and would give them what they were looking for.

"I speak English. Hablo Español. I speak English and Spanish. Hablo Español y Inglés. Sorry, but I don't speak French." I was trying so hard to communicate with them. I pointed at things on my pack, I tried rudimentary sign language. I wanted so badly to know what they were thinking.

"I'm sorry, I speak English. I don't understand you."

One of the older boys—who had run ahead and stopped in my path—looked intently at me as I spoke. He stopped speaking and was very clearly thinking. After I had run by, and after the younger boys had stopped running, he found his voice.

"*Run, Forrest, run!*" he screamed at the top of his lungs. Shocked, I turned around and started clapping. He and the rest of the children laughed and shrieked. We had finally communicated.

Somewhere in the middle of Morocco, miles from the closest road, there must be a little mud hut that has the town's only electricity. I imagined a small two-in-one television/VCR combination unit propped up on a counter; I wondered how many times the village children had watched Tom Hanks run across America, catch shrimp, and play ping-pong.

I snapped open my compass case to look at myself in the small pocket mirror. I had no doubt that, with a week's beard, I looked a great deal like Forrest Gump to those children. I was, after all, a tall white man who had not bathed and was numb to the elements. I was running for no reason other than because I could. *I was running.*

I gave the children a thumb's up as I ran off into the distance. I wondered how many other Hollywood movies they had seen, and as I thought about their Western clothes, I wondered what they thought about the United States, if anything at all. Our politicians would have us believe that the citizens of the world hate us for our foreign policy, but I saw nothing of that sort in those children.

I saw kids, wearing clothing that they had likely been given by traveling missionaries, who were struggling to survive on a daily basis. That a world-renowned race was running through their village was likely the most exciting event in years, and when they did enjoy their occasional contact with American technologies and ways, they just enjoyed it as a way to distract themselves from the toils of daily life. My guess was that to them, the United States was a place somewhere that produced all sorts of incredible things that they only occasionally experienced. But when they did, it was fascinating.

The stage concluded with miles of compact, rocky terrain. I ran at an incline over small rolling hills for nearly an hour. The temperature approached unbearable. It must have been at least 110 degrees; it could have been 130. Steam rose from the rocks and distorted the mountains in the distance.

It was 12:30 p.m. Somehow I had managed to run for 210 minutes without breaking down, but now I was miserable. The repetition of the rocky hills caused my mind to drift, and I could not help but focus on the pain.

Ian the Mountain Goat jogged up alongside me.

"How's it going, Ted?" he asked. His floppy, 360-degree adventurer hat bounced up and down on his head. As always, he cradled a 1.5 liter water bottle upside down in his arm.

"Is it over yet, Ian?" I responded. In my present position, I was probably in tenth place for the stage, but I knew that I had nothing left. There would be no surprise cache of energy this time. I would suffer to the finish line.

"Run with me?" he offered. "C'mon." It was genuine; it was exactly what I had tried to do for him during an earlier stage. I knew then how he had felt at the time. I envied his strength but knew that no amount of encouragement could help me to keep up with him.

"I can't, man. I'm dying."

"You'll catch me soon," he responded. That too was the encouragement I had offered him.

"I doubt it," I grunted. "Are there any sand dunes up ahead?" I was able to muster a laugh.

"All right, man. Finish strong. Keep it up."

I watched apathetically as two more runners passed by. It upset me that they had caught me, but I had nothing left to chase them down.

I reached the top of a small hill, and the terrain transformed from rolling hills to a rock flat. The finish line was a mile in the distance. I had white sweat streaks all over my chest. My feet had swelled so much that they were rubbing against the insides of my shoes, despite the fact that I was wearing shoes a full size larger than normal to compensate for the heat. But there it was: the finish before the finish. If I could make it there, only eleven miles would remain in the event.

Footsteps pounded behind me. It was two Frenchmen in matching orange shirts. I had seesawed with them throughout the race (they had been two of the group of nine that had been lost in the sand dunes on the first and third stages), and we were ranked close to one another.

I looked at the finish line and looked back at the Frenchmen. The closest was only a few steps away; the second was another ten yards. With my mind drifting from incoherent thought to incoherent thought, I had an idea that made perfect sense to me. I was able to bargain with myself: I would split the difference and allow one of the Frenchmen, but not both, to beat me.

It made no sense. Either I should have felt so bad so as not to care if they passed me or, if I had the energy to compete, I should have been unwilling to give ground. I should have been determined to beat them both, but instead I constructed a theory that it would be okay to have one orange man in front of me and another behind—but that it would be uneven to have both of them on either side.

One of the Orangemen ran ahead, and I stuck with him. His

compatriot struggled to keep up, and after a few minutes I found myself suspended perfectly between the two. In my delirium, it seemed a perfect balance—one short, orange Frenchman fifty yards in front of me, and a second an equal distance behind. And that is the way that we crossed the finish line.

I had finished the stage in fifteenth place—which placed me fifteenth overall. I had run a marathon in stifling heat, with a backpack, over sharp, rocky terrain, and after having run 115 miles over the previous few days—and I had finished it in well under four hours.

I screamed at the top of my lungs as I tried to remember back over the day. I could remember feeling poor at the start. I could remember the view from the hill. And I could remember my Forrest Gump experience. But I could remember nothing else. Somehow I had become a machine, running a marathon distance at the fastest pace of any stage during the race. I had run 15% faster than I had on the first day, when my legs were fresh.

I screamed again. *Now*, I thought, *the race is really done!* With only eleven miles remaining on the following day, I realized that I could break my leg and likely limp my way to the finish.

I looked to the left and saw a middle-aged white woman with two young children, about ten years old. They were speaking what sounded like French; the boy was waving a Swiss flag. They were sitting on the wooden box where I had spent many of my afternoons welcoming in some of the other runners. I wondered who they were, where they had come from. I decided to find out.

"Hi." It did not occur to me that they might not speak English. Luckily for me, the woman responded.

"Hello," she said, with a thick accent. "You are done very quickly. Very impressive. Where are you from?" Her children jogged over to be close by. They wanted to listen to the stranger.

"The United States."

"American? Oh, very nice. We are from Switzerland."

"Yeah, I noticed his flag." I pointed at the boy, who smiled and blushed from the attention.

"You look dirty," the young girl said, also in broken English. Her mother shot her a look, swatted at her, and said something in French that no doubt scolded her for her manners.

"Oh, it's okay. I'm very tired and *very dirty*." I looked at the young girl, knelt down, and said, "I haven't had a shower in a week. That's pretty gross, huh?"

She nodded, and her mother laughed. She explained that she was waiting for her husband, their father, who was running the race as well. Evidently the race organizers were willing to sell family members a package to visit loved ones as they finished the marathon. She explained that they had paid a great deal to be out at the sixth bivouac to wait for their father.

"Do you think that your dad is crazy?" I asked. I had a big smile on my face and was hoping that the children would understand my humor.

The boy nodded a little and laughed. "He will look dirtier than you because he is not as fast."

We sat and talked awhile. In broken English, the children tried to express how proud they were of their father. They struggled to find the words, but they were able to talk about how, though they thought he was crazy for running in this heat, they could not wait to tell their friends back home. The woman analyzed me; it was obvious that she was trying to figure out how well her fifty-year-old husband would be faring if a thirty-one-year-old looked as bad as I did.

"I'm sorry," I apologized. "How bad do I smell?" I realized that I had inconsiderately thrust myself into their breathing space.

The woman laughed. "Pretty bad, but that is okay. No need to worry about it."

Eventually they departed. The race organizers called them over to a Land Cruiser, and the children said goodbye. It was time to drive out into the desert in search of their loved ones. There were a total of six trucks and about forty family members. They wore hats and fanned themselves; they carried water bottles; the children clung to their mothers and whined. I grew tired just watching them suffer.

I looked out into the distance and could see my tent mate Jeff chugging along. He was making good time, and he certainly was finishing strong. He sprinted in, and though I could not see his eyes, his black glasses told the entire story: *I am a stud.* His arms pumped rapidly, and his shoulders were square.

We walked back to the tent together, stopping to collect our afternoon's water ration. We shared our experiences, marveling at how well we had been able to run. The day had been miserable, but we knew how each other felt. Given how much we had been through and how sore we were, we were amazed that our bodies had allowed us to run so fast. He too had run his fastest pace of the event.

We talked about the boys in the village who had called me Forrest Gump. We talked a little about sociology and politics, noting how nice it was to have an intercultural exchange that seemed genuine—not dominated by some government agenda to portray others as foreign. We were Americans, they Moroccans, and we all were happy just to have the opportunity to high-five and laugh with one another.

Our experience, however, was radically different from what Andrea and Karen experienced in the same village later in the day. They arrived late in the afternoon with a proclamation:

"What heathens! Oh my God, can you believe those horrible children?!"

"I know, eh? What horrible jerks," Karen responded.

Jeff and I exchanged looks. Confused, I assumed that we were talking about different kids.

"What kids are you talking about?"

"Those disgusting punks back in the village that we ran through just before the final checkpoint," Andrea responded. Karen said essentially the same thing at the same time.

"What happened?" Jeff asked. He was concerned; it was obvious that both gals were upset.

"What didn't happen, eh?"

"Oh, they're just disgusting, horrible kids. I can't believe their parents don't scold them."

"Right, eh? I mean, it's not like they don't have anything else that they could be doing."

"Wait," I said. I was still stuck on the notion that we were talking about the Forrest Gump crowd—the same children who had cheered for me, held my hand, and run alongside me. "You're talking about the kids back in the village with the crops and palm trees?"

"*Yes!*" both of them screamed. It was obviously not a ruse.

"Oh my God, they're heathens!" Andrea yelled. Jeff and I again exchanged glances, wondering if they would fill us in on the details.

"What did they do?" Jeff asked.

"Oh, well, let's see," Andrea sarcastically said. "It would have been nice if they had just screamed at us, which is all they did at first."

"Oh, yeah, the screaming was the pleasant part."

"But after screaming at us, they decided to start spitting at us, which was gross."

"I would have even been happy with them just spitting at us," Karen responded. The two of them were rapidly firing comments back and forth. They were angrily wrapped up in the story.

"Yeah, then they started grabbing us. One of the boys grabbed my butt, and then a few more decided that would be fun. Then one of them got his hands up the front of my shirt!"

"Are you serious?!" Jeff's jaw dropped and the whites of his eyes were fully visible. "They were actually grabbing you guys? What did you do? Didn't anyone make them stop?"

Karen laughed—not a rude laugh, but a laugh that nonetheless suggested Jeff's naiveté. "Yeah, that would have been nice, but we were sort of toward the end of the group. There weren't exactly any other runners around to stick up for us."

"Well, there was that one father who scolded one group of the boys," Andrea interjected. "I was thankful for him, but none of the other groups of boys had any parents around."

The conversation went on for another ten minutes, with Andrea and Karen describing in greater detail how the boys had molested them. Neither of them was at all restrained in expressing their contempt for the children in our host country. I listened in disbelief as they blasted the children whom I had praised not so long ago. These were the same boys for whom I had felt fondly.

Our experiences had been radically different. No doubt, it was for a simple reason: I was a man, and they were women. I was engaged in an event—and was dressed accordingly—that made sense for men. It involved physical effort, sweating, struggle, and triumph. My legs and arms were visible, and I was required to be alone for long stretches of time.

I thought about the few Moroccan women I had seen out in the desert. Unlike the women in western dress in Casablanca and Ouarzazate, these women were fully or mostly covered. I remembered that they had averted their eyes as we approached. They stood behind the men or boys with whom they traveled.

I contrasted this to Andrea and Karen—active, without a male escort, legs and arms exposed, and dressed in a way that is incompatible with certain worldviews. I felt sorry for them. It was a horrible way to distort the cultural experience we were having—but I was not particularly surprised. Under the circumstances, with what I had seen along the way, it made sense.

***

Just before nightfall, the sun perched upon the mountaintops and glowed a neon pink. I walked with Bruno, the producer from ABC. Far away from the bivouac, Matt and Clarissa were waiting, and the camera pointed toward the desolate, dry, and uninhabited hell that was the Sahara Desert. My mind drifted, and I remembered my father telling me of Newton Minnow, FCC Chairman in the 1960s. Television, it seemed, was indeed a vast wasteland.

Bruno and Clarissa asked if I would be willing to participate in a "retrospective" interview. I thought it odd, given that "retrospective" referred to the past, and though the end of the race was a mere sixteen hours away, I very much felt that I was still in the midst of the experience. Until I had a shower, a cooked meal, and a bed, I would consider "retrospective" to be a bit premature.

Still, as I sat on the compact sand (my butt positioned carefully between two jagged rocks), I was overcome with a surreal sensation that the Marathon Des Sables was no more. I looked directly into the sun so that the camera would see a well-illuminated face. They asked about the first day, the dunes, my diet, how much weight I had lost, and what the event had meant to me. They wanted to know if spending more than a week suffering in the desert had changed me.

The footage that they would later show on national TV (on "World Nightly News with Charlie Gibson") showed me, unshaven, talking about how I wanted nothing more than a Coca-Cola and four cheeseburgers. I would later joke with my friends that the sentiment perfectly encapsulated who I am—and that is true to a point. But the sound bite did miss a bit of the message that I had tried to convey as my final Saharan sunset fizzled in the distance.

It was and is a cliché, but I told them that I could offer no words to explain what the experience had meant.

I tried to refocus the discussion away from my performance—I was currently in fifteenth place overall and would eventually finish in sixteenth—but they seemed interested in talking about how I had managed to go from never having run an ultra marathon to competing with some of the world's best. I admitted that the success was a bit overwhelming, but I wanted them to understand that my ranking was unimportant in the broader picture.

There was Jeff Arricale just a few tents down. He took nearly twice as long to complete the event, but his purpose was so much greater. He had raised tens of thousands of dollars for a medical charity to improve the lives of children—children like his who suffered.

There was Marianne "Bunny" DeMarco, a writer from New York, who offered a continuous string of humorous comments. At any moment, she could brighten the mood for all of us. She could commiserate and entertain with the same sentence.

Georgia talked about her kids and her love for her husband. With it, she intertwined a series of comments about her own pride and determination. Though she had been defeated this year, she would finish the Marathon Des Sables the following year.

There were countless faces—Andrea and Karen, Jeff, Brendan, Jay, Toby, Mark, Laurie, Mike, Peggy, Michelle, Leigh and George, Andrew, Steve, and so many more. Each had a different past and perspective, but we had all shared the same experience. This is what made the experience so much different from any I had ever had. My competitive spirit was overshadowed by my desire to share the memory with people from all walks of life.

There was something unexplainable that happened during that week in the desert. We had run at different speeds, but we had run the same course. We had felt different pains, but we had shared the heat. We had struggled at different points, but we took solace in knowing that we were not alone in our suffering.

There is a bond that forms between people who know what it means to struggle, persevere, and succeed. As we cringed, limped, smiled, or ate, we could look one another in the eye and know that nowhere else in the world could we find someone who would understand the moment.

I talked with men and women, young and old, short and tall, parents and bachelors. None of the titles mattered; none of our experiences from back home had carried over into the desert. There was something magical about being suspended between reality and death. We all had blank slates and enjoyed the peace that went along with not having to fill them—even if it was just for a short while longer.

I tried, despite my discomfort, to communicate all of this to ABC. But I understood why Charlie Gibson eventually chose to air only the cheeseburger comment: the meandering rants of a man who admits having no words to describe an experience make for bad television.

I returned to the tent to the sound of music. The race organizers had flown in members from the Paris Opera to perform in the middle of the bivouac, and they played their stringed instruments and sang under the open sky. It was so out of place, this thing of beauty stranded in the wilderness. It made no sense that 800 runners who had suffered for so long, lost so much weight, and been denied even life's simplest conveniences, would be allowed to enjoy the music of some of the world's best musicians.

And yet, in another way, nothing could be more fitting. The Marathon Des Sables had been all about the juxtaposition of the ugly and the beautiful, the sensible and the absurd, the possible and the impossible. We had been forced to be self-sufficient (for the most part), but the race organizers had provided just enough of a connection to our known world to continually remind us just how stark our circumstances had become. I could not understand her words, but the singer's voice was as beautiful as our feet were ugly.

So my thoughts drifted as I drifted to sleep. I reflected on the various stages, and a slight breeze blew through the tent as the woman sang a melodious version of John Lennon's *Imagine*. I wondered just what the world might be like if everyone could experience what we had gone through.

16
The Final Stage

If I had learned anything during the entire experience, it was that my body was exceptionally resilient. Each morning I had been able to move beyond discomfort—and excel in the process. I had fared far better than I had ever imagined possible, but as the sun slits slipped through our tent that morning, I had to begin learning all over again how to move.

My neck and shoulders were stiff and pulsing in pain. My mouth dry, I reached slowly for my water bottle, but a jolt of electricity shot up my entire arm. I let it rest and reached with the other arm, but I felt a sharp pain near the elbow. I decided that rolling over would be more productive.

I rocked myself leftward, and as my tailbone left the ground, I realized that pressure had been the only thing keeping my lower back from throbbing. My left hip popped as I rolled on top of it, and my head fog returned in the process.

"Oh man, my feet are a bloody mess," Andrea announced to the entire group. I looked across the tent and realized that everyone else was already awake.

As I lay suffering, they sat eating.

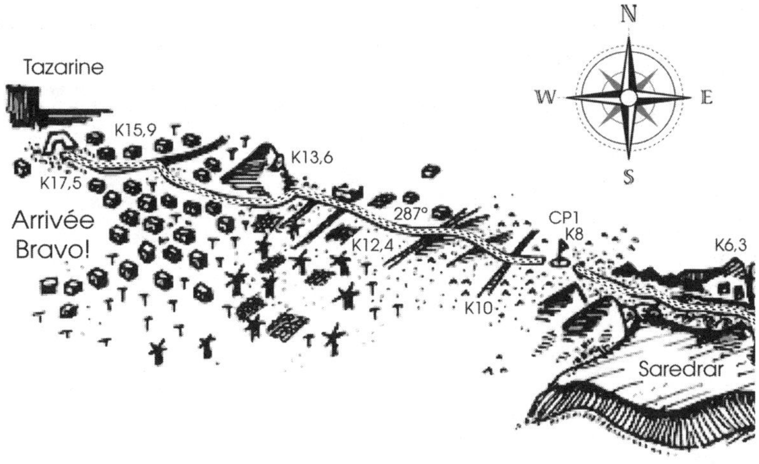

"Are you guys *excited*?!" It was Georgia. After getting past the disappointment of having to withdraw from the race, she had become a source of encouragement for us. Part of me appreciated her enthusiasm that morning; the other part wondered if I could survive it.

"I'm going to go nice and easy the entire day, eh?"

"You said it. I'm right there with you," Andrea concurred. She and Karen had traveled nearly every step of the race together, and the final day would be no different.

"I'm feeling pretty good," Jeff offered. It was almost a question, as though he was still negotiating with his body to determine what he would be allowed to do. "Can you guys believe that this is it?" he added.

Karen and Andrea nearly collided with one another from across the tent as they hurried to answer him. The two of them were clearly excited; Jeff was cautiously optimistic; Georgia was energetic; and Michelle, Brendan, and I had yet to utter a word. For Michelle and Brendan, who had been reserved much of the trip, that was normal. I had run my mouth enough so that others expected my participation.

"Hey, Teddy, how's it going over there?" By her tone, it was obvious that Georgia already knew the answer, but we both knew that I deserved a little ribbing.

I offered a slight groan but nothing more. The gals chuckled a bit that the loudmouth, singing, quick-running Californian wanted to cry but was unwilling to expend the energy necessary.

Jeff vocalized a little concern, but I suspect that he was laughing a bit as well: "You all right, man?" It was the obligatory question that someone had to ask.

I tried to sit up, and my vision blurred a bit, so I closed my eyes. Unable to keep my eyes open long enough to read the numbers written on the bottle caps, I asked which bottle of water was mine. Someone handed me a bottle, and I unscrewed the cap and took a drink. It hurt to swallow, and I kept my eyes shut because it felt better that way.

"That bad?" It was Jeff again, this time a little more concerned. I thought about the competitors who had been airlifted to safety in a helicopter and the man who had died the previous year. I realized that I needed to make it very clear to my tent mates that I was not seriously sick.

"Uh," I started, "I'll be okay." The words were coming out in short bursts. "I feel pretty crummy, but it's only eleven miles today, so I'll be okay by the time we get started."

I rotated my back a little, and it popped a few times. I extended my knees, and after a few minutes of whining—and being appropriately made fun of for it—I felt good enough to take a stroll.

The toilet holes seemed farther than they had been the night before. Though they would occasionally move (because the Berbers would dig new holes and cover the old ones), I had no doubt that it was not the distance, but my perspective that had changed.

About fifty yards from the tent, I stopped and looked around. I realized that I had become one of them—the zombies that hardly shuffled their feet as they struggled to move around the camp. I surveyed the landscape. It was still very early, and no one was moving much. Only a handful of people were up and about; most of them carried wadded-up toilet paper in their hands.

That morning should have been a special one. It should have been an opportunity to reflect on the experience, talk with others about what we had enjoyed most, and savor the final miles into Tazarine. We had run 142 miles over six days, the entire time imagining how satisfied we would be on the final morning. And yet, having reached that moment, I could not even manage a smile.

That morning there was nothing about the experience that I enjoyed. Two days prior I had reached a sickening point of needing a shower. Twelve hours after that I had gotten sick and had lost all desire to run. Less than a day prior, I had needed an inexplicable intervention—perhaps an act of God—to run as I had on previous days. As I circled the tent, I itched nearly everywhere. I scratched my scalp and face, and I wanted desperately to remove whatever filth had built up inside of my ears. I felt as though ants crawled all over my body. I was certain that I would fall ill following the event.

"Last day, buddy. You ready to rock?!" It was Mike from a few tents down. He was a veteran of the Marathon Des Sables, which made me cringe. The thought crossed my mind that I would never return. Looking at his smile as he slapped my back, I could only assume that he did not hurt as much as I did. If he had, I convinced myself, he never would have completed his registration form—let alone boarded another plane bound for the Moroccan Sahara.

"Mike, I am so done with this race. It's over. I'm finished."

He said nothing.

"I mean, I have absolutely no desire to be here anymore," I continued.

His smile faded, and a perplexed look crossed his face. It was obvious that he was excited, and it was equally obvious that he was struggling to understand how it was that I was not overjoyed to have arrived at the final day. His face spelled half surprise and half concern.

"You gonna be all right?" As with Jeff, it was obvious from his tone that he was concerned.

There I was, more miserable than I had ever been, and there he was—genuine, caring, and decent. The entire picture was so different from every world I had ever known. Despite injuries and illnesses, competitors at the Marathon Des Sables watched out for one another. None of us had anything we could offer to cure another's ailment, but we could give our support. I nodded my head in recognition, thankful that I had found people with whom I would be proud to go into battle.

"Yeah, man," I said. "I've never felt so bad in my life," I began. But, not wanting to be the negative voice at our camp, I quickly thought better of it: "But I'm glad that we're almost done. I'll be okay. You're looking good, though."

Mike's face again transformed back to his perplexed look. His eyes squinted and his cheeks pushed toward his nose as he shook his head rapidly from side to side.

"Oh, no, I'm in all sorts of pain," he smiled. I incredulously stared back. He was something out of a masochism convention. "I'm hurtin' everywhere," he smiled wider. "But it's okay. It's the last day, and that's a good thing. Good luck today, Teddy!" He slapped my back and walked off toward the toilet pits.

For a brief moment, I tried to convince myself that mood was all a matter of perspective. I realized that Mike *did hurt* as much as I did—but that perhaps he had just developed a healthier perspective. However, as I felt the grinding in my hips, the churning in my abdomen, and the pulsing in my skull, it became easier to believe that Mike had just lost his mind.

For the final day, I had not brought freeze-dried blueberry granola—an omission for which I was grateful. I reached for my double portion of Pop-Tarts and cringed as I thought of them touching my tongue. Both pouches had been reduced to chalky pebbles. I grabbed a bottle of water and tried as best I could to swallow.

An orange Frenchman walked by; I recognized his bib number. He was the fellow who was a mere fifty-two seconds behind me in the overall standings. He was either lost or had made his way to the other side of the camp specifically to search me out. I was impressed by the thought that it might have been the latter. I knew that I did not have the energy to think about trying to run down other competitors.

I dreaded the starting line that morning. What had started as an adventure and morphed into a series of obstacles had now become a joyless burden. There was considerably more energy at the starting line than there had been in days, but I was clearly out of place.

Patrick Bauer and his translator bellowed out instructions, congratulations, birthday announcements, and proclamations about how important the race has become for him. He offered plenty of clichés—odd, given how *atypical* an experience this was—but people cheered nonetheless. He talked about how the Marathon Des Sables enabled people to really live, showed us who we really are, and enabled us to find the beauty in both nature and humanity. I had heard it all before—in middle school, during an assembly with a poorly paid motivational speaker who grasped at words the way that infants reach for shiny objects.

I shook my head and rubbed my face. *How negative I had become!* I tried to remind myself that I had already run more than 140 miles with hundreds of people from around the world. I tried to convince myself that I would look back on this day forever and recall how incredible an experience it had been. Yet, despite the fact that I knew how important and impactful the experience had been, I could not bring myself to enjoy the moment. The desert had broken me; I could no longer feel anything but discomfort.

As the runners screamed along with that morning's countdown, I caught sight of the orange Frenchman who was fifty-two seconds behind me in the overall standings. He bounced up and down, had a smile on his face, and shot off the line at a rapid pace. He clearly wanted my ranking, and though I knew that there was no way that I could defeat him, I decided to try. If for no other reason than the purity of sport, I owed it to him to put forth my best effort. I sprinted across the line and ran on his heels, telling myself that I would run as hard and as fast as necessary to keep up with him until

I simply could not continue.

The pace was simply blistering. We ran the first two miles in under fourteen minutes, with much of the terrain being loose sand and slightly uphill. Though my pack was nearly empty, it still rubbed. It also bounced around quite a bit, making it awkward to run quickly.

The orange Frenchman began to pull ahead. He was still not fifty-two seconds in front of me, but I could no longer hit him with a football.

I ran on will—to a considerably greater extent than I had done on previous days. With no desire to run, no desire to finish, and no desire to stop, I simply plodded along in hopes that I would at some juncture meet a point where it would be possible to smile again.

By the time I reached the only checkpoint of the stage—a poorly organized assemblage of trucks and water bottles—I had lost sight of the orange Frenchman. I looked at my watch and realized that I had covered the more than five and a half miles in forty minutes. I had been running at faster than thirteen kilometers/hour, which was 20% faster than any of the stages I had run during the entire race. And yet, despite my considerably faster pace, I could no longer see any of the runners with whom I had grown accustomed to running. They were far ahead of me, flying toward the finish.

A few runners in front and behind me elected not to stop at all at the checkpoint. With the stage a mere eleven miles long, many of us would finish in less than ninety minutes. The 1.5 liters of water with which we started was more than enough for someone to cover that distance. Despite this fact, I grabbed my ration of water. No doubt it was out of habit, the paranoia of a man who had so many times during the race asked his tent mates if they had any leftovers.

Catre-son-catre-van-dooze, I thought to myself. "Catre-son-catre-van-dooze," I said aloud in an attempt to reconcile the pain with the purpose.

With my shoes feeling as though the padding had been ripped out of them, my feet hit the ground like bricks on the beach. I scanned the horizon with the dirty brown mountains that promised death and suffering. The foreground was a bit more inviting. There were more frequent weeds shooting out of a sandy clay mixture. Up ahead I could see a row of drooping crops next to a man-made clay wall. Overhead was a power line. It signaled civilization.

I turned a corner around a small hill and could see rows of buildings in the distance. No doubt this was Tazarine, and I turned onto a road of compact dirt, sand, and shale. Crops lined the road, and I could see some children and a woman just ahead. I was surprised that they were standing idle on the outskirts of town, but then again, it was Sunday. Or was it Monday? I thought about it a bit and concluded that it was probably Friday, but I was unwilling to bet on it.

I waved to the children as I passed. In stark contrast to the kids out in the middle of nowhere, they said nothing. I wondered if it was pity on their part. Did I appear to be suffering that much? They just shaded their eyes and watched as I lumbered over the top of a small hill and back down the other side.

There were scattered buildings now. I saw a clothesline to my right; white towels hung in the open air. There were three small goats just to the left, and from somewhere I could hear a radio playing softly. The town seemed to officially begin a few hundred yards ahead. There was a cross street and a street sign, along with wall-to-wall two-story buildings lining the dirt road.

As I crossed the road, I saw a toothless old man sitting in a doorway. An Arabic Coca-Cola sign hung overhead, and he offered an assortment of bagged foods for sale. He was reading a pamphlet.

Catre-son-catre-van-dooze.

A stocky runner came up behind me and passed. I had seen him during other stages. He was wont to wander far off the course. He was also one of the infamous nine, along with me, who had twice gotten lost in the dunes.

He sprinted ahead, not noticing the woman sweeping her sidewalk or the teenage girls twenty feet above leaning out the window. He was following the red circles that had been painted on the sides of buildings as directions—as though there was any other way to go but straight ahead.

It was a dusty, simple, third-world town. The people were poor, and life was hard. But for me it was sensory overload. Accustomed to seeing open plains, dunes, and blue skies, my mind became clouded from the cramped quarters, the shaded road, and the high clay buildings.

***

I thought again about my sister. It had been a week—or had it been two or three?—since she had supposedly gone to Utah. It struck me that I had no idea what had happened. Had she made it to Utah, or had she refused to board the plane in Sacramento? Had she gotten through the Denver airport and made her connection? Had she gotten drunk on the plane or in the airport?

I tried to imagine her out in the Utah desert, but the image was blurry. It reminded me of the way that Michael J. Fox's character experiences a near loss of identity as he struggles to get his future parents to meet in *Back to the Future*. I could only see part of my sister, part of myself.

I wondered if she had trekked through the desert and found a small town along the way. Had she struggled in the middle of nowhere, only to round a bend, come up over a hill, and see a few silent children? Had they looked questioningly at her or welcomed her?

I wondered if she had come into a town of mud huts—or would they have been made of splintering wood? Had there been a toothless man under a Coke sign? I imagined Amy, thirsty and hungry, staring at the man's wears and cringing at the dirty sacks and dried meat.

"Do you have any Luna bars or anything?"

The man briefly looked up from his pamphlet and squinted at her. Amy walked away frustrated.

I could not tell if she was appreciating the experience; she looked like I felt: uncomfortable and uncertain as to how life was supposed to feel at that moment.

"This is totally stupid," I could hear her say to no one in particular. She stood alone, walking away from the rest of the group and refusing to participate in whatever she was supposed to participate in. The others in her group ignored her. They were too tired to focus their energies on someone else.

"*Amy, this isn't stupid!*" I yelled. She continued walking, not even glancing in my direction.

"*Amy!*" I had no idea what was happening, and I had no idea what I was doing. "*Amy, take advantage of this. Please! Don't blow it!*" I was yelling, but I had surprisingly little emotion. I was numb. She did not appear to be listening, and I had little doubt that she would ignore my pleas even if she could hear every word.

***

Without warning, I stumbled and nearly fell to the ground. I had gone from compact dirt to a freshly paved road. No longer was I in a narrow chute surrounded by buildings on both sides, but on a four-lane road bisecting a reasonably busy street.

A group of men yelled and then sighed as I nearly fell. Gathered around a small cart of wares, they were pretending to work. I had no doubt that they would spend much of their day watching the runners come into town. I waved to them to let them know that I was all right, but I wondered how far I had run while thinking about Amy.

The street was a busy one, and pavement markings instructed us to run in the shoulder. Cars whizzed by, shopkeepers yelled to convince passersby to stop in, and tourists sipped coffee in roadside open-air eateries. Others ate "tangines," a typical Moroccan-style dish consisting of steamed meat and vegetables in a clay pot.

I then remembered the road book. Pavement meant that I was only seven-tenths of a mile from the finish line. Instinctively, I increased my pace. Under normal conditions, I would have finished in four minutes. The cars and restaurants and little Coca-Cola kiosks made me understand that the end really was near—not in the way that I had tried to convince myself during previous stages or before the marathon day had even begun, but for real. The pavement was my Pavlov's bell. It told me that I would get what I wanted.

Some people pointed now, and a few cheered. I ran alone, and though everyone in town understood why I was there, it was obvious that I did not fit in. The other tourists wore sandals and carried handbags. They had Polo shirts and pressed khaki shorts. My hat was bright red and paper thin, with a long, dangling flap; they wore stylish, brimmed hats. Not a single one of them had water bottles with straws attached to his torso.

I ran with longer strides now, pressing through the center of town and looking into the distance. I wanted to see the white inflatable finish line. I wanted to see the sponsors' logos and the ten-foot-tall red fabric fan blades with the New Balance logo. The streets were narrower now as more and more people lined the sides. There were a few parked cars, but none were trying to make their way this far into town.

I turned a corner at the end of a block and saw it. What a contrast it was to every other day. Hundreds of people had packed around the finish line to cheer the runners as we arrived. There was no sand, no mountains in the distance, and no black tents set up in a dusty, lonely ring. It was a party. At the end of all previous stages, I could see the race organizers for hundreds of yards as I approached. They stood alone, bored, and waiting for us to arrive. As I approached today's finish, I could not distinguish the race officials from the throngs. They were obscured by screaming children, hopeful family members who had traveled to see their loved ones finish, and locals who were no doubt prepared to sell me things.

***

A month after the Marathon Des Sables, ABC World Nightly News ran a segment that showed me crossing the finish line side by side with Ian the Brit. I watched that three-second portion of the segment over and over again—not because I was vain, but because I was surprised to see a smile on my face. As I sprinted in and crossed the finish line, I was beaming, grinning ear to ear. Short of raising my arms in triumph and thanking God, I could have been an Olympian winning gold.

The reason that this confused me so is that, at the time, I felt nothing—except a small amount of disgust. As I broke the plane of the finish, I had successfully completed "the world's toughest footrace" in sixteenth place, having run 153 miles over six stages. It should have been a moment of exaltation. Nothing I had ever done athletically compared to that moment, and yet I felt absolutely nothing but a small amount of anger and frustration—almost resentment—at having to complete the experience.

Sitting on the couch watching ABC, with a month's perspective behind me, I finally realized why I had not felt a stronger sense of satisfaction. I was not angry because of the race—though I would never wish my filth on anyone—but, rather, because I had reached the end. As satisfying as it would be to enjoy a shower, eat a freshly prepared meal, and sleep in a padded bed, I knew that these pleasures would come at the expense of the bonds I had formed out in the desert.

Standing at the finish line, waiting to walk through the chute lined with screaming people, I shook my head in disgust and cursed the event that had been so painful so as to completely sap my ability to enjoy the satisfaction of victory.

Later I understood that I would miss the commiseration. It would be impossible upon my return home to get together a group of seven people, remove all cell phones, slow down, and so completely immerse ourselves in living.

Later I realized that part of me would miss freeze-dried slop. Sure, I would enjoy the bounty awaiting me at the hotel, but our future meals would come so easily that we would not appreciate them on the same level.

***

"Ted! Ted! How do you feel?" It was the ABC News crew. As usual, Bruno the producer lingered behind, watching.

"What's going through your head right now?"

I thought back to our initial conversation—when I had awkwardly flubbed my response—and for the first time in a week had similar concerns as I stared into the giant black eye. Nothing profound came to mind.

"I'm gonna get a Coke," I responded. I had seen the unintelligible Arabic signs on the way into town, but I recognized the color and the arch on the logo. All of the people, the music, the signs, and the screaming meant nothing to me. I could enjoy none of them, but I did know that I wanted a Coke.

"Okay, okay, that sounds like a plan," she responded. She was suspended between understanding and disappointment. "Can we talk to you in a little bit?"

"Yeah, sure, absolutely," I nodded as I wandered away.

By the time I had returned to the finish line twenty minutes later—armed with four liter-sized bottles of Coca-Cola that I had paid for by handing a local shopkeeper a wad of bills and walking away—it was even busier. Another hundred runners had finished, and I recognized more and more people.

I saw Georgia and her husband, Monte, who had traveled to see her at the finish. We exchanged a few words that I could not remember. I was selfishly focused on the Coke, enjoying the sweetness even though the carbonation burned my throat as it went down.

Off to the side, I could see Jeff, Brendan, and Michelle sitting up against a rock wall. They were eating the sack lunch that the race officials had handed us as we finished.

"Hey guys," I said as I approached.

"Hey," they said in unison. They were far more interested in their food, which, under the circumstances, made sense. Like me, however, they seemed numb. There were some celebrating athletes—locals playing violins and tambourines as racers danced—but our contingent was subdued.

"You know," Jeff said, "I would have thought that after running 150 miles, I would have been happy to get any sort of food. But I've got to be honest. I'm still sick of this Moroccan bread."

He held up the six-inch round disc, about an inch thick, and then flung it back into his bag.

"They got any of those little French cheeses in there?" I asked. Coca-Cola was suiting me just fine for the time being, but I knew that I would eventually want something.

"You're in luck, but they only give you one."

"I'll live. I'm not even hungry."

We sat against the wall, in the shade and quiet, watching others finish, scream, and cry.

"Well, can you guys believe that it's done?" Brendan asked. It was half statement, half question.

"I'm sure that I'll look back on this moment and have fonder memories," I responded. "But, to be honest, I'm really happy that it's done, and I can't even begin to explain how ready I am for a shower."

"What bus number are you on?" Jeff asked. He held up a white ticket.

Confused, I shrugged and reached a hand into my pockets. Sure enough, I too had a white ticket. No doubt I had picked it up when I had gotten my sack lunch, which I cradled in my left arm.

"Bus number one. 11:20 a.m."

"We're on bus number two at the same time," he responded. Michelle and Brendan nodded along. It was only fifteen minutes away, but no one was particularly worried about making it.

After the fourth and fifth stages, I had been overcome with excitement and pride. I had screamed at the top of my lungs. They had been battle cries worthy of *Braveheart*; but upon finishing I had no desire to even whimper.

Beyond my Coca-Cola, all I could think about was returning to Ouarzazate. Perhaps, I thought, some sense of life would return after I had showered, put on clean clothes, and seen modern comforts.

That was it. The race was over, and I was a slug.

Looking back, it was definitely a missed opportunity. I should have sat and savored the moment a bit more. I could have removed my shirt, enjoyed the slight breeze, and gotten sunburned. I could have bought a round of beers for the race organizers, danced, or kicked a soccer ball with the local children.

I should have thanked God for having had the opportunity to compete and extend myself. I should have thanked Him that I had made it alive.

Pride and perspective would have to wait. At that moment, I had nothing left to offer, nothing left of value. I was a cut-down stump, but one thing was certain: I had given all I was capable of giving.

17 Ooh, That Smell

Body odor can be as fascinating as it is disgusting.

For the most part, we are immune to our own scent, however foul it might become. But when another reeks of death and shame, we are quick to revolt and wonder how someone could ever allow himself to descend to such a level.

Such had been the case at the bivouac. I had told my tent mates that I was surprised at how little I could smell from our tent—but I had been quick to joke that the French areas should be quarantined.

We simply become numb to our own funk.

My freshman year in college, my roommate hailed from Bulgaria. He commented during our first day together that, since he had taken a shower the previous day, he did not need to take another shower for three more days. He honestly had no idea that his scent was debilitating. The thought never crossed his mind that others had been breathing into their shirts during lunch or holding their breath as he passed in the halls. It had never crossed his mind that wiping sweat from his brow was a bad thing to do with the towel that he planned on using for that next shower.

I have played sports all of my life—in high school, college, and beyond—and men especially are prone to disgusting rituals that can produce horrible odors. I had teammates who refused to wash socks for an entire season. Others took pride in farting in small, closed spaces or shoving their dirty underwear in a teammate's face.

But never in twenty-five years of competitive athletics had I smelled anything even close to as repulsing as what awaited me on the bus.

The race organizers had arranged for luxury coaches—air conditioning, individual high-backed seats, and overhead storage. After a week in the desolate Sahara, they were an indulgence—complete with a bathroom and flushable toilet.

However, though the race officials had arranged for comfort, they failed to provide nose pins.

Imagine walking into a closed room of nearly eighty-five degrees with forty different versions of the smelliest man you have ever encountered in your life.

I gagged as I stepped onto the bus. I knew that I had to be a contributing factor—perhaps worse than others—but I could not believe how disgusting the cumulative odor had become. Two men at the back had removed their shirts. Another close up had raised his shorts to massage his quadriceps muscle. I looked around and saw endless flesh, and it might as well have been rotting meat.

The Frenchman to my right was a skunk steak.

The Australian to my left, no doubt a kangaroo filet in the process of turning green, was fighting with the Jordanian, his long, sinewy neck resembling a giraffe.

Ian the Brit, now the rotting corpse of a Mountain Goat, was in the middle of the bus, sitting alone. I wandered his way, said hello, and sat down. I figured that I might as well be able to talk to my seatmate during the three-and-a-half-hour drive. I wonder what type of rotting animal he had pegged me for—a jackass, perhaps?

We were spoiled, curdled milk. We were fuzzy green cheese and month-old eggs sitting in the sun. Sulfur—a pure, gaseous scent that at least had the benefit of being consistently nauseating—

would have been preferable to our own body odor.

Most of us had been warned by race veterans. They had told us that the final bus ride was an exercise in holding one's nose for as long as possible—and then learning to breathe only through the mouth. I wanted to wretch. I sipped my Coca-Cola and was temporarily relieved to smell the sugar. I looked at my sack lunch and recoiled at the thought of eating anything in the bag.

There was a small wedge of cheese, no doubt a pungent chunk of Limberger. I saw a small sack of beef nuggets and a cup of lentils in a deep grey mush. Even the bread I imagined as taking on characteristics of something that was decaying and competing for my nose.

Maggots would have been in heaven—incapacitated, no doubt, by the sheer number of options. Like children at a buffet, they would have scurried around the bus, wanting so desperately to stop and partake in a particular course—only to be ripped away by an uncontrollable force drawing them elsewhere.

A fly buzzed back and forth overhead; overloaded by sensory inputs, he died in midair and fell to the floor.

I looked around the bus, which I shared with the race's elite runners—the top forty finishers. I wondered who would be smelliest—the faster or the slower runners. On the one hand, I could imagine that the elite runners were better conditioned and thus less prone to sweat and smell. On the other hand, so many of them had pushed themselves so hard and in such miserable conditions that their bodies surely would have forced out every foul substance. The slower runners had been in the sun longer; perhaps they had stewed longer in their own filth—or perhaps they had baked off the smell by spending more time in the black rock ovens.

During the three-and-a-half-hour drive, I spoke with Ian about running and life. We both were dating Americans and struggling through long-distance relationships. His girlfriend, in Seattle, was a bit farther a trip than my 140-mile drive to Sacramento. Nonetheless, we shared an understanding of what it took to maintain a relationship that could not be watered daily. We talked about the importance and value that contact took on (we savored what time we did get to spend together) and commiserated that solving problems was difficult a continent or bay away.

Ian, it turned out, was an exceptional runner—albeit an amateur. He had run dozens of marathons (to my four), racking up an impressive list of victories and accomplishments.

He had attempted the Marathon Des Sables in 2006 but had failed to finish. Like so many other competitors that year, he had succumbed to the heat and humidity. More than 20% of the field had dropped out due to high humidity and a virus that traveled around camp. He simply could not make it.

He had wanted to return in 2007, but the British group often sells out years in advance.

This year—2008—then, was Ian's chance for redemption. He had told the French media covering the event that he would not only be finishing, but would be "the top Brit"—quite a prediction for a group that sent hundreds of competitors. But not only was he the top Englishman, he also finished thirteenth overall.

Thinking back to his discussion of his own triumphs and running exploits, it would have been easy to believe that he was bragging. But that notion never crossed my mind. He never came across as arrogant, but rather he just spoke about his life. He was as modest as an exceptional athlete could be, and I found myself genuinely liking him.

However, despite the fact that I was enjoying his stories, I could not help but be repulsed by his odor—or was it the man to my right? I could not be certain, but smelling whoever it was made me want to apologize to everyone on the bus. I knew that if they smelled bad to me, I most likely offered them an equally disgusting odor.

It is unfortunate that a picture cannot capture scents; I would have asked someone to preserve that moment as a reminder of what not to be. Without that extra-sensory photo, I can only remind myself that while sitting on that bus, I found myself thinking about how much more pleasant it would be to drive through Coalinga—one of California's largest cow farms and manure plants. Imagining the drive I had made many times, I took a deep breath and felt relieved, albeit temporarily, by the smell of dung baking in the summer sun.

18
Drifting Away

As our bus pulled into Ouarzazate, rain poured down, sending the local inhabitants scurrying for cover.

That region of Morocco is a land of dust, sand, dirt, and grime, but the water that spilled onto the landscape that day was warm and fresh. God spoke to me about irony and symbolism, and the streets ran thick with rivers of golden-brown sludge. It was just what I had imagined my shower looking like. I could not see my legs beneath a thick, matted mess of dust, sweat, and sunscreen.

We stood awhile in the rain, tasting freedom and enjoying the purest substance to touch our skin in more than a week.

"It's done, huh, buddy?" It was Mark, the speedy Brit who shared the American tents. He had finished this year's event, overcoming his 2006 withdrawal.

"Unbelievable," I paused. "Thank God."

"I can't tell which I want more—a shower or a meal."

"I'll tell you what, I'll take both," I answered.

And yet, there we stood, outside our hotel, in the pouring rain. We discussed the small matter of our pre-race baggage, which we had left at our pre-race hotel a mile down the road. It had our clean clothes, deodorant, and shaving gear. We decided to delay gratification awhile and walk down to grab them.

The walk was a perfect ritual. Out in the rain, I felt as though we were partaking in the town's cleansing process. The sides of the streets ran with mud, only to reveal fresh black pavement underneath. The scraggly roadside trees drank, and the wild dogs in the empty lots jumped in circles and played with one another.

We were all being offered a clean start.

Back at the hotel, I had to remove the Elastoplast tape from my spine and sides. It seemed an eternity since Ed and Terry had instructed me in its placement. Despite its assistance, I had developed open sores around my sides and rubbing down my spine. Removing the tape might have been the hygienic thing to do, but it stung as a fellow runner ripped it off.

My shower, as a consequence, was rejuvenating but painful. The hot water scalded my wounds. I scrubbed anyway, soaping myself three times in hopes of finally feeling clean.

I had arranged to meet Mark back in the lobby for a meal, and we walked across the street for a four-course indulgence at four in the afternoon. My stomach churned as I shoveled in potatoes, beef, carrots, and sticky buns. I drank beer and chuckled as Mark consumed one Coca-Cola after another.

Three hours later, we were all eating again. The hotel had arranged for an all-you-can-eat buffet, and more than 100 of us congregated and tried our best to exhibit manners as we piled our plates high with chicken, breads, soups, and marinated olives. We ate as though afraid that it would be our last meal.

That night I spoke with Andrew again, my roommate before the race and one of the most inspirational and sad stories of that year's Marathon Des Sables. He had rested since his disqualification following the third stage, but he still walked with a pronounced limp. He beamed as we talked about the race. After congratulating me, he declared that he would return when he was better trained and could better afford the cost of the experience. At twenty-one years of age, he had plenty of time; I was happy for him that he had developed such a healthy perspective and was determined to persevere. It again reminded me of my cynical and dismissive attitude toward life at his age.

Things seemed to be in hyper-speed that day. We talked, laughed, and drank beer, but we could not seem to capture the moment. I wanted so much to hang onto those hours so that I might fully appreciate what it meant to sit in a chair, have a beer, not repulse others with my scent, and enjoy air conditioning. But the day was over despite my internal protests.

Sadly, the following day proceeded in the same fashion. The race officials had arranged for a race expo at one of the hotels, and we spent our day walking through there, returning our flares to the organizers, buying commemorative T-shirts, and eating golden-foiled ice cream bars sold by children with push-carts. Nothing, however, seemed to stick. I was caught in between pride and disbelief, exhaustion and motivation, inertia and change.

Not even lunch—at an empty hotel with only the winner, Mohamad Ahansal, and his friends at a neighboring table—made much sense. The race was behind me, and though I had no desire to return to the pain of the desert, I could not hold onto anything.

Most of all, I just wanted time to stand still. Everything was moving too fast, and I was far too slow to process my surroundings. I wanted the world to stop so that I could just observe it. I wanted to be able to pinch myself without fear of missing critical information.

But that was it. Day slipped into night, the Internet cafes in Ouarzazate shuttered their doors, and even our last supper together seemed to pass without our participation. I kept reaching for the present, but some force ushered me along.

After nearly two years of obsessions, six months of grueling training, and a week of the most embedded misery imaginable, I was done. I was pleased that it was over, but I had expected a greater level of excitement. Mostly, however, I just felt deflated. The thought of ever returning to compete in the Marathon Des Sables again made me sick.

And yet, as we boarded the plane to leave Morocco, and as my new friends spread out across the plane for the flight back to New York, I realized that I would miss our time together.

I would have a comfortable bed at home and all I could eat, but my thoughts kept returning to our commiseration. I had leaned on them, and they on me, so that we might learn something more about ourselves as we struggled to survive.

As we left the plane and said our goodbyes at the JFK baggage claim, I wondered when I would see them again. And, though my hips popped as I walked and pain shot through my legs, I wondered: *Might I be able to do it faster?*

Postscript

As it turned out, the Marathon Des Sables was indeed the paradox that I had been told to expect: it was the toughest footrace in the world, and yet, something that anyone could accomplish. Athletes of all ages and capabilities arrived from the edges of the earth with different objectives but a common mission. Women in their sixties and men in their twenties cried together because they could not express their feelings in words.

I would recommend it to anyone who has ever thought that doing the impossible, if just once, is something worth adding to the resume. Finishing the race in sixteenth place—which garnered me a small amount of press on ABC News and a few running-oriented blogs—in no way changed my life. I experienced no epiphany and made no deep conclusions about my existence. But finishing the Marathon Des Sables with newfound friends certainly added to my perspective. I learned to further appreciate the value of hard work and determination, and I impressed myself along the way with my own ability to persevere.

The course changes every year, so it is impossible to offer words of advice or encouragement beyond generalities. Finishing requires a training regimen that borders on life-consuming, with half as many hours out on trails as in the office. I spoke with one finisher who claimed to never have run more than six miles per day during training. Though I genuinely believe him to be telling the truth, I also believe that he may be the only one of six billion living people to be capable of accomplishing such a feat.

If you are interested in the event, visit the race's Website at www.darabaroud.com and click the little British flag for the English version of the site. Americans, Canadians, and

Australians can visit www.dreamchaserevents.com, which is the official regional race representative. Jay Batchen and Lisa Smith-Batchen are two of the nicest folks in the world, but be careful: their enthusiasm is contagious. You might just find yourself training for a future year's event.

Fin.